Natural Religion

Natural Religion

A *None's* Journey of Religious Discovery

Davis Baird

WIPF & STOCK · Eugene, Oregon

NATURAL RELIGION
A *None's* Journey of Religious Discovery

Wipf & Stock
An Imprint of Wipf and Stock Publishers
199 W. 8th Ave., Suite 3
Eugene, OR 97401

www.wipfandstock.com

PAPERBACK ISBN: 979-8-3852-3988-7
HARDCOVER ISBN: 979-8-3852-3989-4
EBOOK ISBN: 979-8-3852-3990-0

VERSION NUMBER 06/17/25

Photo of Earl C. Davis at Bowdoin College (chapter 2, figure 13) used by permission, courtesy of the George J. Mitchell Department of Special Collections & Archives, Bowdoin College Library, Brunswick, Maine

To Earl Clement Davis (1876–1953) and
Annie Foster Dodge Davis (1880–1964)

To feel the deeper undercurrent of this great pulsating humanity, to swim valiantly in the great current of human progress, to feel the call of the finite to its universal consecration, and to fulfill, joyously, in pain and in pleasure, the great function of human life—that is life. —Earl Clement Davis, "The Travail and Pain of Human Life"

Contents

List of Illustrations and Tables

Illustrations:

Tables:

Preface

> If there is any validity at all to religion, it must rest upon a foundation which is valid, not only in our modern world of machines and science, but which was valid in the day of the Puritans and the Lollards; in the day of Gregory the Great, and the first missionaries among our barbaric forefathers in Europe. It must rest upon a foundation that was valid in the Roman Empire and in Egypt and will be valid a thousand years hence as well. Back of all the forms which, in the name of religion, mankind has ever created, there is the unconquerable faith and courage that has created them; faith that there are permanent values in human life and that courageous fidelity to those values has its root in the nature of things.[1]

1. Curiosities

WRITING THIS BOOK HAS been a voyage of discovery for me, discovery of a grandfather I never knew, and discovery of an approach—his approach—to religion I didn't know was possible. It began when I finally had the time and mental space to begin reading the manuscripts, mostly sermons, he left behind. They were gathered almost randomly in an old trunk I inherited through my mother. Where to begin? How to proceed?

1. Davis, "Results of Protestantism" (1931), 8. All quotations from Davis are taken from the typed transcriptions available in the Earl Clement Davis digital depository. These transcriptions preserve Davis's original spelling and grammar.

Of course, I knew *of* my grandfather, Earl Clement Davis. I knew that he was a Unitarian minister, and that he had been the minister of the Unitarian church in Petersham, Massachusetts. Until I started this work, I was always a little uncertain about when he died. Did he die in 1953 or was it 1959? I got that straight—1953, May 19, to be exact. He died eleven months before I was born and I was named after him: my slightly unusual first name, Davis, his surname. His widow, Annie Foster Davis, née Dodge, moved in with her daughter, my mother, after he died. So, I knew her somewhat—at least insofar as a toddler/young child knows someone. She died when I was ten.

But knew close to nothing about their lives, their beliefs, their world. When—or where—either of them was born. I didn't know when or how they met, nor when they got married. I didn't know—beyond Petersham—where or when my grandfather was a minister, or what his background was that led him to the ministry.

My parents, who argued about everything, did seem to agree that Earl Clement Davis was a good and lovely man, that Annie Foster Davis was a good and lovely woman, and that they had a good and strong marriage. This always prompted some curiosity in me. Who were these people that my parents—who disagreed about everything—both loved?

Religion has always been peripheral in my life. Clearly my mother had some kind of a religious upbringing, being the daughter of a minister. And it had an impact insofar as she was a member of the local Unitarian—subsequently Unitarian Universalist, or UU—church. But she never attended services. Although she did serve as chair the Parish Committee, the first woman to do so. She did not expect her children to attend services, and I never did. I have never felt like something was missing in my life, but I always had a tingle of curiosity. Professionally, as a practicing philosophy professor, I felt I should know something about religion. As the grandson of a minister, I should know something.

The demands of life pushed these curiosities to a back corner of my mind. Preparing classes—lots of logic, including statistics, history and philosophy of science. Writing and publishing to gain tenure and ultimately promotion. No real room in there to explore religion or my grandparents. The last eleven years I served as Clark University's provost, an administrative job that grabs every hour of the day, with the last year and half in COVID with its added challenges.

Then I retired, and suddenly, I had time and mental space. I opened the trunk and began. Pretty randomly. Pick a manuscript and start reading.

2. *Thanksgiving*

Earl C. and Annie F. Davis had four children—John, Foster, Byron, and my mother, Mary. This much I knew. And I had many cousins. Although, until I got going with this research, I couldn't have named them all, nor was I clear about each familial line. They were all, but for one, older than me. My oldest cousin, Jock Davis, is nineteen years my senior. We gathered as a big family for Thanksgiving. This was *the* exciting holiday of the year for me, and for the family at large. It was a tradition that Earl and Annie started. Here is a picture from Thanksgiving 1948 at the Petersham parsonage:

Davis Family Thanksgiving, Petersham, Massachusetts, Parsonage, 1948
Earl and Annie Davis, upper left
John, oldest son (1906–59), far right
Foster, second son (1908–58), seated, far left
Byron, third son (1912–98) tallest, back row middle
Mary, daughter (1915–87), just to the right of Byron

Along with spouses and thirteen grandchildren, and a dog. My sisters—Brinna (b. 1939, nine years old) and Anne (then named Nancy) (b. 1941, seven years old)—are on either side of my mother. And my brother, Douglas (1945–2017, three years old) is in my father's arms while my father looks up into the sky at something—what?

By my middle teenage years, it was just too big. We separated into two Thanksgiving gatherings. One Thanksgiving gathered those descending from Foster and Byron—whose wives, Alice Merritt (1912–84) and Patsy Merritt (1915–92) were sisters. Two brothers married two sisters. A second Thanksgiving gathered those descending from John and Mary. But every so often we would come together in a massive, all-in Thanksgiving extravaganza. Here is a picture from Thanksgiving 1987, the year my mother died:

Extended Davis Family Thanksgiving, Lexington, Massachusetts, 1987

Thomas Malthus in action. Given how much my grandfather admired "personality" and the importance of life, growth—and family—I am confident he would have been very happy to see his robust family line, here thirty-four years after his death. But this gets way ahead of my story.

I share these bits about the Davis family Thanksgiving for several reasons. First, Earl and Annie started something. They created a family identity—the Earl C. and Annie F. Davis family identity—a family identity that engages both patriarchal and matriarchal lines. My "Davis" family identity does not eclipse but stands fully beside my "Baird" family identity. This identity is tied to the power of the personalities of Earl and Annie. There must have been something about them. Something that I might uncover in my grandfather's writings.

Related to this, I have felt some obligation to make my grandfather's writings available to the wider family, my siblings, my cousins and all their "issue." I carried the trunk of my grandfather's writings with me for years—decades—before I began work with the documents. But I did peak occasionally. Once, in 2001, as a sixtieth birthday present for my sister Anne, I transcribed a few of the texts. I picked randomly, and my time was limited so I choose shorter texts. One of these earlier texts that I transcribed was titled, "The Thirst for a Living God," all of three typed pages.[2] My digital transcription made the rounds of the family. My cousin, Mark Davis (b. 1948—the baby in the arms of his mother, Patsy Merritt Davis—fourth from left in the 1948 Thanksgiving photo), was so moved by the sermon that he arranged to re-deliver it on October 1, 2017, at the Petersham Unitarian church, where our grandfather finished his ministerial life.

There was family interest in the materials. To make these materials available, I didn't just read them. I scanned them, transcribed them, edited them and posted them online.[3] These materials are also being archived by Clark University in its digital commons.[4]

3. Getting Organized

As I found the manuscripts in the trunk, many were "on their own," their pages bound together by various means—a loop of string, a brad, a straight pin:

2. Davis, "Thirst for a Living God" (191Xa).

3. See Baird, "Earl Clement Davis."

4. See "Earl Clement Davis Papers" (1893–1953). I am very grateful to Clark's head librarian, Laura Robinson, for her support of my work, and to the librarian, Katie Stebbins, who did all the work to get these materials into the Clark's Digital Commons.

Some Helps by the Way.
Scripture:-
Text:

Not to grovel in the dust, not to fly in the air, but to walk erectly, strongly, and

(14) Sermons I.
Scripture. Proverbs. 31–26
Text. Text Proverbs 26–20
Subject: Feed the whole man.

I suppose that we all love days when it seems to us that

The Hope For a New Age.
Thanksgiving expressed in terms of Hope.
Electro-motive Force.
Motive Power.
Momentum of a stream.

Some of sermons—perhaps fifteen to twenty of them—were in envelopes with the title and date of the sermon on the envelope:

Creedless Church. A Plea for.
Outline of Address in Pittsfield, Mass.
In connection with ordination, 1905.

There also were collections. I particularly loved the self-bound booklets of sermon notes from Davis's time in Petersham:

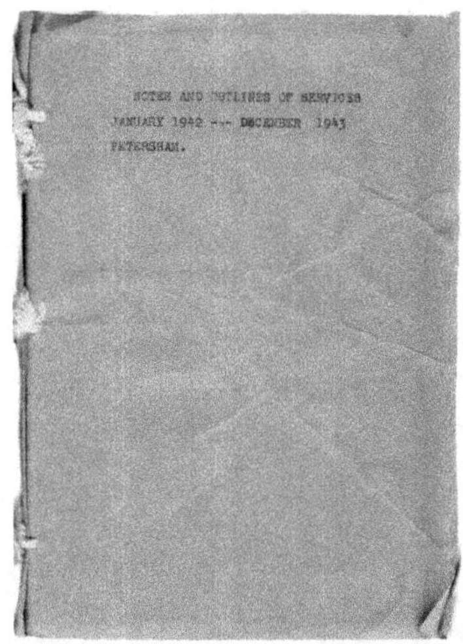

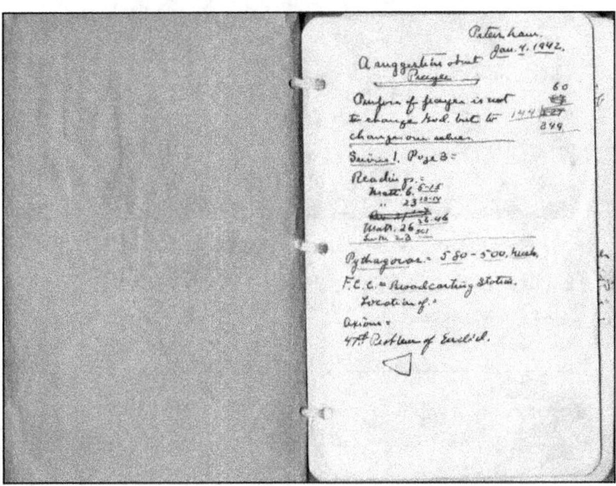

And there was an over-full typewriter paper box with "Pittsfield Mostly" written across the top.

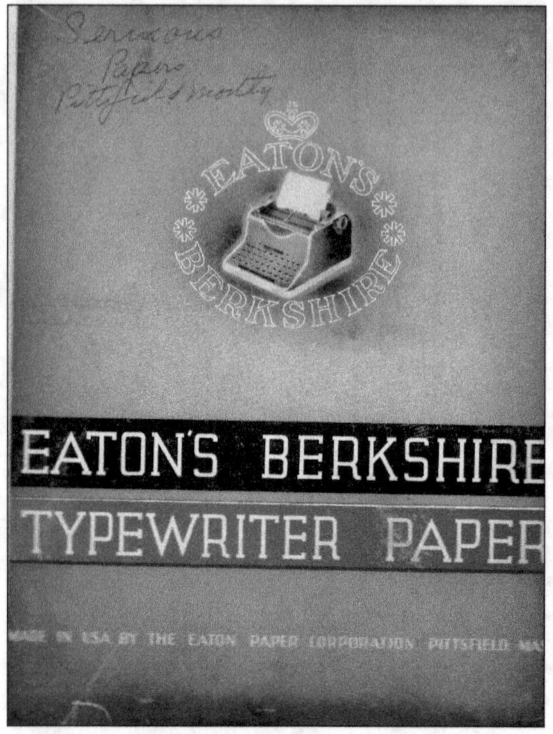

It was filled with several blocks of texts—each an inch think of string-bound pages of sermon texts:

Keeping back a part of the price.
August 30 '08.

This strange little tale connected with the history of the early christian church, is a delightfully human document. Apart from certain obvious exagerations that are intended to add to the dramatic effect of the story this incident is so characteristic of a certain type of a person that one can almost see how this Annias looked as he came walking up to the apostles and laid his money at their feet. Indeed it seems worth our while to take time to recall this situation just for

There was no obviously correct way to approach this. At the beginning I picked randomly. With some of the typed texts I tried to scan them directly into digital texts. This proved problematic with a very large number of errors that needed correction. In the end, I typed or retyped everything.

At the outset, I couldn't face the huge blocks of texts. So, I started with the—many—singleton manuscripts. Most of these were complete beginning-to-end sermons or essays. Some were just notes—for example, there was a single page of notes for Davis's April 7, 1905, ordination at the Unity Church in Pittsfield, "A Plea for the Principle of a Creedless Church."[5] I decided to prioritize the full text manuscripts. This way I would be in a better position to understand the notes.

The handwritten texts took some time. It became clear that Davis got a typewriter sometime in 1907. All the texts prior to 1907 were handwritten—except his Harvard thesis, "A Prophet of Democracy,"[6] which was typeset. After 1907, most of the texts were typed, frequently with handwritten edits. It seemed a good idea to tackle the earlier texts first so I could get some sense of the development of his thought. So many of the handwritten manuscripts were done early. They became easier as I got to know his hand.

Most of the texts were sermons. But not all. There were some—fascinating to me—collections of historical texts.[7] For example, eight handwritten lectures on the "Origins of Modern Religion, Modern Charity and Modern Labor Problems"; written in 1905, it discussed the development of charity, labor, and religion from about 1300 CE.[8] I came to understand that these collections supported the religious education he offered his congregation. There were a couple of publications; one surprising publication from 1910 alerted me to my grandfather's socialist commitments, "Socialism: A Reply to The Common Assertion That the Socialist Movement Is Atheistic, Irreligious, and a Menace to the Family," published by the Pittsfield Socialist Local.[9]

As I got into the daily swing of transcribing, editing, and posting online, I came to realize that I needed a way to organize what I

5. Davis, "Plea for the Principle" (1905a).

6. Davis, "Prophet of Democracy" (1904a).

7. See, for example, Davis, "Rise and Development" (1906a) or *Origins and History* (1916a).

8. Davis, "Origins of Modern Religion" (1905c).

9. Davis, "Socialism: A Reply" (1910a).

was dealing with. I started with a simple spreadsheet that listed key facts—and a brief abstract—about each manuscript. This didn't quite prove enough to keep my head wrapped around what I was learning from my grandfather. So I started to write about what I was learning. I transcribed and I wrote, I wrote and I transcribed. This helped me organize and understand what was learning. But as I transcribed more, I would have to go back and rewrite, for I would learn something new—something surprising—that changed things.

4. Surprises

When I began, I thought I would learn something of my grandfather's views about religion, which to my mind meant something about God, Jesus, heaven, etc. In the end, I did learn about his views on these topics. But not before some other topics, which emerged as more important to Davis.

My first surprise was how focused Davis was on governance. Consider the title of his Harvard thesis mentioned above, "A Prophet of Democracy."[10] The thesis concerned John Wise (1652–1725) who was the minister of the church in Ipswich, Massachusetts, from 1683 until his death. He was an early advocate of the rights of the colonists, specifically arguing against taxation without representation, a position for which Wise was arrested and fined in 1687. I, of course, connected this phrase, "no taxation without representation," to the American Revolution of 1775. It turns out it had an earlier pedigree.

Davis's history collection, "The Rise and Development of the Congregational Polity and Spirit,"[11] began to enlighten me about his concern with governance. Who gets to say what one should believe about God and other religious matters? Growing up in a largely secular way, in a country that—presumably—enshrines the separation of church and state, I had never paid much attention to this question. But reading these manuscripts reminded me of all the conflict and strife, religious wars, fought over this question. For Davis, the most important religious development came out of the Reformation, which initially for Christians challenged the authority of the Pope. Various intermediary answers were tried—including the king/queen for Anglicans, but also the authority of the Bible.

10. Davis, "Prophet of Democracy" (1904a).
11. Davis, "Rise and Development" (1906a).

For Davis, this transition ultimately landed with each individual: We are each individually responsible for deciding what to believe about God and other religious matters. There is no other or higher authority.

Davis characterized the transition from ancient and medieval times as a transition from revelation, authority, and obedience to discovery, freedom, and consent.[12] There is more on this in the book that follows. But the point here is that governance was—is—foundationally important to religion. Once I had become familiar with my grandfather's thinking, this made good sense. But it was a surprise at the outset.

My second surprise was the centrality of *change* to Davis's thinking. It was only after I started to work on the big blocks of typed texts in the typewriter paper box—"Pittsfield mostly"—I ran headfirst into change. There I found Davis's sermon for May 9, 1909, "The Travail and Pain of Human Life: What Can it Mean?"[13] The sermon addresses what philosophers call "the problem of evil": How can there be evil in a world with an omniscient, omnipotent, and benevolent God? Davis's answer was change. God didn't finish the job (whether in six or seven days or otherwise). The world was still being made. It still is being made.

For me, as a resident of the secular scientific world, a world initiated with "the big bang," that the world was changing was too obvious to bear notice. But Davis's sermon made me pause to consider the significant implications of this fact of change. If the world is not finished, if it is still changing, evolving, then we should not expect a perfect world. The evil we find in the world became, for Davis, our marching orders: There is work to do, work to make the world better. Our work.

Change was a palpably obvious feature of the times my grandparents lived through, and, indeed, something our current time shares with that of my grandparents: small village craft industry life to artificial intelligence and nanotechnology. Modernity, through the scientific revolution and the industrial revolution, ushered in the world of change we became accustomed to.

Like governance, once you recognize it, change is both obvious and important. Beyond being Davis's solution to the problem of evil, change demands institutions—including religious institutions—that can manage change. Davis spoke at some length of the need for religion to keep up, to remain relevant and useful. Traditional worship was not enough.

12. Davis and Kopf, "Democracy Versus Authority" (1936).

13. Davis, "Travail and Pain" (1909a).

In light of the importance of change in the modern world, my third surprise was the importance of the Bible for Davis. I had put off to last a large set of manuscripts Davis wrote in 1916 on the *Origins and History of the Bible*,[14] fourteen lectures comprising well over two hundred full-size typed pages, with extensive references from first-rate biblical scholarship. I suppose I shouldn't have been surprised. He was a minister after all. But his emphasis on modernity, on change, on individual responsibility to think through religious questions, all suggested to me that a two thousand-year-old text might not be so central or important in his thinking. Wrong!

There were many other surprises along the way: Davis's commitment to democratic socialism and his involvement in the labor movement during the first two decades of the twentieth century. I also learned that he spent five months at Camp Devons in Massachusetts during 1917–18 providing religious support for the troops training to enter World War I.[15] To make some extra money he spent some time as an "investigator" (as far as I can tell this was in the nature of market research) for the full-fashioned Hosiery Industry of Philadelphia.[16]

A different kind of surprise was Davis's attachment to rural life, almost to the point of romantic idealism. Among his writings was a 1916 manuscript, "The Other End of a Shad Dinner."[17] I admit I did not know what a "shad dinner" was until I learned from the manuscript that it is a fish dinner. The manuscript first describes a spring 1916 night out in Boston with his wife Annie; they had a shad dinner. The manuscript then moves to their 1916 family summer vacation on an island in the Kennebec River in Maine.[18] In addition to farming, islanders supported themselves catching and selling shad to Boston restaurants among other places. Here was the "other end" of his shad dinner. Davis had a deeply romantic attachment to the way of life on the island.

> Is that life we found at the Island a bit of the Utopian past, the tail to the shad, whose head carries us to the city with its hurry,

14. Davis, *Origins and History* (1916a).

15. Davis, "Five Months at Camp Devens" (1919b).

16. These details are outlined in Davis's Unitarian Ministerial Personnel file, now kept in the archives at the Harvard Divinity School Library.

17. Davis, "Other End of a Shad Dinner" (1916b).

18. Various internal clues allowed me to identify this island as Swan Island, now a state nature preserve, which lies a little upstream from Bath and opposite Richmond, Maine.

> and its pressure its loss of the poise and the dignity of life in the senseless round of activity. Or is there, in that Island life, a permanent element of human achievement to the attainment of which we must arrive thru the malaise of our confusing modern city life. Which end of the shad dinner would you rather take part in, the end that caught the shad and produced or the end that consumed the shad?[19]

Perhaps ironically, a few years after Earl and Annie's 1916 vacation on Swan Island, the island was vacated by its longtime permanent residents. It was no longer economically viable to live there.[20]

5. Natural Religion

As I wrote and transcribed, I went through various titles. The first complete draft of this book was titled, *Discovery, Freedom, and Consent,* and it focused on the governance surprise. A different pass, prompted by *change*, was titled, *An Epistle to Nones.* But after working through Davis's work on the Bible, a more salient feature of Davis's thought emerged for me. Of the Bible, from the scholarship he attended to, he concluded that it was not the revealed word of God. Rather, it was—is—a natural book, "naturally produced and naturally transmitted."[21] Similarly, he wrote of Jesus as a natural man, not some supernatural element of the Trinity. And he found God in nature, human nature included. He focused on heaven on earth, not in some other "supernatural realm." Even his views on immortality were curiously tied to human life in the natural world. He rejected the supernatural. His approach to religion was natural, through and through.

Davis concluded a 1931 lecture he gave—likely to other ministers at a conference of protestant ministers—on "The Results of Protestantism" as follows:

> If there is any validity at all to religion, it must rest upon a foundation which is valid, not only in our modern world of machines and science, but which was valid in the day of the Puritans and the Lollards; in the day of Gregory the Great, and the first missionaries among our barbaric forefathers in Europe. It must rest upon a foundation that was valid in the Roman Empire and in

19. Davis, "Other End of a Shad Dinner" (1916b), 14.

20. Rossel, "Other Swan Island."

21. Davis, "Results of Protestantism" (1931), 6.

> Egypt and will be valid a thousand years hence as well. Back of all the forms which, in the name of religion, mankind has ever created, there is the unconquerable faith and courage that has created them; faith that there are permanent values in human life and that courageous fidelity to those values has its root in the nature of things.[22]

At the core of Davis's faith—his view of the validity to religion—was faith in "permanent values," values that have their "root in the nature of things": *Natural Religion.*

22. Davis, "Results of Protestantism" (1931), 8.

Acknowledgments

THINKING AND WRITING ABOUT religion has brought me to entirely new and unfamiliar terrain, not a comfortable place for my academic self. And yet I found my grandfather's writings so compelling and so strangely timely that I have not been able to resist.

My first debt then must be to my grandfather, Earl Clement Davis (1876–1953), a man I never knew, but a man with whom I now feel deeply connected—thanks to the fact that he saved some of his writings. This book is my journey into his thinking.

And I would not have these writings if not for the fact that his widow, Annie Foster Davis (1880–1964), kept his writings when she moved out of the Petersham parsonage. And, similarly, my mother also kept them. And so, they rested undisturbed in my parents' house for two decades. And again, I have benefitted from the good fortune that my siblings and I kept them. Almost four decades further on, I have been able to read and work with these century-old writings.

Still, I have had to question the wisdom of writing about these religious topics with my absolute lack of background. While my grandfather's writings appeared to me reasoned, informed, sensible—they felt like I could trust them—what did I know? Several people then have encouraged me here.

On that score I must start with my wife, Deanna Leamon, who—unlike me—had a religious upbringing and has insightful intuitions about religion and life. As I shared what I was reading from my grandfather, she insistently urged me to share it more widely. She has been the foundation of my hope that there might be something here that others would respond to. Supportive, encouraging, loving, I could not ask for a better helpmate.

Fortune played a huge role in a friendship my wife and I have enjoyed with Alice Valentine and her husband John—JZ—Zeugner. Alice is a—now retired—Clark University professor; she was the Clark Japanese program. JZ is a—now retired—professor of humanities at Worcester Polytechnic Institute. It just so happens that JZ is both deeply interested in and widely read in religious history and thinking. Furthermore—and here is my great good fortune—he was willing to read and comment on drafts of all the chapters. He has helped this project in innumerable ways: Pointing me to important texts (a few of which found their way into this work); catching embarrassing bloopers; suggesting different approaches to organization; but most fundamentally he encouraged the work. He did this, despite the fact that I am pretty clear that he found my grandfather's outlook overly rosy. I don't think he bought my grandfather's idea that the problem of evil can be resolved by noting that the world is not complete, that there is work to be done. He would respond that no amount of good work will erase the evil in the world. Evil is and will be a profound problem. And, yet he encouraged the work. I could not be more grateful.

I started reading my grandfather's writings after I completed my service as Clark's provost and joined the Clark faculty. For this first, post-provost year Clark gave me a sabbatical. This allowed me time to completely focus and concentrate on my grandfather's writings. After years as provost, working with deadlines-on-deadlines and distractions-on-distractions, this was a great gift, and I thank Clark for this time.

The project did not begin as a book project, but rather as an editing project. I wanted to preserve my grandfather's writings. I scanned them. I transcribed them and I edited the transcriptions. What to do with the results? Laura Robinson, Clark's University Librarian, was enormously helpful here. In addition to encouraging the work she provided Clark's digital commons[1] as a suitable archival destination for the work. Catherine—Katie—Stebbins, Clark's Digital Projects Librarian, then did an enormous amount of work preparing and adding Earl C. Davis's papers to Clark's digital commons.[2] I am deeply grateful to both.

Librarians at the Harvard Divinity School Library also have been tremendously helpful, pointing me to vast troves of religious literature

1. See https://commons.clarku.edu/digitized_materials/.

2. See "Earl Clement Davis Papers."

from the time my grandfather was a student there and as a minister, particularly liberal religious literature. They also made available to me my grandfather's personnel file, which is kept at the Harvard Divinity School Library. Ultimately all the original texts by my grandfather will find their way to being preserved by the Divinity School Library.

Part of the motivation for editing my grandfather's writings was to make them available to my extended family, to my grandfather's "issue." My cousin, Mark Davis, mentioned in the preface, was enthusiastic about this project and helped with some of his own research on our grandfather, and with his IT expertise. My sisters, Brinna Ann Sands and Anne Clement Baird, have confirmed and affirmed my sense that there is something important and compelling in our grandfather's writing. They also had the benefit and privilege of having known him when they were young. Here was one direct window for me into the person who wrote all these sermons. When the task of scanning my grandfather's pages began to overwhelm me, my sisters also provided financial support for me to hire a student scanner.

There have been a few other early readers, all of whom helped in ways large and small, one of whom deserves special mention. Mike Lavin went to graduate school with me. Ultimately, he pursued a career in psychotherapy, not academic philosophy. Our paths largely separated. For reasons unknown to me, he reached out by email as I was hip-deep in writing this book and he became a tireless dependable reader of the chapters as they got done. And as emerges in the afterword, he brought a very important perspective to religious practice that had eluded me. I thank him for this and his support and friendship.

Writing is not easy, and writing about an unfamiliar subject certainly is not easy. All the encouragement I received from these people and many others has been essential. Beyond the writing is publishing, and here again I entered unfamiliar terrain. Who or what kind of publisher would be interested in this work? I had no clue. John Zeugner again came to my rescue, with many suggestions, including Wipf & Stock, with whom he has published. Perhaps most important he simply urged me forward: Send the material out.

I have learned a tremendous amount from my grandfather. It has been exhilarating coming to appreciate him and his times, his perspective on the world. His melding of religious, social, ethical and political matters, all informed by a deep appreciation of history, has profoundly moved me, changed my own thinking. Knowledgeable about the past, still his primary concern was with the future. He saw great things in the future, not technological things—although he was excited by the rapidly advancing technology of his day—he saw great advances for human flourishing in the future. In this he was a man of his "progressive" times. We "postmoderns" are less confident. But as a matter of choice are we not better facing the future "not with fear and despair, but in faith and confidence, buoyant in spirit, strong in purpose, keen to contribute to the age to come whatsoever of the Life Spirit dwells within each one"?[3]

3. Davis, "Not Revelation" (1947a), 5.

Chapter 1: **An Epistle to *Nones***

> However great the past may have been, in remote ages or in more immediate centuries, whatever of wisdom may have been gleaned from the experiences of the centuries, the startling truth faces us that we, the living and the generations to come after us, are the vital agents through which that life spirit, call it by whatever name you will, moves out of the past into the age to come.[1]

1. Nones

My mother's father, Earl C. Davis, was a Unitarian minister from 1905 until his death in 1953. My father, nominally brought up Baptist, did not attend church. He was a scientist and entrepreneur who, as it appeared to me as a youngster, had little time for or interest in religion.[2] My mother clearly identified with the Unitarian church of her father and she served on our local Unitarian church's parish committee, but she did not attend services. Perhaps she felt she had done enough attending services growing up with her father's weekly sermons. Perhaps this was a consequence of her marriage to my father. The upshot for me was that church was never part of my life growing up.

I had friends of many faiths and as middle-schoolers we would discuss religion. But I didn't know where I stood. If anything, Unitarian,

1. Davis, "Not Revelation" (1947a), 5.

2. In 1936 my father founded a company, Baird Associates (subsequently Baird Atomic, subsequently Baird Inc.) that made scientific instruments. I have written about some of this work in my *Thing Knowledge*.

but what did that mean? I have a vivid memory, from sometime in my middle school years, of asking my mother, "What *do* Unitarians believe?" Her response, coming promptly and in her sharply pointed way: "There is no creed!" Whatever that meant! It was as if I had asked a forbidden question, and I left it at that.

And I grew up with no membership in any religious institution and no religious affiliation. Today such people are called "*nones*." I am a *none*. I didn't know I was a *none* until, for reasons I'll come to, I began to read widely in religion shortly after I left my work in academic administration in July 2021. I learned about *nones*. It is a kind of deflating label, *nones*, nothings, a kind of void, and we know nature abhors a vacuum. Yet, I've never felt a void, or an urgent need to let something fill up some empty space in me. I am a curious person, and I have greatly enjoyed learning more about religion. But still I have not attended religious services or joined a church. I may yet, but for now—2024—I am still a *none*, and not unhappy about it.

When my son was young—very likely when he was in middle school himself—he asked me about religion and God. The memory I have of this moment is indistinct on particulars, but clear on my realization that I had no good answers for him. I was embarrassed. Surely an academic philosopher should have *something* useful to offer on this topic. I had nothing. It is not that I feel some kind of spiritual void at the core of my being. Rather it is that I should have some understanding of religion and its claims to our attention. Something to offer my son. I had learned from my mother that church somehow is important. I just didn't know why.

It turns out that *nones* are ascendant. In the second, 2023 edition of his book, *The Nones: Where They Came From, Who They Are, and Where They Are Going,* Ryan Burge estimates from various statistical studies that, as of 2023, the *nones* constitute about 30 percent of the population of the United States, a number that has been growing significantly since the 1970s—when the *nones* were perhaps 5 percent of the population—and particularly in the decade after 2010, with growth from the mid-teens to 30 percent of the population.[3]

Jessica Grose, *New York Times* opinion writer, wrote a very interesting series of editorials in 2023 about the twenty-first-century phenomenon of Americans moving away from religion. Grose was upfront with her own stance:

3. Burge, *Nones*, 27–31.

> As I started my reporting, my own feelings about the rise of nones were somewhat ambivalent; I'm Jewish and still have a strong cultural identity, but I'm not observant. I don't miss shul and have little desire to return, yet I feel a bit heartsick about not passing down Jewish rituals with more consistency for my children.[4]

I don't have even this ambivalence. I was brought up in a secular way. There are traditions I hope I have passed on to my son, but they are more about thinking rationally, mindfully, open to new experience and information, different points of view—along with some quirky family Thanksgiving rituals. I don't miss religion.

So why am I writing about *nones*, about religion? Why "An Epistle to *Nones*"? While I've never felt a void, or an unmet religious need, I have found something in my recent reading that has struck a chord. Not something that has upset my *none*-ness so much as something that has offered a way of thinking about religious questions that squares with my commitments to the natural—not supernatural—world, to reasoned discussion, to learning from experience, to being open to different points of view.

When I say "thinking about religious questions" I mean thinking about such questions as: Why are we here? What about God, or Jesus? Where do good and evil come from, and what can we do to diminish evil and increase good? What—if anything—happens after we die? What is faith, and what role should it play in a world of evidence and reason? How can we manage deeply depressing and challenging personal and societal setbacks? I began this work during COVID lockdowns. This was a difficult, depressing time, a time that shook even my generally optimistic outlook.

Questions like these have frequently been answered by religion. God provides answers. But then, for me anyway, this immediately begs the question of what is God? How do we know there is a God? Organized religions provide differing answers. But I've never found these answers compelling. Typically, they turn on some supernatural element that is discovered by revelation. Experience and reason need not apply. Instead, lean into faith in that revelation. But one person's revelation can be another person's hocus pocus. And we have no good way to resolve such differences. Religious wars have been the result.

4. Grose, "What Churches Offer."

These religious questions are hard. I have lived most of my life trying to avoid them. And most of the time this is not difficult, just focus on the job at hand. Let the big mysteries of life figure themselves out. Life as a *none*.

2. My Grandfather, Earl Clement Davis

I was drawn into reading and thinking about religion by my grandfather, Earl Clement Davis. Born on June 3, 1876, he died May 19, 1953, eleven months before I was born. So I never met him or knew him. But the things people said about him were positive and loving. My parents, who agreed on little, agreed he was a wonderful person.

In 1981, when I graduated with my PhD in philosophy of science, my mother gave me her father's academic robes. They appeared as "generic" doctoral robes, all black with three velvet stripes on each sleeve. For many years I wore them to commencement exercises, until, as I was told by a tailor, the cotton had become so rotten that they could neither be repaired or saved.

The author in 1981 wearing Earl C. Davis's 1904 graduation robe

The note that my mother wrote with the gift says:

> From Earl Clement Davis
>
> To his namesake, Davis Baird
>
> I wish you two had known each other—you would have had much to enjoy, and he would have been very happy and proud. (Me too!) Much love, M.

I already knew I had been named after my grandfather. The story I learned as a young person was that both my mother and my aunt Patsy became pregnant shortly after my grandfather's death. Both children were named after their recently deceased common grandfather. My cousin got his first name, Earl; I got his last name, Davis.

More important than the—now long gone—academic robes, I inherited through my mother an old trunk full of my grandfather's writings. I've been carting this trunk around for decades while I pursued my academic career. The trunk started its career in Petersham, Massachusetts, as my widowed grandmother vacated the Petersham Unitarian parsonage in 1954. It came with her to my parents' home in Lexington, Massachusetts. Sometime after both my parents had died, probably around 1990, it came to me in Columbia, South Carolina, where it sat while I continued with my academic career at the University of South Carolina. In 2010, it moved with me to Worcester, Massachusetts, when I took up the job of provost of Clark University.

The trunk that carried Earl C. Davis's saved manuscripts

In 2021, when I left my position as provost of Clark University, I finally had time to open the trunk and read what was inside. My mother was right: my grandfather and I "would have had much to enjoy." He brought to his sermons a historian's sense of the importance of the past and its bearing on the present, and a philosopher's appreciation for principle and argument. My own academic work in the history and philosophy of science and technology shares these commitments. He was completely committed to experience, evidence, and reason. Revelation and the supernatural had no part in his religion. I was surprised at what I was reading.

My voyage of getting to know my grandfather began out of curiosity. Who was this person after whom I was named, and what did he think? I also felt a kind of obligation to my larger family—the "issue" of Earl C. Davis and his wife, Annie F. Davis—to make his writings available to them. Over the past two plus years I have scanned, transcribed, and edited the trunkful of his writings, well over three hundred documents. The results are posted on my website.[5] They are also being preserved in Clark University's Digital Commons.[6]

As I worked through my grandfather's writings, satisfying my curiosity about him, I found myself asking the religious questions that I had heretofore avoided. Remarkably, he shared some of my misgivings about organized religion—but not about the importance of religious questions. From his point of view, thinking about the deep mysteries of life, about good and evil, about life and death, is a human necessity. It just happens, whether we do it consciously and mindfully or not.

Thinking about these questions is hard, and people try to avoid it—I have tried to avoid it—but the questions are still there, quietly nagging in the background, as life tumbles forward. In my grandfather's view, each individual has to find their own answers. If the answers from a religious organization do not work, so much the worse for the organization. But the questions, the human hopes and fears, aspirations and challenges, these questions, all remain.

I was surprised by what I was daily reading and editing. While I have no doubt that we would have disagreed—argued—about many details, had we the opportunity, there was much about my grandfather's

5. See Baird, "Earl Clement Davis."

6. See "Earl Clement Davis Papers."

approach to religion appealed to me. It is an approach that could appeal to a *none*.

3. Finding Hope

I began doing this work when the world was eighteen months into the COVID pandemic. I had spent a trying year-and-a-half helping to manage Clark University through the onset of COVID. This was challenging, exhausting work, as we had to reimagine and reimplement most of the basic elements of a small liberal arts education. Small, intimate, in-person classes were out. Remote learning was the thing. Research resources had to be available digitally. Students—and faculty and staff—were suffering.

After I left that role, and while the pandemic continued to wreak havoc, surprisingly I found that editing my grandfather's sermons was a tonic for me. I became addicted to them, to my daily dose of how to think positively about the future in the face of a bleak present. My grandfather did not offer a saccharine or false positivity, but rather something that felt genuine, something even a skeptical philosopher—or a *none*—could find persuasive.

One of the first sermons I worked on had the—for me—rather opaque title, "Not Revelation but Discovery; Not Forms but the Holy Spirit." My grandfather wrote it in 1947, in the aftermath of World War II: sixty million people dead, the Holocaust, anticolonialist revolutions, the treacheries of Joseph Stalin's Soviet Union. My grandfather wrote about how people were

> discouraged by the current confusion of the world, the wars, the revolutions, the slipping standards of what we call religion, the animosities of a divided Christendom, the conflicts of religions. How sad, how devastating. We are on the down grade, slipping from bad to worse. We have lost the faith once delivered to the saints. Oh, for the good old days, Revive the past, return to the doctrines and methods of an age that is gone.[7]

I was astonished; these words could have been written today. Certainly, as I was daily reading the "COVID numbers," and hoping for release from this scourge, the past looked pretty good. Add to this the war in Ukraine, the war between Israel and Hamas, and, yes, things don't feel good.

7. Davis, "Not Revelation" (1947a), 1.

My grandfather would have none of this counsel of despair. Don't look to the past. Look to the future. Life is always moving forward. My grandfather, while deeply knowledgeable about the past, was always looking to a better future. Not a future made better by some external divine intervention, by some savior, but a future made better by us, the living, and our commitment to a better future:

> Age after age we have discovered some bit of insight into the nature of that life stream in which we move from age to age, but its steady flow, its unexhausted power still calls us, not from the past but from the age to come. However great the past may have been, in remote ages or in more immediate centuries, whatever of wisdom may have been gleaned from the experiences of the centuries, the startling truth faces us that we, the living and the generations to come after us, are the vital agents through which that life spirit, call it by whatever name you will, moves out of the past into the age to come. We should face it all not with fear and despair, but in faith and confidence, buoyant in spirit, strong in purpose, keen to contribute to the age to come whatsoever of the Life Spirit dwells within each one.[8]

The *none* in me has some skepticism about his concept of "the life spirit," a skepticism I come to in the pages that follow. But the core point here—that "we the living and the generations to come after us" are responsible for ensuring a better future, that for generations and generations past, our ancestors have risen to this responsibility, and they have done so in the face of challenges more daunting than those that face us today—that resonated with me.

We can do this. We must do this. It will take work. It won't yield instant gratification. It is being human, being part of, and contributing to, the ongoing process by which the future emerges out of the past. We are part of this life stream. We find hope when we see and understand ourselves as part of this bigger story, human history, or as my grandfather put it, the unexhausted power of the ongoing life stream.

4. Truth and Authority

My grandfather was enthralled by science and industry, and the progress made possible by scientific discovery. He found my father's scientific

8. Davis, "Not Revelation" (1947a), 5.

entrepreneurial work fascinating, exciting—clearly a reason *both* of my parents were attracted to him. In 1950, he wrote his fifteen-year-old first grandson, Jock Davis,

> It has been great fun living in an age that has done so much in the way of invention. One day at the Baird Associates I had in my hand a bit of apparatus that was shot up into the air at White Sands a distance of 106 miles.[9]

I hadn't expected this from a religious person. Religion is frequently presented in opposition to science, an opposition that seems to emerge out of methods and sources of knowledge. Standard canned approaches to the history of science frequently represent religion holding to ultimately indefensible positions in the face of scientific progress. One thinks of the conflict between the Catholic Church and Galileo or the conflict between Darwinian evolution and the book of Genesis.

Religious discovery—so I believed—arrives by revelation, or supernatural intervention—God speaking to us—or perhaps spiritual intuition. Religion, it seemed to me, invited interminable and unresolvable differences of opinion and conflict. Different people will hear God differently, if they hear God at all, if God even exists, if God speaks to us.

Science, while it lives in differences of opinion, has widely agreed-upon ways to resolve differences of opinion, through publicly sharable experience and experiment. Conflict resolution by revelation and authority is not part of the picture—at least not part of the *ideal* of scientific discovery. But then here was my grandfather, enthusiastic about scientific discovery, finding no conflict between religion and science, indeed finding the discoveries of science exciting, feeding his religious interests.

My grandfather found a different conflict behind the supposed conflict between science and religion. He found a conflict between freedom and authoritarianism.

In a sermon my grandfather gave in 1942, the tercentenary of Galileo's death, "From Copernicus to Galileo," he tells the story of the conflict between the Catholic Church and the idea that the earth revolves around the sun.[10] In his telling we learn of Nicolai Copernicus

9. Davis, Letter to Jock Davis (1950). Jock Davis is the son of John—Earl and Annie's first son—and Priscilla Davis. During the late 1940s my father's company, Baird Associates, designed the spectrographic instruments that were put into V2 rockets captured from Germany at the end of World War II. These instruments provided the first data on the chemical composition of the upper atmosphere.

10. Davis, "From Copernicus to Galileo" (1942a).

(1473–1543) and the publication of his 1543 book *On the Revolutions of the Heavenly Spheres*; we learn of Giordano Bruno's (1548–1600) being burned at the stake for supporting Copernicus's ideas; we learn of Galileo Galilei's (1564–1642) struggles with the church and his observations of the heavenly bodies with the newly discovered telescope. And we learn that it was not until 1822—180 years after Galileo's death—when the church finally "allowed" the printing and publication of works treating of the motion of the earth.

Why was this history important to Davis? He wrote,

> Some appreciation of this first great conflict between authority and freedom, between dogma and truth, is necessary in order to appreciate the nature of the conflicts, the character of the forces interested, and above all the fundamental principles involved in the problems of modern life. For after all, while the questions of the facts at stake in the controversy over the problems of astronomy are important, the fundamental principle of importance was whether truth should be a source of authority, or authority the alleged source of truth. That conflict is still on, and with increasing intensity is being forced into our range of vision today. With surprising ignorance in various forms, and clothing, the old beast of authority is being presented to us as the panacea for all our evils, social, individual, intellectual, moral, and artistic. History has demonstrated the viciousness of this kind of a master.[11]

The story of Copernicus, Bruno, Galileo, and the Catholic Church is not a story of conflict between religion and science, but a story of conflict between authority and truth, "whether truth should be a source of authority, or authority the alleged source of truth." It was important for Davis to recall this conflict in 1942, not because it exposes weaknesses religious belief, but because "the old beast of authority" was active in Davis's world of 1942. And, alas, our world of 2024.

For Davis, the method of science was *the* route to truth and to human freedom:

> More important than the defense of any fact or dogma, or any doctrine, is the loyal persistent, fearless devotion to this method of science. Following this we have broken down pretty nearly all the old dogmatic standards of feudalism. It has been our cloud by day and our pillar of fire by night that has led us forward

11. Davis, "From Copernicus to Galileo" (1942a), 2.

> through the centuries. It is our guide now. We are dealing with subtle problems in our day, but the principle is the same, the open mind, ready for new truth, ready to risk that truth in the open arena. To this principle, to this method above all else we are dedicated.[12]

To this principle—the principle of having an open mind ready for new truth, and ready to risk that truth in the open arena—above all else, Davis was dedicated. This was astonishing to me. This was an approach to religious questions that I could find congenial, an approach that might work for a *none*—and at least this *none*.

Work in the history and philosophy of science has shown without doubt that power and authority have played central roles in the resolution of scientific differences. Science as practiced is not free of the "beast of authority." But the *ideal* of science, of truth as a source of authority and not vice versa, remains. It is this ideal that brings an element of tragic interest to incidents in the history of science that have not lived up to this ideal. And it is to this ideal that above all else Davis was dedicated.

For Davis, putting authority ahead of truth was the problem. This was his biggest concern:

> Today as yesterday the principles are the same. Authority comes to us with many beautiful raiments, but behind them all the skeleton in the closet of civilization.[13]

Davis found authority in what he called "authority religion," a form of religion he vigorously resisted. But he also found authority in monarchical systems of government, or fascism, or indeed, Soviet State Communism. He found authority in certain forms of unfettered capitalism, what he sometimes called "the monarchy of money." Authority comes in "many beautiful raiments." The conflict he saw was not between science and religion, it was between authority and open-ended, ongoing discovery—scientific discovery by experience and experiment.

12. Davis, "From Copernicus to Galileo" (1942a), 7–8. In my religious ignorance, the curious passage Davis uses, "It has been our cloud by day and our pillar of fire by night," was new to me. It is from Exod 13:21–22; it describes how God led the Israelites from slavery and exile in Egypt to the promised land.

13. Davis, "From Copernicus to Galileo" (1942a), 8.

5. Bearing My Burden

Davis's approach to religious questions was unlike any I had previously encountered. Now, my initial curiosity about my grandfather and his religious beliefs began to morph into something different, more philosophical, something closer to my professional life. What kind of answers to religious questions flow from this principle of discovery, from having an open mind "ready for new truth, ready to risk that truth in the open arena"? What kind of a God emerges from this approach to religion and religious belief? It seemed almost entirely contrary to what I had unreflectively believed about religion. Religion based on scientific discovery, how could that work?

The book that follows began to take shape as these questions pressed themselves upon me. I took up the various questions that my grandfather's approach to religion seemed to raise, questions about God, about Jesus, about the Bible, about heaven, the afterlife, about faith.

In one of his early sermons in 1904, "Man's Responsibility,"[14] Davis argued that each person must find their own way to their religious and moral lives. Taking it on authority—again, the problem—authority from some other source, whether it be "God," the Bible, Jesus, a church's religious creed, is not sufficient. The biblical text for the sermon is Gal 6:5, "For every man shall bear his own burden." With my grandfather's help, I began to bear my burden.

6. Discovery, Freedom, and Consent

While the principle of discovery—not revelation—is the foundation of Davis's approach to religion, two additional principles—freedom and consent—join with discovery. As I will show in greater depth, for Davis, the purpose of religion and religious practice is to promote the most abundant life possible for all living human beings. Davis characterized an abundant life in terms of discovery, freedom, and consent. Humans—all humans—should be afforded the greatest freedom to live their lives, to discover their worlds, to pursue their ambitions and ideals.

Freedom, for Davis, was at once both individual and communal. If my individual freedom interferes with your individual freedom—if I am allowed to force my freedom on you, to force your obedience without

14. Davis, "Man's Responsibility" (1904c).

your consent—we do not have full human freedom. Freedom and consent work together to allow us *together* to carve out a path of maximal individual and communal freedom.

Davis was reverently proud of American democracy, which he contrasted with authoritarian forms of governance. In a proper democracy, American democracy running right as he thought of it, everyone has a voice. We come together, not necessarily in agreement, but in engagement, to find the best way forward for all, to find a maximal path of individual and communal freedom.

Discovery, freedom, and consent—as opposed to revelation, authority, and obedience—this, I learned, was the basis for my grandfather's approach religion, indeed his approach to life. It lies behind all his sermons.[15]

Heaven on earth—not heaven in some afterlife—was Davis's concern. He was deeply concerned about and attentive to constraints on freedom and systems of obedience. He came of age with the Civil War and slavery a part of living memory. He was well aware of "the race problem." So too with the enfranchisement of women; Davis's wife, Annie Foster Davis, was an active suffragette in the first years of the twentieth century. And then there was the emergence during the nineteenth century of a brutal international capitalism. Workers were being denied freedom and consent, and labor problems, with multiple violent worker strikes, were prominent. My grandfather was an active, vocal socialist in response. To be clear, he was a *democratic* socialist, seeing no conflict between democracy and socialism. But socialism was the political route he saw to curbing the excesses of capitalism, to curbing the monarchy of money.

Unfortunately, the problems Davis was concerned with—race, enfranchisement, economic inequality, the excesses of capitalism—do not feel dated. The particulars are different, but the more I read my grandfather's writings, the more they felt relevant to current times. The

15. This view is perhaps most forcefully expressed in a 1936 paper he cowrote with Carl Heath Kopf. They conclude this paper, "In short, the sweep of the social economy of our time is away from the totalitarian order of the middle-ages with its concepts of Revelation, Authority, and Obedience, towards an order whose distinguishing concepts are freedom, discovery, and consent. In spite of atavistic reactions, in both Church and State, the future is with freedom, discovery, consent. The intellectual, the scientific and the religious advance of centuries combines with events in the political and industrial order towards the realization of this tendency. Within the field of religion and values, as elsewhere, the principles of freedom and fellowship, tested in experience, are valid guides to which complete allegiance may be given." Davis and Kopf, "Democracy Versus Authority" (1936), 10.

old beast of authority, with its many beautiful raiments, continues to challenge us.

7. An Epistle to Nones

Among the books of the New Testament are a group of "Epistles," letters offering support and guidance to some group, such as the apostle Paul's various epistles to Romans, to Corinthians, to Galatians, etc. The Scripture reading that Davis used in his 1947 sermon discussed above was from Heb 3:1–15, another of the Epistles of the New Testament. In the sermon Davis writes:

> The Epistle to the Hebrews . . . is a living document if one takes the trouble to penetrate the meaning of it in terms of the situation to which it was addressed. . . . Written sometime between 80 and 90 A.D., during the reign of Domitian, by an unknown person to those refugee "Christians" who came together in Rome, this amazing document was an appeal to the wavering and frightened and discouraged folk living amid the terrors of their day. . . . They had been through the terrors of the reign of Nero, they had suffered all sorts of humiliations and indignities. They had survived, some of them, and now, half a century after the death of Jesus, they faced another persecution. . . . The old enthusiasm had weakened. . . . Freedom had not come. Paul's belief in the immediate return of Christ to redeem his world was to many of them a broken promise. Why cling to such vague and unrewarding beliefs? Why not take their fun where they find it? Why not forsake the lost cause of freedom and faith? After all one has to live in the world as it is. To face another persecution, well, what for?
>
> How like the world of today? Change a few words and phrases, names and localities, dogmas and teachings, and the Epistle to the Hebrews comes alive. It has something to say.[16]

The Epistle to the Hebrews, as Davis understood it, offered some solace, some reason for hope, some reason for those discouraged first-century "Hebrew-Christians" to keep the faith. The epistle's message was one of commitment to the future, to the idea that "we the living and the generations to come after us" create the future. We the living are responsible for ensuring a better future.

16. Davis, "Not Revelation" (1947a), 2–3.

Still true today. Over eons of history, "we the living" have risen to this challenge. Current life may not be perfect, but it is better than life hundreds of years ago. It is better because of the efforts of past humans committing to the future—our present. And so, today we too can commit for future generations. Following the Epistle to the Hebrews, Davis found hope in seeing oneself as part of this never-ending path out of the past into the future. A pathway of progress, as he saw it.

My grandfather's writings have been an epistle to me, providing a pathway through religious questions that takes the questions seriously, offering serious plausible answers, while also taking seriously the possibility of—indeed the historical fact of—learning more as we gain more experience in the world. Learning more about the natural and social worlds we live in *and* learning more about these religious questions. Answers to questions, religious questions included, are never final. We learn more day-by-day, century-by-century. My grandfather's "epistle" has offered me a pathway of hope for the future, hope based in seeing myself as part of a centuries-long process, a process out of darkness into light, and yet a process where we are always confined to stumbling around, doing our best, in a dim half-light. No panacea. No finished product. Only an ongoing process which gives meaning and hope to our daily toil.

And so, with humility and thanks to my grandfather's wisdom, I am sharing some of my grandfather's thought, his epistle to me, a *none*. What follows is a kind of dialogue between a Unitarian minister and a *none*. It is not a call to return to some religion, some established church, synagogue, or temple. Instead, it offers a way to think about religious questions, a way to live in our ongoing, rushing, demanding, difficult world. A way to live with hope for the future, to live with an understanding of one's place in the life stream with its unexhausted power moving out of the past into the ages to come.

8. The Arc of My Story

What *do* Unitarians believe, I asked my mother. When I started this project with my grandfather's writings, I wanted answers to this question. I anticipated learning about my grandfather's stances concerning the Bible, Jesus, God, heaven, life after death, faith, etc. I was curious what he would have to say about these topics.

The first big surprise was Davis's focus on governance. How should religious questions—religious differences—be resolved? Who gets to decide—if anyone? Out of these concerns came Davis's emphasis on the transition from medieval revelation, authority, and obedience to modern discovery, freedom, and consent. Modern people should have the freedom to think through these issues for themselves—individually and collectively. Indeed, they have the responsibility to do so.

One thing I know from previous philosophical investigations, the path usually is inward: What lies behind this view, and then behind that view? The path is more like peeling an onion, layer by layer. I started down this road expecting answers to the question I asked my mother. Instead, I found governance. I found "modern" discovery, freedom, and consent. But behind governance I found something more fundamental still: change. The modern world is a world of change, not stasis. Behind "discovery, freedom, and consent," is change itself.

The modern world emerged out of a more static medieval world. There was a series of convulsive and massive changes starting with the humanism of the Renaissance, and sweeping forward with scientific discovery—Copernicus, Galileo, Newton, Darwin, etc.—the Reformation and the complicated emergence of Protestantism. The industrial revolution.

Davis lived in a world of change, and he sought ways to embrace change. This prompted governance, with discovery, freedom, and consent. But there is more to change. Change implies that things are not finished; this is where my story begins, chapter 2: The Unfinished Universe.

That the world is changing is an empirical—experienced—fact. The massive sweeping changes of the modernizing, industrializing world that Davis inhabited in the transition between the nineteenth and twentieth centuries were breathtaking. Not surprisingly, these changes were hugely anxiety provoking. And the pace of change has not let up. The twenty-first century continues forward with breathtaking, awe-inspiring, and anxiety-provoking change. Will artificial intelligence bring the end of humanity?

This fact of change underlies everything. It is not going away. More than discovery, freedom, and consent, it is change, ongoing, accelerating, bewildering change, that characterizes the modern world. Our world, even if we occasionally call ourselves "postmodern."

Davis was excited by the changes underway in the modern world. While the sources of change are many and complex, for Davis, the most essential point was that humans have a role in directing change. The fact that humans can imagine a better world, that we have aspirations and ideals, is essential. As we imagine a better world, so we can take steps to create a better world. We can make positive change.

Change is difficult—emotionally and socially, but also conceptually. Davis saw positive change. But by what measure do we conclude that the changes taking place are positive? This question gets particularly challenging when we realize that the concepts themselves are changing. Davis was confident and optimistic about the changes underway being positive. Recent generations have been less confident, less optimistic. This is part of the dialogue that chapter 2 opens.

Davis spoke of the ideals of truth, beauty, and goodness, and how they drive positive change. In an unfinished universe, a universe where human ideals help direct human actions, and where human actions can make for a better world, it is the human ideals that matter most. This, then, is my next stop, chapter 3: Truth, Beauty, and Goodness.

Davis was encouraged that with our ideals of truth, beauty, and goodness, we would find ways to direct change, to improve the unfinished universe. He saw this happening in his day. The move away from revelation, authority, and obedience to discovery, freedom, and consent was—in his view—a big advance for humanity. He saw this in the increasing industrial productivity that offered ways to support each individual human personality to live more abundant lives. He saw his modern world in contrast to the nasty, brutish and short[17] lives of most medievals. To him, this justified his optimism. Truth, beauty, and goodness were winning—even if too slowly and with setbacks every step of the way.

Today we are less confident that truth, beauty, and goodness are winning. Indeed, we are less confident of what truth, beauty, and goodness are. Part of what characterizes the "postmodern world" is a loss of faith in human progress.

Davis would not be surprised. Recall his reading of the Epistle to the Hebrews, an "appeal to the wavering and frightened and discouraged folk living amid the terrors of their day." "Keep the faith," said the author of the Epistle to Hebrews. "Keep the faith," said Davis to the discouraged people of his day who had just come through World War II with all its horrors. Keep the faith, even today. We can create a better future. This is the continuing dialogue about change of chapter 3.

17. A phrase frequently quoted from Thomas Hobbes. See his *Leviathan*, 84.

Finally, with these inner elements of the onion exposed—change and human ideals—Davis's approach to more standard religious questions, the questions I started with, begin to make sense.

Davis rejected supernatural answers. The approach to religion he advocates is thoroughly "natural," grounded in the world of experience, and the processes of finding truth through experience and experiment, but also in recognizing that what we learn can be overturned by future learning. Change happens to what we know too. Humility and openness to different points of view characterized his approach.

I begin with the Bible in chapter 4: A Natural Book. Since Davis drew from the Bible to discuss other topics—Jesus, God, heaven, life after death, faith—we need to understand how he viewed his source material. Davis argued—persuasively to me—that the Bible is a natural book, written by humans, not supernaturally revealed truth.

Similarly, Davis argued that Jesus is a natural human (chapter 5), not a uniquely divine element of the Trinity. Indeed, from Davis's point of view, it is Jesus' humanity that underlies his greatest appeal and power. It is Jesus' powerful human personality that Davis was most impressed with.

God, too, is natural for Davis (chapter 6). Indeed, God *is* nature—including human nature, human personality, as Davis put it. Davis's pantheism is subtle and interesting, with genuine commitments to the importance and power of human personality.

Whatever heaven might be, it is heaven on earth (chapter 7)—"natural heaven"—that interested Davis. How can we take steps to move toward heaven on earth? This was the question that he focused on. This, also, was where his democratic socialism was anchored.

For all these religious matters—the Bible, Jesus, God, heaven—Davis offered natural interpretations. Nothing supernatural. He even found a way to describe immortality naturally, immortality here and now (chapter 8).

The natural world—the rewards of experience, the operations of science—do not provide guarantees. New discoveries will displace old—even cherished—beliefs. Here was Davis's faith, faith in the natural world, faith in human ability to learn from the natural world (chapter 9). Not a credulous faith, not an arrogant faith, but a humble faith, and yet a genuine commitment, a commitment to the natural world and to the human possibilities for its improvement. No final answers here, but an approach to answers that I have found helpful, encouraging, supportive, an approach that avoids the supernatural—what I call "Natural Religion."

Chapter 2: **The Unfinished Universe**

> The universe is not made, but is being made, it is not completed but is in the midst of a great process of evolution whose beginning we cannot even guess at and whose day of completion is infinitely remote.[1]

1. Annie and Earl

SOMETIME AFTER MY GRANDFATHER died in May 1953, his widow had to vacate the Petersham, Massachusetts, Unitarian parsonage she had been living in for twenty years. Annie Foster Davis, née Dodge, my grandmother, came to Lexington Massachusetts, to live with her daughter—my mother—bringing with her, among her life possessions, the trunk of her husband's writings. She lived with us until the early 1960s when her progressive dementia required more expertise and care than my mother alone could provide. She was moved to a "rest home" not far from our house. I remember tagging along with my mother's visits to the rest home. I have only a few other memories of my grandmother. I was too young. I remember making shadow figures on the wall with our hands, a rabbit, a dog, that kind of thing. That was fun. I remember her as gentle and calm. She died on Christmas Eve, 1964, age eighty-four.

I do have a very vivid memory from my grandmother's funeral service in January 1965. Someone noted that she found it remarkable to have lived from the time of horse and buggy to space flight. That description

1. Davis, "Travail and Pain" (1909a), 2.

of her lifespan has stayed with me. My ten-year-old self-thought, "Horse and buggy!" That was unimaginable. The world I lived in was "modern," with cars and color televisions and jet airplanes. Horse and buggy was television fiction. Evidently not for my grandparents.[2]

Annie Foster Dodge was born in 1880 outside of Philadelphia. After her father died when she was ten, she, her mother, and her siblings moved to Billerica, Massachusetts. They took in lodgers, one of whom, in 1897, was the new principal of the local public high school, the Howe School. The principal, Earl Clement Davis, had just graduated from Bowdoin College; he was twenty-one years old, and had his first full-time adult job.

At the end of his first year, in June 1898, Davis, as principal, signed the diploma of the young woman in whose home he was lodging, Annie Foster Dodge.[3] Evidently, a relationship had developed, and they shared "an understanding." But Earl first wanted to be clear and confident of his life purpose, his "calling."[4] Here are pictures of Earl C. Davis—in his 1897 Bowdoin graduation photo—and Annie F. Dodge in 1898, age eighteen:

2. In a March 2, 1950, letter to his 15-year-old—oldest—grandson, Jock Davis (son of John and Priscilla Davis), Earl C. Davis wrote, "I used to ride horse-back quite a lot. We had a black horse named Dick. He liked to buck me off."

3. You can see the diploma at the digital "Earl Clement Davis Papers" archive: https://commons.clarku.edu/before_1902/2/.

4. In a birthday note to Annie for her sixty-eighth birthday in 1948 Earl wrote, "The baby girl of some few years ago grew into a teenage High School girl with a braid of hair hanging down her back, and, as I remember, a cute little fir cap on her head. Then she became a disturbing, gay dance-loving teacher. Then she promised to share a life with a poor embryo person parson. So, she kept her promise through some hard, but happy years, for him at least. She turned out to be a much beloved and respected mother, and then a wonderful adored and understanding grandmother. Through the years she has continued to grow into a really great person, and hardly a day passes that she does not reveal some surprisingly new quality of a loving and loveable person, and a most companionable mate in the world. So happy birth to you, dear sweetheart of mine, on this May 5, 1948."

Earl C. Davis's Bowdoin graduation photo from 1897. Courtesy of the George J. Mitchell Department of Special Collections & Archives, Bowdoin College Library, Brunswick, Maine

Annie Foster Dodge, high school graduation photo, 1898, age eighteen

The retiring principal of the Howe School, Samuel Tucker, and the also retiring minister of the local Billerica Unitarian church, Christopher Coffin Hussey, had been in their respective positions in Billerica for several decades; they had developed a close relationship, both personally and institutionally. So, when Davis arrived as the new principal of the Howe School, and Minot Simons, a recent graduate of the Harvard Divinity School, arrived as the new Unitarian minister, their relationship was "hard-wired."[5]

While I have no evidence beyond some tidbits, my sense is that my grandfather's relationship with the local Unitarian minister, Minot Simons, helped to set his sights on the ministry—in particular, the Unitarian ministry. In ministry paperwork he describes his religious upbringing as "somewhat Methodist." He enrolled in the Harvard Divinity School full-time in 1902, leaving his post as principal. For the next two years he studied in pursuit of a Bachelor of Sacred Theology, or "STB" degree, which was the normal training at the time for the ministry. He graduated in June 1904.[6] He successfully sought his first ministry, the Unity Church of Pittsfield, Massachusetts, where he was ordained on April 7, 1905. He served there until 1919.[7] In the following graduation photo, Earl C. Davis is seated far left, wearing the academic gown I later wore:

5. The information I have about this period in Earl C. Davis's and Annie F. Dodge's life is quite limited. What I report here I found in an unsigned 1953 obituary for him. You can see the obituary at the "Earl Clement Davis Papers" archive (https://commons.clarku.edu/funeral/3/).

6. You can see the diploma the "Earl Clement Davis papers" archive (https://commons.clarku.edu/education/1/).

7. Surely not a coincidence, the Unity Church in Pittsfield was founded in 1887 with William Wallace Fenn (1862–1932) as its first minister, serving from 1887 to 1890. Ultimately, Fenn went on to a faculty position at the Harvard Divinity School, where he served from 1901 until his death, and where he was dean from 1906 to 1922. Fenn was one of Davis's first teachers and Davis was "one of Fenn's boys," as the coterie of students who surrounded and worked with Fenn were called. See Park, "Address at the Memorial Service," 7: "His boys. They were very dear to him, and he was very dear to them." In this same volume of memorial essays, Davis contributed the "Alumni Tribute," 33–38. Fenn and Davis remained close to the end of Fenn's life, and indeed Davis remained close with Fenn's son, Dan Huntington Fenn Sr. (1897–1989) who also became a Unitarian minister and an administrator in the American Unitarian Association. His son—grandson of William Wallace Fenn—Dan Huntington Fenn Jr. (1923–2020) was one of the last surviving members of President Kennedy's White House senior staff and the founding director of the John F. Kennedy Presidential Library—and in a strange "everything-is-connected" quirk of fate, a resident of Lexington Massachusetts, and member of the Lexington Unitarian Universalist church, the closest thing to the church of my youth.

Earl C. Davis with his 1904 STB graduates from Harvard Divinity School. Davis is seated far left.

Meanwhile, Annie Dodge, after graduating from the Howe School, enrolled in the State Normal School in Lowell, Massachusetts—now the University of Massachusetts, Lowell—where she got a teacher's certificate in June 1900.[8] She took a teaching job in Merrimac, Massachusetts.

Five years later, with his degree in hand, and a permanent position as minister of the Unity Church in Pittsfield, Earl was ready, and he and Annie were married on June 28, 1905. They moved to Pittsfield where Earl took up his ministry and together they started their family with their first child, John, arriving April 16, 1906, followed in turn by Foster, 1908, Byron, 1912, and my mother, Mary, 1915.

2. Horse and Buggy to Space Flight

Sixty years later, at my grandmother's funeral, I would be struck by the fact that she had lived from horse and buggy to spaceflight. To a ten-year-old, sixty years is an infinity. Horse and buggy? She was old. Now, sixty years further on, as a seventy-year-old man, sixty years is long, but clearly not an infinity. Indeed, thinking of the span of history, sixty years is short.

8. You can see the diploma at the "Earl Clement Davis Papers" archive (https://commons.clarku.edu/annie_dodge/2/).

And in that short span, the lifespan of my grandparents, life changed fundamentally, horse and buggy to space flight.

"Modernism" by an academic name. Modernism saw rapid changes in science, technology, industry, capital markets, global trade—and everything else in train. The world became flat, in Thomas Friedman's vivid phrase.[9] Friedman focused on the twenty-first-century globalism, but it was at the dawn of the twentieth century when globalization first accelerated.

From his perch in Pittsfield, Earl C. Davis could see the impacts of modernism—positive and negative. Goods from all over the world were now available in what a few decades earlier had been a small, isolated village in western Massachusetts. General Electric opened a major manufacturing facility in Pittsfield in 1903—a development that in the years ahead would have very significant implications for my grandparents.

Science and industry were advancing rapidly. The discoveries of science were revealing much about our world and our place in it, while in the process putting traditional religious beliefs and practices on the defensive. Industry made enormous strides in productivity, raising the quality of life for many, while also creating ongoing labor problems, with numerous strikes across the country, including at General Electric's Pittsfield plant in 1919.

The politics of the country were sharply divided, and there was a growing interest in socialism as an alternative to the brutalities of the capitalism of the day. Davis was an active socialist during his years in Pittsfield, including, in 1911, running for and losing election as an alderman of Pittsfield on the Socialist ticket. After the election Davis spoke to the local newspaper for the Pittsfield Socialists:

> I am entirely satisfied and pleased with the socialist vote. Most people do not understand that the socialists are looking for a steady, intelligent gain. . . . It seems to me that from the vote of the election and from what we know of the spread of socialist thought in the city, that 550 or thereabouts represents very fairly the number of voters who are sufficiently advanced in their political thinking to cast a socialist vote. You will see a gradual and steady growth. The socialists, so far as I have learned their opinions, are very much pleased.[10]

9. Friedman, *World Is Flat*.

10. "Socialists Pleased," 9.

By the end of the 1910s, prompted in part by World War I and in part by the Russian Revolution, the United States government launched a vicious response to "a red scare," with socialists and labor agitators taking the brunt of the violence.[11] Famously, Eugene V. Debs (1855–1926) ran for president five times on the Socialist ticket (1900, 1904, 1908, 1912, and 1920). He ran his fifth campaign for president from prison, where he had been incarcerated for voicing dissent over the United States' entry into World War I and thereby violating the Sedition Act of 1918; he got 3.4 percent of the vote.

Davis's writings, particularly his sermons, articulated a pathway through modernism, a forward-looking religious response to the rapid, exciting, disturbing changes that characterized the times he was living through. He celebrated science and its progressive nature, its ability to drive change with discoveries, and to find new truth. He preached a form of "natural religion," religion stripped of its supernatural elements. He welcomed the achievements of industrialism, as they paved a pathway out of poverty toward prosperity. But he emphasized the moral imperative that this pathway had to lead to prosperity for all, not just the fortunate few. His approach to religion looked to a future that recognized what he called the primacy of "human personality," the fundamental moral, social, and political importance of every individual human soul. He was optimistic that the future would bring more freedom for all humans.

3. The Unfinished World; the Undiscovered Future

On May 2, 1909, Davis preached a sermon, "The Travail and Pain of Human Life: What Can it Mean?"[12] The focus was on what philosophers call "the problem of evil": How can a theoretically omnipotent and benevolent God allow evil to exist in the world? For centuries the problem of evil has been one of the principal arguments against the existence of such a God. It still is.[13]

Davis acknowledged the pervasiveness of the world's problems, the obvious reality of evil. His conclusion, however, did not concern God's existence. Rather, he concluded that the making of the world was not finished:

11. See Hochschild, *American Midnight*.

12. Davis, "Travail and Pain" (1909a).

13. For one recent discussion, see Goff, *Why*, ch. 4.

> While we may not hold literally to the statement that God made the world in six days and rested on the seventh in the full assurance that he had completed his work, we still cling tenaciously to the idea that the universe is a completed article, finished and ready for use. But if you stop to think of it there is not one single scrap of evidence that such is the case. Everywhere is incompleteness and constant change. In the small bit of the universe that we know of there is nothing that is complete and final. Even the earth is subject to constant change and development, nature in every root and branch is alive with changing forces, man in his thought, his manner of living, in his ideals is so hopelessly incomplete that many would have us think that all life is the sheerest mockery. . . .
>
> Do not all the facts that we know of this universe in which we live, do not all the facts of human life and the inner impulses of the human soul, do not all the facts of the history of humanity and its long process of development declare to us beyond a venture of a doubt that the universe is not made, but is being made, that it is not completed but is in the midst of a great process of evolution whose beginning we cannot even guess at and whose day of completion is infinitely remote?[14]

Not a scrap of evidence that the universe is the completed article. Everywhere is incompleteness and change, and the "day of completion is infinitely remote." Whatever one may conclude about God, the existence of evil, in Davis's view, was part and parcel to the incompletion of the world. There was—is—work to be done.

The world is being made. This is a process, and significantly, a process that humans participate in. Indeed, humans play a special role in the ongoing making of the world:

> Insofar as man rises above the commonplace animal existence, he does so in response to an irrepressible impulse to realize a truer, grandeur view of life than he has yet lived. Before him is the vision of truth unknown, of goodness not yet realized, of beauty as yet undreamt of. To feel the deeper undercurrent of this great pulsating humanity, to swim valiantly in the great current of human progress, to feel the call of the finite to its universal consecration, and to fulfill, joyously, in pain and in pleasure, the great function of human life—that is life.[15]

14. Davis, "Travail and Pain" (1909a), 2.
15. Davis, "Travail and Pain" (1909a), 6.

For Davis, our purpose on earth was to fulfill an irrepressible impulse to realize a better—a truer, more beautiful, more just—world. Here is our role in the ongoing making of the world. Our efforts to improve the world take us forward to a world in the future, a world not yet realized, a world not yet fully defined, "as yet undreamt of."

Put aside for the moment the question of the truth of the idea that humans have an irrepressible impulse to realize a better world, that humans "bring a vision of truth unknown, of goodness not yet realized, of beauty as yet undreamt of." The fundamental fact here is change itself. In the 1947 sermon, "Not Revelation but Discovery; Not Forms but the Holy Spirit," discussed in chapter 1, Davis asked us to "try to fathom" "this thing we call life,"

> its depth and its power, irresistible in its uncontrolled ferocity, or magnificent and majestic in its disciplined and intelligent best. . . .
>
> Some have dared to say that this strange and mysterious power that we feel within is like unto the power that we discover in all nature and all mankind, in all things everywhere, moving on, through age after age, toward an undiscovered purpose.[16]

God did not finish the job in six days. The making of the world is underway—perhaps will always be underway—and change, change with uncontrolled ferocity, change that can be disciplined and intelligent, change in all things everywhere, change through age after age, change toward an undiscovered purpose, change is our experience of the world.

The "discovery of change" was a major element of nineteenth century. As geology emerged as a discipline it became clear that the earth was both much older than previously appreciated and that the earth had undergone massive changes over its history. Dinosaurs had come and gone. The universe itself was not some kind of "steady state system," but was itself changing, mutating, evolving over time. And then there was the big bombshell of Darwin's theory of evolution, a theory of change in biological forms. Humans—and all other creatures, plants, lifeforms—were not created as finished, perfect products by some singular supernatural act; rather they all evolved over eons of time through a process Darwin described as natural selection. Variations occur and those variations that are best able to live and reproduce carry forward into future generations. The process is repetitive and ongoing. Beyond

16. Davis, "Not Revelation" (1947a), 1–2.

reproductive success, however, there is no goal here. Darwinian natural selection is not directed in that sense.

Davis's view of life combined the undirected power of natural selection with the human-directed power of our beliefs, desires, aspirations, and ideals. Our efforts to realize our aspirations, active through all human history, adds direction to the undirected power of natural selection. Among these aspirations, Davis found universalizing desires for ideals of truth, beauty, and justice. His faith—or is it his observation?—was that humans have these aspirations, these ideals, and that these ideals are the source of human efforts through history to make things better. This is why he believed there is a direction to the unrelenting change we observe and live with.

That there has been change over the millennia is now an obvious fact. But has there been progress? Can we reasonably describe the change Davis observed as progress, as change *toward* "undiscovered purposes," "an undreamt-of future"? How can we know this change will be change for the better? Davis's historical process was directed, directed by human purposes and values. Are there in fact "universalizing desires for truth, beauty and justice" in humans? And, if so, have they been responsible for human progress over the millennia?

Sometimes we capture this idea with the phrase "the arc of history is long, but it bends towards justice."[17] This is a beautiful sentiment, but are our values stable enough through history? Has our purpose remained true? Considering these uncertainties, one wants to know how stable are these (claimed) human desires for truth, beauty, and justice? Progress, it would seem, would require some stability in these concepts.

4. Change and the Problems of Progress

My grandfather was committed to accepting the reality of change, to rejoicing in this reality, and to working to find ways for us to manage change productively. Here I found that my grandfather and I share something.

17. This phrase likely originates with the nineteenth-century Unitarian minister, Theodore Parker (1810–60) who wrote in a sermon, "I do not pretend to understand the moral universe, the arc is a long one, my eye reaches but little ways. I cannot calculate the curve and complete the figure by the experience of sight; I can divine it by conscience. But from what I see I am sure it bends towards justice." See Parker, "Justice and the Conscience," 84–85. More recently the phrase has been adapted and used by Martin Luther King Jr. and Barack Obama, among many others.

While my grandfather was concerned about religious responses to change—including institutional religious responses to change—I have been concerned with change in science and technology.

My philosophical education came in the wake of Thomas Kuhn's 1962 *The Structure of Scientific Revolutions.*[18] Kuhn opens with this sentence: "History, if viewed as a repository for more than anecdote or chronology, could produce a decisive transformation in the image of science by which we are now possessed."[19] That image was an image of pure progressive—accumulative—science, truth being added to truth, year by year, century by century. By contrast, Kuhn saw periods of "destructive construction," where whole blocks of previously accepted "truths"—old scientific theories—would be discarded in favor of alternative conceptions. Successive replacement, not addition, was the picture Kuhn took from history.

Kuhn went on to spell out a theory of scientific change. He introduced the terms "normal science," "paradigm," "anomaly," "scientific revolution," finally resulting in "new normal science." For a generation, the field of history and philosophy of science debated the details, with proposals and counterproposals and a quite refreshing lot of history of science. But the key point here is change. Think Newton to Einstein: theories change, the concepts we use change (from the force of gravity to the curvature of the space-time continuum), the experiments we perform change, the instruments we use to make the experiments change. Everything changes. Progress—if it exists—is not simply additive.

It has been common to think of science as a prototypical progressive part of our culture. We know more now than we did one hundred years ago, two hundred years ago, one thousand years ago. Certainly, my grandfather believed this. I believe this. Yet the fact that science does not progress in an additive way, but through successive replacements creates two problems: a conceptual problem and an institutional problem.

Conceptually, it is challenging to spell out the respect(s) in which we know more in an ongoing whirlwind of everything changing—including the very concepts we might use to spell out in what sense we know more now than we used to. The concepts do not seem stable enough. And yet

18. Kuhn, *Structure of Scientific Revolutions.* My dissertation adviser, Ian Hacking (1936–2023), was heavily influenced by Kuhn; he wrote the introduction to the 50th edition of *Structure of Scientific Revolutions*, vii–xxxvii.

19. Kuhn, *Structure of Scientific Revolutions*, 1.

quite obviously we do know more today than we did years ago. This has been a challenge for philosophers of science, about which more below.

Institutionally, ongoing change requires institutions to adapt to new contexts. In science, we are accustomed to institutional change. New scientific societies and their associated journals emerge—e.g., the International Society for Computational Biology, founded 1997, and its journal, *Bioinformatics*, founded in 1998.[20] Others disappear or transform—e.g., the American Eugenics Society, founded in 1921, became the Society for the Study of Social Biology in 1973, and now is the Society for Biodemography and Social Biology.[21]

In religion, institutional responses to change have been more convulsive and divisive. Think of the Reformation. How religious institutions responded to change was a primary focus of my grandfather.

My grandfather rejected religious creeds—statements of belief that a given denomination adopts—because they are not built to respond to change, to new experience. At best they capture what some people hold to be true at a moment in time. At his ordination at the Unity Church in 1905, Davis launched his career with "A Plea for the Principle of a Creedless Church."[22] In the outline for the sermon—there is no full text—he answered the question, "Why should not a creed be retained in the church today?" by noting, among other things, that "it is intellectually impossible."[23] It is impossible because of change—new experience should prompt new beliefs, and consequently people are unlikely to—indeed, shouldn't—hold a set of beliefs fixed forever.

In response to the question, "What attitude should we take?" Davis offered three responses:

1. The free and open church, where the spirit may have free play.
2. In regard to intellectual truth, we ought to be willing and ready to favor all things. Hold fast to that which is true. Scientist. The historical club. Same method in church.
3. We have no moral right to any artificial barrier.[24]

20. When it was initially founded, *Bioinformatics* was titled *Computer Applications in the Biosciences.*

21. See "American Eugenics Society."

22. Davis, "Plea for the Principle" (1905a).

23. Davis, "Plea for the Principle" (1905a), 1.

24. Davis, "Plea for the Principle" (1905a), 1.

Davis argued that religious change should follow the same method as scientific change. Furthermore, each person had—*has*—the right to express and practice religious truth as they find it, "no moral right to any artificial barrier." Of course, with this right comes a responsibility, a burden to bear, to carefully think through and practice one's religious responses to/in the world.

5. What Shall We Do with the Heretics?

On December 21, 2022—a few days into my initial work on this book—Ross Douthat, opinion columnist for the *New York Times*, published "The Americanization of Religion." The column was in part a reflection on how, in his view, the religious landscape in America had shifted in the decade after his 2012 book, *Bad Religion: How We Became a Nation of Heretics.*[25] In his 2022 piece he concluded that

> our longtime national impulse toward *heresy*—toward personalized revisions of Christian doctrine, Americanized updates of the gospel—has finally completed its victory over older Christian institutions and traditions.[26]

With the result that the religious landscape is now

> dominated by popular Christian ideas that have "gone mad," as G. K. Chesterton once put it, "because they have been isolated from each other and are wandering alone."[27]

We've entered a post-Christian world, a label that "fits the overall trend in American spirituality more than it did a decade ago."[28]

Douthat describes all this churn in religious thinking as a "national impulse to heresy." Heresy sounds bad, and no doubt in Douthat's view it is bad. Davis took a different view. He urged us to welcome and celebrate the heretics.

A century earlier, in February 1923, Davis preached a sermon addressing heresy.[29] Early in the sermon he noted that on February 17, 1900,

25. Douthat, *Bad Religion*.

26. Douthat, "Americanization of Religion," 1 (emphasis in the original).

27. Douthat, "Americanization of Religion," 1. The quote from G. K. Chesterton is from his *Orthodoxy*, 53.

28. Douthat, "Americanization of Religion," 3.

29. Davis, "What Shall We Do" (1923a). The manuscript for this sermon did not

> the scholars of the world gathered in the City of Rome, for the purpose of dedicating a monument to Giordano Bruno. Upon the very spot where the monument was erected, this same Giordano Bruno had been burned at the stake on February 17, 1600, because he had taught certain ideas concerning the Universe, that are now taught in every public and private school and college in America. . . . That is really the essence of this heresy business.[30]

In addition to the double anniversary tied to Giordano Bruno, Davis wrote about heresy in 1923 because of a case current at the time. A disagreement had arisen between the Reverend Percy Stickney Grant, Rector of the Episcopal Church of the Ascension in New York City, and Bishop William T. Manning of the Episcopal Diocese of New York. Evidently Reverend Grant had come to hold and teach views that varied from those accepted by his church, specifically concerning the deity of Christ, the miracles, and the Apostles' Creed. Bishop Manning ordered Reverend Grant to resign or recant.[31]

Davis noted that the Catholic Church has an accepted system to dealing with such differences of opinion:

> The pope is the authority provided by Christ (or God) to pass upon these differences. The priest has no original power. He teaches as the Church instructs. That is logical and sound, provided the premises of the Catholic Religion are accepted."[32]

For the Protestant churches—including Reverend Grant's and Bishop Manning's Episcopal Church—the controversy exposed the lack of such a process for resolution:

have a specific date. But given the double anniversary—Bruno's execution and the statue erected in his honor three hundred years later, February 17, 1600, and 1900—likely this sermon was delivered on the Sunday close to the 17th, perhaps February 25, 1923. The manuscript does note that Davis also read this sermon in Petersham, Massachusetts, on September 25, 1949.

30. Davis, "What Shall We Do" (1923a), 1.

31. From 1893 until he resigned in 1924, Percy Stickney Grant (1860–1927) was the rector of the Church of the Ascension. In addition to the concerns mentioned in Davis's sermon, Reverend Grant also courted controversy with his socialist views, views with which Davis would have been sympathetic. Grant also sought to marry a divorcée, Rita de Acosta Lydig, and Bishop Manning refused to authorize the marriage. Bishop William T. Manning (1866–1949) was the United States Episcopal Bishop of New York City from 1921 until 1946.

32. Davis, "What Shall We Do" (1923a), 3.

> We have no mechanism, no policy, no real standards, no one to speak with authority, no court of high appeal. The reason is that we have really thrown overboard the whole system of authority religion, or religion as a supernatural revelation.[33]

Davis noted that many Protestant churches have formal creeds, but he dismissed them "as survivals of ancient controversies":

> They are interesting, but they have no significance beyond that of being expressions of the beliefs and opinions once held by a group of men and women.[34]

And yet creeds provide the basis for charges of heresy. They are

> the sources of most of the contentions, and about which the heresy hunters gather. Four hundred years of protestant history has demonstrated that the halfway measures of sectarian creeds land us in utter disintegrations, and confusion. Our hundred or more protestant sects, competing and quarrelling over words and creeds, and those hundred sects now facing still further division and conflict, do not present a spectacle particularly reassuring or dignified.[35]

Authority religion avoids this—but at the cost of accepting the premises of supernatural revealed religion. Given the history of errors of these "revelations"—Giordano Bruno!—this was a concession Davis was unwilling to make. What then is the option?

Davis found the solution to this competing and quarrelling over words and creeds in a different direction. Instead of branding people with whom one disagrees as heretics, and casting them out, bring them in. Learn from them. He called for a "spirit of broad toleration that will permit and encourage fellowship amid the widest diversities of opinions and beliefs."

> Let us widen the circle so that it will include the erstwhile heretic, and instead of trying to brand him as an outcast and person to be shunned, let us seek him out that we may learn what he has to tell us of life. After all, had it not been for the heretic we would still be living in caves, victims of fear and superstition. Along the pathway of history, the paths have been blazed by the heretic. Is

33. Davis, "What Shall We Do" (1923a), 3.
34. Davis, "What Shall We Do" (1923a), 4.
35. Davis, "What Shall We Do" (1923a), 4.

> it not time that we were intelligent enough, even if we are not generous enough to give him his full place.[36]

For Davis, far from being a danger to religion, the heretics were the essential drivers of progress—including religious progress. In Davis's view, religion needed to stay current, forward looking, accepting and responding to new knowledge and new human conditions, and not restrained by dogmas that emerged in times when there was no inkling of where humans would be in the centuries ahead.

What then of Chesterton's 1908 complaint of a religious landscape "gone mad"? Davis was certainly aware of this challenge, and likely aware of Chesterton's book itself. In Chesterton's view, religious seekers had gone mad "because they have been isolated from each other and are wandering alone."[37] Davis would say that it is through thoughtful, open dialog within the many and various individual congregations that tomorrow's religious truth is found and forged. It is a social effort, not an individual effort. Christianity has not gone mad; rather the churches provide an avenue for this work. People are not "wandering alone":

> If we are going to have creeds and authority religions let us have the real thing as set forth in the Roman Catholic Church, and not these small makeshifts. The time is here not for the revision of creeds, but for the abolition of creeds from ecclesiastical machinery, and a fellowship based upon broad toleration, with a frank and full recognition of differences of opinion and belief bound by a common tie of purpose.[38]

As he wrote in another essay, "Permanent Characteristics of Liberal Religion,"

> Faithfulness in inquiry, clarity in thought, and candor in expression have become individual moral values than which no other is more needed at the present time.[39]

We find truth not by forbidding views with which we disagree, but rather by engaging exactly these views.

36. Davis, "What Shall We Do" (1923a), 4–5.
37. Chesterton, *Orthodoxy*, 53.
38. Davis, "What Shall We Do" (1923a), 5.
39. Davis, "Permanent Characteristics" (No Date-a), 7.

6. American Pragmatism

In the fall of 2022, I concluded my teaching career with a seminar on American Pragmatism. I started with pragmatism's founders Charles Saunders Peirce (1839–1914), William James (1842–1910), and John Dewey (1859–1952). I wanted to teach this seminar because, among other things, pragmatism directly addresses the big discovery of the nineteenth century, change.

The problem of change began to emerge as a pressing issue for philosophers during the Renaissance. For Davis it was the Reformation. Old, long-established beliefs and practices were challenged and discarded. The early responses sought some underlying unchanging element behind the "surface changes."

Famously, René Descartes (1596–1650) responded by seeking a bedrock of certainty, something that could not be discarded, a belief that could not be doubted—I exist as a thinking, doubting—being.[40] Of course, philosophy being a highly contentious discipline, not everyone agreed. What followed was an intensely generative period of philosophy, with multiple efforts to find some bedrock certainty behind all the change, that is, to ground change in something unchanging. This period, known to philosophers as "modern philosophy," had some philosophers—commonly referred to as "British empiricists"—seeking solutions in the certainties of experience; others—"continental rationalists"—followed Descartes in seeking solutions in ideas that couldn't be wrong. At the end of the eighteenth century, Immanuel Kant (1742–1804) famously developed a hybrid of empiricism and rationalism. All along, the project aimed at finding some bedrock certainty, something to hang one's hat on, in the face of change.

In the nineteenth century, C. S. Peirce rejected the project of seeking some bedrock of certainty behind all the change. Instead, he argued that all our beliefs, including our best science, are always fallible, subject to future rejection in light of future experience. At a given moment we may hold certain beliefs. But future experience can change this.

What, then, should we believe? Peirce seriously considered the idea that we should adopt certain "truths" as bedrock, irrefutable truth, "creeds." But Peirce rejected this option—which he called "the method of tenacity"—*not* because it might have us believing falsehoods as truths, but because, he argued, it simply wouldn't work:

40. Descartes, *Meditations*.

> But this method of fixing belief, which may be called the method of tenacity, will be unable to hold its ground in practice. The social impulse is against it. The man who adopts it will find that other men think differently from him, and it will be apt to occur to him, in some saner moment, that their opinions are quite as good as his own, and this will shake his confidence in his belief.[41]

The method of tenacity—creeds—ultimately invites Davis's "hundred or more protestant sects, competing and quarrelling over words and creeds." As Peirce noted, "the social impulse is against it." Peirce and Davis agree, creeds cannot work.

Instead of seeking some bedrock certainty, Peirce relied on the *method* of science.

> To satisfy our doubts, therefore, it is necessary that a method should be found by which our beliefs may be caused by nothing human, but some external permanency—by something upon which our thinking has no effect. . . . Such is the method of science.[42]

This could sound like a simple solution to the problem of change: Apply the method of science and accept the result as truth. But at any point in time—any point in history—our experience is always incomplete, science is always incomplete; further experience, new scientific evidence, may reveal mistaken beliefs. Our beliefs—including those based in science—are always fallible, subject to being abandoned because of future experience and evidence. Peirce's confidence in—faith in—the *method* of science was about its ability to self-correct. Future experience—some "external permanency"—will alter and improve what we believe. If there is final truth to be found, it will be the method of science that—eventually—finds it. Unfortunately, at any given point in time our experience will always be incomplete, and so our knowledge will always be fallible. The method of science may find final truth, but we may never know it has done so.

William James and John Dewey were less impressed with Peirce's approach to truth. James saw Peirce's idea of final absolute truth—what the method of science would ultimately yield—as something of a will-o-the-wisp:

> The "absolutely" true, meaning what no farther experience will ever alter, is that ideal vanishing-point towards which we

41. See Peirce, "Fixation of Belief," in Menand, *Pragmatism*, 16.

42. Peirce, "Fixation of Belief," in Menand, *Pragmatism*, 16.

> imagine that all our temporary truths will someday converge. It runs on all fours with the perfectly wise man, and with the absolutely complete experience; and, if these ideals are ever realized, they will all be realized together. Meanwhile we have to live today by what truth we can get today and be ready tomorrow to call it falsehood.[43]

Peirce's move to the scientific method—as a way to define and ascertain ultimate truth—put this desirable concept of truth out of reach, for we will never attain "absolutely complete experience."

James's essay, "The Will to Believe," argues that, for certain important matters—religion included—it can make sense to "accept as true" certain propositions even in absence of full evidence, that the withholding of belief—of a potentially true, but unproven, doctrine—can be as damaging as believing something that is false.[44]

And yet, problematically, James's willingness to speak of the "truth we can get today" as tomorrow's possible falsehood, undermines what we expect of truth. Truth is—or should be—eternal: true today, true tomorrow, just *true*. Unchanging! Dewey tried to avoid this dilemma by speaking instead in a phrase only philosophers, or perhaps lawyers, could love, "warranted assertability."[45] None of these philosophical solutions is fully satisfactory, and debate did not end with Dewey. Philosophy continues contentiously to wrestle with these issues.

Pragmatism became current—particularly at Harvard where James taught—while Davis was studying for the ministry at Harvard. Davis quoted James at the conclusion to his September 19, 1909, sermon, "Two Great Principles of the Modern World":

> A conception of the world rises in you somehow, no matter how. Is it true or not? you ask.
>
> It *might* be true somewhere, you say, for it is not self-contradictory.
>
> It *may* be true, you continue, even here and now.
>
> It is *fit* to be true, it would be *well if it were true,* it *ought* to be true, you presently feel.
>
> It *must* be true, something persuasive in you whispers next; and then—as a final result—

43. James, "Pragmatism's Conception of Truth," 150.
44. James, "Will to Believe."
45. See Capps, "Pragmatic Theory of Truth."

> It shall be *held for true*, you decide, it *shall be* as if true for *you*.
>
> And your acting thus may in certain special cases be a means of making it securely true in the end.[46]

This quotation, from James's 1909 book, *A Pluralistic Universe*, captures an element of James's earlier essay, "The Will to Believe." For James, it was acceptable, in certain instances, to believe something, even in absence of full evidence.

James was particularly interested in special cases where one's belief can lead to actions that make the belief become true. Consider the ideals—truth, beauty, and justice—that Davis identified as the essential elements behind how humans direct the progress of the world. Believing in these human ideals—believing that the world can be better in certain specific idealistic ways—leads to human actions that can in fact make the world better, better specifically as the ideals represent it. Belief in the ideals would seem to make the ideals become true.

For Davis, change was simply a fact of life. Change involves fallibilism, what we have accepted as truth may need to be reconsidered in light of new experience. Creeds cannot work. We must drop the attempt to find bedrock truth, and instead rely on the ongoing application of the scientific method to lead us on a self-correcting path towards truth. We may never know if we get there, but the point is ongoing progress, not completion. The unfinished world always continues to be made. And critically, humans—with their fallible beliefs and ideals—are part of the process of this ongoing making of the world. Indeed, following James, belief in the progressive power of these ideals can become a self-fulfilling prophecy.

7. The Congregational Polity

Davis wrote at length about the history of the protestant churches, including the arrival in the New World of religious refugees, the Pilgrims in Plymouth (1620), the Puritans in Salem (1629), and the many others that followed. The Pilgrims and the Puritans held different religious beliefs, with differing religious practices. As they struggled to survive in the New World, they also struggled with each other's differences. The history of

46. James, *A Pluralistic Universe*, 328–29 (emphasis in the original). I discuss Davis's sermon, "Two Great Principles of the Modern World," in more detail in ch. 6. For Davis's quote of James see Davis, "Two Great Principles" (1909b), 7.

these early struggles is complex, and was entirely new to me, fascinating to learn, as I read through Davis's sketch of this story.[47]

Two aspects of these early settlers compete and confuse the story. Their religious beliefs drew from John Calvin (1509–64) and challenged both Catholic and Anglican beliefs. Strict Calvinism is not a liberal doctrine. But the polity of the Pilgrims and the Puritans—how they responded to differences of opinion—was distinctly liberal. Davis wrote,

> We are not to think that these people, who sailed in the Mayflower, were liberal in their thought or in their interpretation of historic Christianity. On the contrary, they were steeped in the most rigid Calvinism, and their separation [from the Church of England] in no small degree represented the extreme defense of Calvinism, as opposed to the Catholic Church and the English Church. But the spirit of Free Inquiry and Universal Priesthood had been the power that had broken away from the Catholic Church and established Calvinism, and even though Calvinism be the shell, the real meat of the nut that came to New England in the Mayflower was that Spirit of Free Inquiry.[48]

Free inquiry and universal priesthood. Each person is free to inquire about religious truth, *and* there is no specially endowed or anointed class of persons—priests—who have special access to religious truth. We all have access, "universal priesthood." These principles allowed the Pilgrims to break with the Anglican Church. But the same principles would further splinter other "free churches" arriving in New England. There were complications on complications. But the key point here, the key point for Davis, was the "congregational polity."

As more people arrived in the New World, the Puritans after the Pilgrims and many more in the years following, theological differences and differences of practice emerged. How to manage these differences? That is where the congregational polity came in. Ultimately differences, congregation by congregation, were allowed. Each individual church asserted its power to determine for itself its religious belief and practice. There was

47. Among Davis's writings are several collections of writings concerning church history, which evidently were used to support the religious education that Davis provided his congregations; see his "Rise and Development" (1906a). A more contemporary source for this history, which also brings it forward to the end of the twentieth century was written by Wright, *Congregational Polity*; see also, Miller, *New England Mind.*

48. Davis, "Rise and Development" (1906a), Lecture IV, 5–6.

no superior authority to contravene an individual congregation's choices. Free inquiry and universal priesthood in action.

While the new settlers adhered to a strict and absolute view of religious truth—with equally strict moral obligations on behavior—they also recognized the need to be open to new revelation. Davis quoted a letter from Edward Winslow (1595–1655) who at several points was governor of the Plymouth Colony:

> We promise and covenant with God and one with another, to receive whatsoever light or truth shall be made known to us from his written Word. But withal exhorted us to take heed what we received for truth, and well to examine and compare, and weigh it with other Scriptures of truth, before we received it; For, saith he, It is not possible the Christian world should come so lately out of such thick Antichristian darkness, and that full perfection of knowledge should brake forth at once.[49]

In his own language, this early seventeenth-century Pilgrim recognized the problem of change and recommends recognizing the fallibility of his congregation's beliefs. Change was coming so quickly that one had to be careful to avoid premature fixing of belief. Future understanding was likely to shift beliefs further. And so, one must be open to change.

The congregational polity allowed for each congregation to engage with each other in a spirit of broad toleration "amid the widest diversities of opinions and beliefs" to find a response to changes underway. For Davis, the solution to the problem of change was found in accepting what we learn from experience, through the scientific method, and in subjecting the implications of these discoveries to open discussion—congregation by congregation—as promoted by the congregational polity.

The congregational polity was essential. For Davis, it was the most important foundational element that the protestant churches brought to the New World. In a 1913 paper he gave to the Connecticut Valley Association of Liberal Ministers—subsequently published in the *Christian Register*[50]—he put the point this way:

> Finally, there is one more element that our experience and inheritance may permit us to make, and failing here, we forfeit all the rest. This most important contribution is our ancient

49. This quotation Davis provides can be found in his "Rise and Development" (1906a), Lecture V, 4. Almost certainly, Davis picked up this quotation, and the surrounding history from Dexter, *Congregationalism*, 404.

50. Davis, "Influence of Democracy" (1913a).

> congregational polity, the democratic organization and democratic administration of our ecclesiastical institutions and affairs. This is the great contribution of New England Puritanism to the political and social development of the nation. In the days when the New England Theocracy, and the English Government threatened to destroy the spirit of local sovereignty it was the insistence by fearless ministers and laymen upon the congregational polity, that gave to us the spirit and the wisdom that carried through the revolutionary war and established the republic.[51]

Davis worried about an erosion in the commitment to the congregational polity, even within the American Unitarian Association:

> In the last few years, the trinitarian body has been moving in the direction of presbyterian polity, or some other semi-authoritative hybrid. In our own fellowship we have been trifling with, if we have not already departed from, our congregationalism. The insidious inroads made by the non-representative missionary body, the American Unitarian Association, upon a true congregational practice is the most dangerous development of our body.[52]

He continued, insisting that the preservation of the congregational polity was more important than any other matter:

> The very root of our liberal faith, the very thing that made possible our development into the richness of modern thought is the fact that we existed organically under this democratic polity of congregationalism, under freedom in thought, and local sovereignty. Any violation of this principle, direct or indirect, is an attack upon the one great distinctive characteristic of our movement. With this congregational polity firmly established

51. Davis, "Influence of Democracy" (1913a), 10–11. Davis's thesis, required for his STB degree, was about one of these "fearless ministers," John Wise (1652–1725) minister of the church in Ipswich, Massachusetts. Wise was an early exponent of the view of no taxation without representation; see Davis "Prophet of Democracy" (1904a). I take up the connection Davis notes between the congregational polity and democracy in chapter 7. Church, *American Creed*, addresses this connection in detail.

52. Davis, "Influence of Democracy" (1913a), 11. Davis was responding to measures taken by Samuel A. Eliot (1862–1950) who was elected to head the American Unitarian Association in 1894 and served in this capacity until 1927. Eliot sought to strengthen the central administration of the Unitarian denomination. Davis's teacher at Harvard, William Wallace Fenn (1862–1932), opposed some of these measures as incursions on the congregational polity, and Davis followed in his wake. Wright, *Congregational Polity*, 101–44, provides an excellent discussion of this period in a chapter titled, "Professionalized Administration 1898–1937/41."

> for a background, we are still a great and prophetic movement. With it choked or destroyed, we are indeed the most helpless and pitiable of cults.

The congregational polity was "the principle that has made possible all the rest. It cannot and must not be lost."[53]

One can see how this highly decentralized approach would lead to multiples of Protestant sects "competing and quarrelling." But we can look at the competing and quarrelling with a different lens. Here we have the robust competition of ideas—argument and counter-argument—along with the tests of experience—the scientific method. Together they lead forward to the success of better ideas, better spiritual ideas, ideas that are better fit to the circumstances, problems and opportunities that present themselves. This is a religion that is responsive to a changing world.

8. Covenants

Davis concluded his February 1923 sermon about the heretics with the following single-sentence final paragraph in quotation marks:

> In the love of Truth and in the spirit of Jesus Christ we unite for the worship of God and service of man.[54]

He did not provide a source—which was true for most of his quoted material. When I first edited this document in the fall of 2021, I included the quotation marks, but I did not chase down the source. On my second pass through this sermon, I did chase down the source. An easy Google search shows this sentence to be the "Ames Covenant" developed by Unitarian preacher Charles Gordon Ames (1828–1912) in 1880 while minister of the Spring Garden Unitarian Society in Philadelphia.[55]

But what is a covenant? More searching and I found some information on the American Unitarian Universalist Association website:

> The free church tradition of which we are a part does not offer up a creed, a certain set of beliefs, that everyone must accept

53. Davis, "Influence of Democracy" (1913a), 11.

54. Davis, "What Shall We Do" (1923a), 5.

55. Charles Gordon Ames (1828–1912) was ordained as a Baptist minister in 1849. He joined the Unitarians in 1858 and served in several Unitarian churches from California to Illinois to the East Coast throughout his life. He was author of several books including *Sermons of Sunrise* (1901) and *Five Points of Faith* (1903) and editor of the Unitarian publication, the *Christian Register,* from 1877–80.

> in order to belong to the community. Instead, the boundaries of our community are determined by commitment and participation. Our central question is not "What do we believe?" but rather "What values will we uphold and how will we do this together?" Our covenant, the promises we make to each other in regarding how we will be a community of faith, is at the heart of what it means to be a Unitarian Universalist.[56]

The UU website goes on to share some of the history—back to the Pilgrims and Puritans—of how covenants became important: "Churches . . . gathered by covenant, a voluntary and mutual promise to walk in the ways of truth and affection as best they were known."[57] Over time, and in keeping with the congregational polity, different congregations adopted different covenants.

The Ames Covenant had become popular among Unitarian churches around the time Davis entered the ministry. Davis preached his sermon on the heretics while he was the minister of the Church of Our Father in Lancaster, Pennsylvania. It is quite likely—nearly certain given the placement of the final sentence of the sermon—that the church had adopted the Ames Covenant. His congregation would have recognized this closing as a reminder of their agreement for how to meet as a religious community. The Ames Covenant also well fit the argument in his sermon about the heretics, that differences of opinion should be handled in a spirit of broad fellowship engaged in free inquiry.

Covenants are not creeds. A creed is a statement of religious beliefs, e.g., the divinity of Christ and/or the Trinitarian conception of God. A covenant is an agreement among congregants to engage with each other in a certain way towards certain ends. A creed fixes belief. A covenant fixes ways and aims: How shall we walk together and towards what goals? A creed assumes a kind of finality—settling matters of dispute—whereas a covenant expects change. A covenant is akin to a statement of method, specifically in how a congregation agrees to carry out its spiritual work.

For Davis, religion needed to move forward, not stand pat in dogma. Religion needed to respond to changes in the world. What kept this forward movement productive, progressive, and not simply dissipating, was the covenant of those walking together in doing this work. The covenant laid out in broadest terms the goals and the "procedural

56. Unitarian Universalist Association, "Leader Resource 1," para. 1.

57. Unitarian Universalist Association, "Leader Resource 1," para 7.

parameters" that the congregation agreed to as they work together on the challenges the world posed.

"We unite," says the Ames Covenant. For Davis, the project and promise of healthy organized religion required engaging our religious and moral issues together in light of the times. "We unite . . . in the service of man," as the Ames Covenant has it, to make the world better—better in terms of truth, beauty, and justice. We unite to think through and engage with the problems that confront us. For the Ames Covenant, "We unite in the spirit of Jesus Christ," which, for Davis, demanded quite specific commitments, principally to the moral and spiritual primacy of humans over other considerations, e.g., money and profits. More on how Davis viewed "the spirit of Jesus" in chapter 5.

9. Are Covenants or Methods Stable Enough?

Today there are many different covenants adopted by different liberal congregations. According to the Unitarian Universalist website one of the most common covenants in use today is that written by L. Griswold Williams in 1933:

> Love is the doctrine of this church, the quest of truth is its sacrament, and service is its prayer. To dwell together in peace, to seek knowledge in freedom, to serve humanity in fellowship, to the end that all souls shall grow in harmony with the Divine—thus do we covenant with each other and with God.[58]

Despite the variations—which represent important differences—all these covenants are variations on a theme: joining together in pursuit of truth and the betterment of life on earth, all the while respecting differences.

Still, the differences matter. This diversity betrays a problem I noted early in this chapter: Are our concepts—even our concepts of method, scientific method, or covenants—stable enough to underwrite progress—not simply change, but progress—over time, over millennia? Davis's picture of the universe in the making, and of the important role humans play in its making, where human ideals of truth, beauty, and justice—and human decisions and actions—underwrite aspirations for the future, could be a progressive picture. *If* these ideals are stable through time. Are they?

58. See Unitarian Universalist Association, "Leader Resource 1." In 1933 Universalist minister L. Griswold Williams (1893–1942) published a book, *Antiphonal Readings for Free Worship*, that included this covenant, still widely used.

Compare, for example, the different covenants of the two Unitarian Universalist churches in my hometown of Worcester, Massachusetts. The Main Street UU church—"The First Unitarian Church of Worcester"[59]—has a simple four-line covenant:

> In the love of truth
> And in the spirit of Jesus
> We unite for the worship of God
> And the service of all.[60]

The covenant was adopted by the congregation on December 18, 1898, and is repeated at each worship service. By contrast the "Holden Street UU Church" has a lengthy and detailed covenant:

> In consonance with the principles and purposes of the Unitarian Universalist Association, we the members and friends of the Unitarian Universalist Church of Worcester covenant to sustain and support a courageous and caring community by. . .

There follows a series of nine bullet points.[61]

59. Prior to the 1961 merger of the Unitarian and the Universalist denominations, the Main Street church was the (first) Unitarian church of Worcester, while the Holden Street UU church was a Universalist church.

60. See Worcester First Unitarian Church, "Our Covenant."

61. See Worcester Unitarian Universalist Church, "Our Mission and Beliefs." Here are the nine bullet points:

- Bringing our best selves to form a welcoming, loving and inclusive community of faith;
- Creating an atmosphere of celebration and worship in a safe environment;
- Providing opportunities where diverse people and points of view are respected and where open-hearted and open-minded discussion of our differences is encouraged;
- Treating each other with kindness and respect;
- Approaching conflicts with a spirit of humility and with the respectful intent for peaceful resolution;
- Engaging in, and encouraging, spiritual and intellectual growth across the lifespan;
- Fostering social justice and positive transformation in our community and in the world at large;
- Growing and maintaining the resources necessary to support the missions and ministries of this congregation;
- Fostering fellowship and enjoying each other and the unique gifts that each person brings to our community.

Obviously very different covenants. The shorter one feels very much from the era of the Ames Covenant. The longer one has more of the sense of a vision and mission statement, the kind of statement that has become common and useful for many—most?—institutions, religious or secular, profit centered and nonprofit. I drafted multiple vision and mission statements in my time as an academic administrator. They help institutions articulate their purposes and reasons for being, and their strategy for future institutional work.

The Main Street UU covenant places Jesus centrally; the Holden Street UU covenant does not mention Jesus. Main Street expresses a love of truth, Holden Street does not mention truth. Both support service to humankind, but the Holden Street Church spells this out in quite specific ways, while the Main Street Church leaves this matter open. The Holden Street Church's statement betrays its time of origin with the emphasis on diversity and inclusion, concerns at the forefront of liberal progressive thinking in the opening years of the twenty-first century. By midcentury, I would expect a somewhat different statement, not a statement that diminishes the concerns of diversity, equity, and inclusion, but a statement that reflects whatever are the most prominent concerns at midcentury.

If the details keep shifting, responding to the prominent concerns of the time, they do not appear stable enough to underwrite millennial progress. And the details are changing. Davis, speaking of the massive change from the ancient world to the modern world, wrote of a complete turnover of ideas:

> Every fact, every experience, every problem of human life presents itself to the man and woman in whom the subtle spirit of modernity is at work, in an entirely different clothing and with an entirely different significance than it presented itself to the man and the woman of the ancient world. Ask your man of the ancient world about his idea of God, his idea of man, his idea of truth, his idea of the universe, his idea of life, his idea of the state and government, his idea of the church, his idea of moral evil, of sin, of death or indeed of any other vital fact or problem of human life. Then compare his answer with the answers that appeal to the modern man as being true, and you will find that there is nothing in common between the two.[62]

62. Davis, "Adventurous Task" (1909c), 1–2.

Davis suggested here that on any important dimension—ideas of God, of man, of truth, of the universe, of morality, etc.—our concepts have changed in the transition from ancient to modern. There is no stability.

My dissertation advisor, Ian Hacking (1936–2023), found the same problem with scientific method. The first half of his 1983 book *Representing and Intervening* (written at the time I was his student) examines various attempts to deal with the problem of change—"Kuhn's problem." He concluded this line of argument discussing Imre Lakatos's (1922–74) response to Kuhn. Peirce proposed scientific method as the way to find ultimate truth. Lakatos pursued this idea with a detailed description of method, what he called "the methodology of scientific research programmes."[63] Hacking suggests even this most sophisticated version of using method to manage the problem of change does not solve the problem:

> It would be wrong to suppose that we can get from this specific kind of growth to a theory of truth and reality. To take seriously the title of a book that Lakatos proposed, but never lived to write, "The changing logic of scientific discovery" is to take seriously the possibility that Lakatos has, like the Greeks, made the eternal verities depend on a mere episode in the history of human knowledge.
>
> There remains an optimistic version of this worry. Lakatos was trying to characterize certain objective values of Western science without an appeal to copy theories of truth. Maybe those objective values are recent enough that his limitation to the past two or three centuries is exactly right. We are left with no external way to evaluate our own tradition, but why should we want that?[64]

Why should we want that? Because we seek some eternal certainty amid rushing ongoing change. Something to hang our hat on. Something to underwrite the idea of progress.

But perhaps that asks too much. We see the future only dimly: "the vision of truth unknown, of goodness not yet realized, of beauty as yet undreamt of," as Davis put it. Undreamt of:

63. Lakatos, *Methodology of Scientific Research Programmes.*

64. Hacking, *Representing and Intervening*, 128. When Hacking writes of the "copy theory of truth" he is referring to the view that a statement is true if it is a faithful copy of the world it describes. But how can words copy things? John Dewey, among others, was entirely dismissive of the "copy theory of truth."

> Half in blind obedience to instincts that are the essential characteristics of his nature, and half in a semi-conscious following of a purpose, he sets out on his long journey over the centuries. . . . Through hardship and toil unspeakable, he has climbed the stairway of the centuries, and . . . today we still find ourselves climbing those same stairways, whose foundations are lost from our view in the utter darkness of the past, and whose uppermost steps are beyond the reach of our wildest imagination. Yet we climb on and on, allured by the light of our radiating visions of truth, goodness and beauty, and impelled by the great power of human life.[65]

It is a matter of our human nature. Whether we can explain it or not—and surely, we cannot, for the future is beyond our wildest imagination—we continue forward.

Is this progress? We cannot answer that question. We cannot prove affirmatively that this process of following our ideals produces progress. But nor can we prove affirmatively that it does not produce progress. For Davis, progress was a matter of faith, faith in what he called "the integrity of the universe." And for more on this faith see chapter 6, Natural Deity, section 8, Pantheism and Two Principles of the Modern World.

Putting aside this question of faith for the moment, we still must acknowledge we live in an unfinished universe; we must expect change, "irresistible in its uncontrolled ferocity, or magnificent and majestic in its disciplined and intelligent best." Change is the one constant of ongoing life. And, at any point in time human aspirations and ideals play a role in the direction of this ferocious and magnificent world in creation. To these ideals, truth, beauty, and goodness, we now turn.

65. Davis, "Inevitable Compensation" (1909d), 4–5.

Chapter 3: **Truth, Beauty, Goodness**

> To every stimulating call that bids us inquire into the truth of life, there goes forth from us a responsive answer. To every alluring well of beauty and harmony from the outside world, there wells up some sense of appreciation, some effort to respond. To every act of heroic conduct there within us the impulse to goodness.[1]

1. Earl C. Davis's Commitments

Earl C. Davis's modern world was changing rapidly, horse and buggy to spaceflight. Humans were—still are—helping to direct its development. If anything, change has accelerated since Davis's day. Recently, we have captured this notion by calling our current geological era the "Anthropocene," the era where human activities are significantly altering all earth's systems.[2] In calling our era the Anthropocene we bring attention to the problem of human-caused climate change. But, perhaps ironically, the term works well to capture one of Davis's key observations: human beings, with our ideals and aspirations—and everything else we carry in our complicated personalities—participate in the evolution of the world. We are contributing.

1. Davis, "Essential Christ" (1922), 4–5.

2. See "Anthropocene." While "Anthropocene" may be in—somewhat—current usage, and some geologists have advocated it as the official name for our current geological era, according to a *New York Times* story in 2024, the International Union of Geological Sciences affirmed a vote by committee to *not* officially label the current geological era "the Anthropocene"; see Zhong, "Geologists Make It Official."

Davis believed our contributions were making the world better. Making the world better, for Davis, certainly included preserving the natural environment, and he would have supported efforts to reverse climate change. But his focus was broader. For Davis, a better world is a world where every human can live the most abundant life possible. These terms are not precise, and I won't here try to spell them out here in detail.

An abundant life is a life of discovery, a life experiencing the world, and discovering its truths, its beauty, its challenges, and its pains. An abundant life, for Davis, included contributing to the good of all, now and in the future. Davis believed that the ideals of truth, beauty, and goodness were built into human personality, and that our responding to them, through them, and with them, is how we made a better world. The process was ongoing. The joy was in the path, in being part of this life. This was where Davis found hope when confronting challenges and setbacks.

These are significant commitments: Commitments to the ideals of truth, beauty, and goodness. Commitments to "human divinity" overcoming "human depravity," both at an individual level and collectively. Commitments to all this continuing into the indefinite future.

Any one of these commitments could turn out to be wrong. Indeed, these commitments seem out of step with our current times, the third decade of the twenty-first century. Do humans respond to the ideals of truth, beauty, and goodness? Are these ideals even stable over time, or across the billions of people alive today? A quip of recent currency—your truth is not my truth—would suggest not. Certainly, it can seem that depravity is winning the struggle with divinity in human personality, and perhaps more important in our collective action. And even if divinity is winning today, what guarantee do we have that it will be winning tomorrow or one hundred years hence? We live in cynical times, apparently out of step with Davis's rosier view of things.

So, these are substantive commitments, commitments for which there is no proof. Davis's faith lay in these commitments. It was not a credulous faith. There was—and is—evidence that humans—some humans some of the time—respond to the ideals of truth, beauty, and goodness, although the exact definitions and the various relative weightings of these and other ideals have shifted over time, over the millennia, and they will continue to shift. Nonetheless, there is evidence that our world—as imperfect as it is—has gotten better. This is the story Steven Pinker tells with boatloads of evidence in *The Better Angels of Our Nature.*[3] But the evidence is not conclusive.

Still, there is much that I find appealing, compelling, in Davis's picture of world. Reading and transcribing his writings nearly daily over the past two-plus years has been a tonic to the depressing news I have encountered daily.

I like his emphasis on discovery, on experience, and I have greatly enjoyed the discoveries I have made reading him. I have never been persuaded by any kind of supernatural revelation, and I have found Davis's rejection of revelation in favor of discovery extremely appealing. I have found his robust admiration for and support of democracy refreshing, a helpful counterbalance to the steady diet of cynicism about government. For all the daily news stories of human depravity—one mass shooting after another—I do believe that many, indeed the vast majority of humans do listen to the better angels of their natures. Even if we are hearing different messages from these angels, we can—and sometimes do—bring these differences into civil, respectful conversation with each other. We can learn from each other. I find that hope for the future is helpful, certainly better than despair.

Still, before getting into the various theological details attached to Davis's commitments, it is worthwhile considering if his cheery outlook was only a creature of his times. Can such commitments work in our darker times? Are our times darker?

2. What about Postmodernism?

Where Davis recognized himself as living in the modern world, today we sometimes say that we live in a "postmodern world." Indeed, according to Wikipedia, some now say we live in a "post-postmodern world."[4] The postmodern world is a world without a "master narrative," no legitimate or true story to tell about the direction of history: How we got here and where we are going. No story of progress.

This sharply contrasts with Davis's story, which is all about the direction of history. Postmodernism rejects Davis's story of emergence of modernism—of discovery, freedom, and consent replacing revelation, authority, and obedience. This is "just" his story, no better than

3. Pinker, *Better Angels of Our Nature.*

4. See "Postmodernism."

any other story. Doubts now surround the objectivity of science. And cynicism is our postmodern stance about the power of our democracy to solve our problems.

With his 1979 book, *Philosophy and the Mirror of Nature,* Richard Rorty (1931–2007) is remembered as the philosopher who brought postmodernism to philosophy in the United States.[5] In a subsequent article, "Postmodernist Bourgeois Liberalism," he defines his terms:

> I use "postmodernist" in a sense given to this term by Jean-François Lyotard, who says that the postmodern attitude is that of "distrust of meta-narratives." . . . These meta-narratives are stories which purport to justify loyalty to, or breaks with, certain contemporary communities.[6]

Davis's story, emphasizing the emergence of discovery, freedom, and consent, is just such a "meta-narrative." It aims to justify loyalty to democracy as a system of government, and American democracy in particular. It also aims to undermine allegiance to systems of authority and obedience tied to supernatural revelation. Discovery, for Davis, provides a surer way to truth than revelation.

Postmodernism doesn't see discovery as a path to the truth. *The* truth doesn't exist in postmodernity. Rorty's *Philosophy and the Mirror of Nature* can be read as an argument against any concept of truth or objectivity that stands apart from the beliefs or commitments of a particular community. Since different communities will have different commitments and beliefs, there will be as many different truths and standards of objectivity as there are communities. Your truth is not my truth.

Rorty puts this point succinctly: We explain "rationality and epistemic authority by reference to what society lets us say, rather than the latter by the former."[7] *The truth* does not explain what society lets us say, rather what society lets us say explains what we call truth and objectivity. Scientific truth exists because certain societies allow it to exist. In another society things could be different. There is nothing special about science to justify its claims to truth and objectivity.

These are not simply abstract philosophical matters. The widespread distrust of the COVID vaccines demonstrate the robust legs of a postmodern view of science—and government. Political polarization, along with

5. Rorty, *Philosophy and the Mirror of Nature.*
6. Rorty, "Postmodernist Bourgeois Liberalism," in Menand, *Pragmatism*, 331–32.
7. Rorty, *Philosophy and the Mirror of Nature*, 174.

dueling information/disinformation campaigns, has done much to drive this distrust. With predictable and—in my view—disastrous results.

Certain aspects of contemporary science have contributed to the current—postmodern—distrust of science. These include widely reported instances of scientific fraud, apparent conflicts of interest with some scientists seemingly beholden to various profit-centered corporate entities—think "big pharma"—and an opaque meritocratic scientific culture that can be experienced as expressing disdain for the nonscientific hoi polloi.

The emergence of "big science" over the course of the twentieth century is well-documented. Big science, with its connections to the military-industrial complex and the health-big pharma complex, looks very different from Davis's science. This, along with the meritocratic nature of scientific training and advancement, moves in the direction of authority and obedience. These days, scientific discoveries are not easy to understand. Davis would remind us that authority comes in "many beautiful raiments" and bemoan a "monarchy of scientific knowledge," sometimes allied with a "monarchy of money."

The postmodernist attack on modernism strikes at the core of the optimistic picture that Davis was attached to at the beginning of the twentieth century. Postmodernism denies a univocal notion of discovery, including scientific discovery. Postmodernism describes an environment that puts community allegiance ahead of a (discredited) notion of truth. "Postmoderns" live in propaganda-sorted alternative community bubbles. Misinformation lives on a par with information, and we have diminished our ability to sort out our differences civilly.

While culturally, postmodernism seems to capture our current sociopolitical moment, conceptually, it seems to me that this postmodernist attack gets lost in its abstractions. Since the time of Plato and Aristotle, philosophers have always struggled with defining "Truth." At that very high level of abstraction, "Truth" is hard, perhaps impossible, to nail down precisely to everyone's satisfaction. But ultimately how persuasive is the idea that we do not know more today than we did when my grandfather wrote, or more than we did when Plato and Aristotle offered their explanations for the natural world?

Is this idea—that we know more today—merely an agreement made by a certain community? This seems completely implausible to me. Consider almost any techno-scientific advance. Heinrich Hertz discovered "radio waves" at the end of the nineteenth century and by the early twentieth century radios proliferated. Here is an example of new knowledge that underwrites a new technological capacity. Radio waves work independent of any community's endorsement. However, we might explain radio waves, there can be little doubt that radios exist, and they exploit our newfound abilities to manipulate and use radio waves.[8] It is much harder for the postmodernist to deny the advance of our abilities to intervene and do things in the world.[9]

While the challenges to our faith in science—fraud, conflicts of interest, an opaque science-knowledge-based meritocracy—would seem to undermine my grandfather's enthusiasm for scientific discovery and his faith in discovery generally, I think just the opposite is true. The fact that we are appalled by scientific fraud demonstrates the power of our commitment to "honest discovery." Similarly with conflicts of interest. These are instances where science has not lived up to the underlying ideals for discovery. Peirce was drawn to the method of science because it offered something external, "something upon which our thinking has no effect."[10] The ideal of the method of science is that it provides an uninterested check on human interests. The fact that we recoil from stories of "scientists" cashing in and muddying the ideal of disinterested inquiry shows that this ideal lives.

The friction between scientific meritocracy and Davis's notion of freedom and consent is more challenging. Contemporary science is complex, and not accessible to everyone. Putting aside the miasma of disinformation and other human failings, we still encounter here a kind of claim to obedience, obedience to science, that is contrary to the ideals of freedom and consent. Here, for me, is a genuine concern behind vaccine denial. Underneath all the grandstanding, dissembling, and outright lying, public health does demand a certain level of obedience and consent to be effective. This is because it operates at a population level, not simply at the level of the individual. To protect a population from COVID—including, of course, the individuals in the population—we need population-level interventions. Obedience.

8. In the late 1880s Heinrich Hertz (1857–94), a German physicist, conclusively confirmed the existence of electromagnetic waves, as predicted by James Clerk Maxwell's theory of electromagnetism. Interestingly, Hertz was also sensitive to how multiple theories, relying on different theoretical commitments about the world—"different truths"—can be equivalently consistent with, and supported by, the empirical facts. He argued for this, a kind of a "proto-postmodernism," in his posthumous *Principles of Mechanics*. For more on Hertz, see my *Heinrich Hertz*.

9. This is one of the principal points of my *Thing Knowledge*.

10. Peirce, "Fixation of Belief," in Menand, *Pragmatism*, 16. See also ch. 2 above.

But here again, have we not in the United States witnessed the underlying power of democratic values—discovery, freedom, and consent—in how vaccine mandates and vaccine denials played out? It has been stressful, ugly, anything but efficient, but multiple voices have been heard, a democratic process has been engaged. Much to the frustration of many public health officials—and others myself included—in the United States we did not implement a pure monarchy of science, of public health. Authority and obedience were resisted. Freedom and consent reigned though this messy democratic process.

3. *Liberalism*

The title to Rorty's, journal article, "Postmodernist Bourgeois Liberalism," is revealing. Rorty wants postmodernism's rejection of objectivity, truth and "meta-narratives." But he also wants what he calls "bourgeois liberal values." He wants the values that underlie American democracy, including discovery, freedom, and consent. But how can we have "bourgeois liberal values" without objectivity and truth? Rorty recognizes this seeming contradiction, writing, "'Postmodernist bourgeois liberalism' sounds oxymoronic."[11] According to postmodernism, bourgeois liberal values are "just" one possible set of values.

Rorty responds, "I hope . . . to suggest . . . that loyalty to itself is morality enough, that such loyalty no longer needs an ahistorical backup."[12] Bourgeois liberalism is "just" our culture, but we can—we should, Rorty suggests—be loyal to it, simply because *it is* our culture. As Ian Hacking wrote (see chapter 2), "We are left with no external way to evaluate our own tradition, but why should we want that?"[13]

We want that because we want some confidence in our commitments, some confidence in the future promise of these commitments. Rorty agrees. He finds this confidence in comparisons:

> Nations or churches or movements are, on this view, shining historical examples not because they reflect rays emanating from a higher source, but because of contrast-effects—comparisons with other, worse communities.[14]

11. Rorty, "Postmodernist Bourgeois Liberalism," in Menand, *Pragmatism*, 332.
12. Rorty, "Postmodernist Bourgeois Liberalism," in Menand, *Pragmatism*, 332.
13. Hacking, *Representing and Intervening*, 128.
14. Rorty, "Postmodernist Bourgeois Liberalism," in Menand, *Pragmatism*, 333-34.

Rorty suggests that we judge "shining historical examples" not based on "rays emanating from a higher source," or, as Davis would put it, based on some supernatural authority. Rather, we judge by comparison. We contrast our bourgeois liberalism with worse examples. American bourgeois liberal democracy is better than the Roman Empire—or autocratic Russia or China. We judge our culture of discovery, freedom, and consent better than revelation, authority, and obedience.

Could this judgment be wrong? Certainly. No one is claiming infallibility here. But Davis would point out that these judgements reflect our ideals. Davis was not claiming a supernatural—external or "meta"—justification for this judgment. For him the fact of such a judgment exposes our deeper aspirations, our hopes, our ideals.

While Davis and Rorty might agree on this point, they sharply diverge on another point. Rorty emphasizes loyalty. Loyalty is "justification enough" for his commitment to bourgeois liberal values. While Davis certainly believed in and supported human empathy and the solidarity of groups struggling for voice in their lives, more important to Davis was courage and independence. Progress happens when people challenge the status quo, not when people are loyal to it. Postmodernism abandons the idea of progress, and this creates a space for Rorty to emphasize loyalty over independence. Davis, by contrast, is committed to progress, and to the importance of independence and courage as drivers of progress. Davis's conception of progress may be well captured with the terms "bourgeois liberal values"—although as a democratic socialist Davis certainly would balk at "bourgeois"—his faith in these values transcends group loyalty.

4. Truth, Beauty, and Goodness

It is our ideals and aspirations that Davis found in human personalities—all our personalities—that Davis believed drove history. Core among these ideals and aspirations are truth, beauty, and goodness:

> To every stimulating call that bids us inquire into the truth of life, there goes forth from us a responsive answer. To every alluring well of beauty and harmony from the outside world, there wells up some sense of appreciation, some effort to

> respond. To every act of heroic conduct there within us the impulse to goodness.[15]

For Davis, these ideals—truth, beauty, and goodness—were somehow built into our personalities, and it is the action of these ideals through our personalities that drove positive change in the world.

But *are* these ideals built into our personalities? Everyone's personality? How did they get there—assuming they are there? Indeed, what precisely are these ideals? Are they the same today as millennia ago? Will they be the same millennia into the future?

Take the last question, are these ideals stable over time? We have already seen that Davis himself did not believe that the ideals were stable over millennia. Davis has pointed out that everything modern differs from its ancient and medieval counterpart, including ideas of God, man, truth, morality, evil, sin, "any other vital fact or problem of human life."[16]

So, if everything is changing—including our aspirations and ideals—surely we cannot expect our current aspirations and ideals to remain the same into the future. Our efforts today—our inevitably incomplete efforts today—to improve things as imagined by our current aspirations and ideals, will never come to completion. Nor will things always continue to get better over time as conceptualized by current aspirations and ideals. In the future our aspirations and ideals will be different. We'll head off in another direction. We can see this happening today as compared with Davis's day. Our conceptions of beauty are different, goodness today comes with a different focus. Postmodern truth certainly is not Davis's modern truth.

Davis's emphasis on discovery provides the pathway through this Gordian knot. Discovery is an ongoing—and fallible—human process. We discover things about the universe, both simple and complex, elementary school addition to protein folding revealed by artificial intelligence. We also discover things about our aspirations and ideals.

The situation with truth, beauty, and goodness is analogous to the situation with postmodern truth discussed above. We can get lost in our abstractions, for it is impossible to find fully satisfactory, final, and universally agreed upon definitions for these terms. As with "postmodern truth," part of living is discovering new and unexpected avenues for

15. Davis, "Essential Christ" (1922), 4–5.

16. See ch. 2. Quote is from Davis, "Adventurous Task" (1909c), 2.

beauty, new and necessary needs for goodness and justice. We realize our earlier conceptions were imperfect at best, if not deeply flawed.

The moral of this fact of change is not that anything goes—and will go—that everything and nothing is true—or good or just or beautiful. The moral of this fact is humility, and a redoubled effort to continue to test and improve what we know of truth, beauty, and goodness—through our experiences and our reflections on these experiences.

> Before us, beginning at our very feet, is the vast expanse of the future. What that future shall bring forth, human minds cannot determine. But I hear the voice of the human soul, still hungering and thirsting after righteousness and justice . . . asking us to come and help. Herein lies the adventurous task of the work that is before us. What specific thing that voice asks of us, we do not know, what we shall be called upon to do, we do not know, but we hear the voice of truth and human love asking us to come and help. We have the sublime faith that to him who has the single-eyed will, the way and the truth shall be disclosed.[17]

As with all of this, it is a matter of faith, that our ongoing efforts at discovery—both about the world, *and about our concepts of the world*—will make progress, progress toward a future "human minds cannot determine." For more on this faith see chapter 9.

5. Divinity and Depravity

Daily, the news media doses us with stories of human failings, mass shootings, governmental gridlock, climate-related disasters, stories of human avarice and moral weakness. "If it bleeds, it leads" is a long-standing motto of journalism. The conclusion that things are getting worse, not better, is preordained by our media production and consumption patterns. The COVID pandemic has been awful, with millions dying, and millions more held apart by "social distancing." Why should we think that our "inner divinity," our aspirations for truth, beauty, and goodness, will overcome—could possibly overcome—our "inner depravity"? The news we take in seems daily to confirm that all the most vile and self-serving elements of our personalities are ascendant. The news we take in, and indeed our own anxieties and self-protective impulses, tell us this

17. Davis, "Adventurous Task" (1909c), 5–6.

is so. Depravity is winning, and we must do everything in our power to protect ourselves from multiple threats that surround us.

A psychologist friend of mine tells me that humans are predisposed to hear criticism much more loudly than praise. Every critical remark speaks with six times the volume of every praising remark. We are built to hear and expect attacks, on ourselves and on those we hold dear. This psychological predisposition likely has some evolutionary value, emphasizing dangers and driving us to take protective action. But it also colors how we see the world, and that coloration can drive a self-fulfilling loop. As the world looks dangerous and people around us seem threatening we build walls and establish distrust.

But humans are complex. Alongside our protective impulses, we also are curious, social, and empathetic creatures. Again, no doubt, features of our evolutionary inheritance. Our curiosity prompts us to learn more; discovery drives us forward. Our social and empathetic natures provide the seeds for our sense of justice and goodness. We can create pathways to trust. Furthermore, we are reasoning creatures that have constructed language and logic, which gives us an additional tool for discovery—about the world, about ourselves, *and* about avenues for truth, beauty, and goodness.

The nineteenth-century Unitarian minister William Ellery Channing (1780–1842) had a large influence on Davis. Channing rejected the deeply pessimistic view of human nature provided by Calvinism, a view of the uniform depravity of humans that was widely held in the Western, post-Reformation, Protestant world. Instead, Channing emphasized another side of humans, a more positive side of human nature. Channing introduced his collected writings thus:

> The following writings will be found to be distinguished by nothing more than the high estimate which they express of human nature.[18]

In 1841, Channing saw this divine side of our personalities and its implications for how to treat humans:

> It is because the human being has moral powers, because he carries a law in his breast, and was made to govern himself, that I cannot endure to see him taken out of his own hands and fashioned into a tool by another's avarice or pride. It is because I see in him a great nature, the divine image, and vast capacities, that

18. Channing, "Introductory Remarks," 57, first published in 1841.

> I demand for him means of self-development, spheres for free action; that I call society not to fetter, but to aid his growth.[19]

Channing saw both divinity and depravity in humans. But he chose to refocus our attention on the good, to support the good, the divinity in humans.

In a 1919 sermon, Davis wrote of Channing,

> His work was always to stir within men that feeling of self-respect, and sense of responsibility, to rouse the latent powers. Never a word of repression, but always expression. He was always urging education, enlightenment, wholesome pleasure, the overcoming of evil with good, not by repressing the evil, but by releasing the good.[20]

For Channing, followed by Davis, evil can be found in our make-up. But so too can more positive ideals, including truth, beauty, and goodness. For Channing—and for Davis—we win by supporting the good in humans, allowing it the greatest opportunity for expression.

The good can—and will, said Davis's faith—win over evil, given a supportive environment and one's effort. Davis writes,

> But there is no dodging the issue over which so much confusion exists today, namely the issue of the relation of environment to individual conduct. He [Channing] relates the two properly and soundly. Both are factors. The good seed cannot grow in sterile and unproductive soil, it cannot grow in the dark. But on the other hand, he realizes full well that given both good seed, and good soil, then to produce good fruits is the result of hard work, of constant and persistent effort. Never does he release the individual from the responsibility resting upon him, a responsibility not only for his own development, but responsibility for providing good soil for the other fellow. This is what he really means by Liberty.
>
> In all relations of life, we are not only bound to make full use of the opportunities that come to us but are under equal obligation to do our full share in guaranteeing to others opportunities such as we have.[21]

Effort is required. Heaven will not be handed to us on a silver platter—or won in some supposed Calvinist divine lottery. We must work for it. A

19. Channing, "Introductory Remarks," 61.
20. Davis, "Channing" (1919a), 5.
21. Davis, "Channing" (1919a), 5–6.

full abundant life for all requires that we work for the good of all, not just for ourselves and those we favor. That is how we overcome evil.

It is worth remembering the context of Davis's "Channing" sermon. It was preached shortly after the conclusion of World War I—the Great War, a war that left approximately nine million soldiers and eight million civilians dead, along with twenty-three million soldiers wounded. It was a horrific display of human depravity. Freedom of expression had been sharply curtailed by "war exigency."[22] A "red scare" was sweeping the United States, denying the rights of expression, marginalizing and imprisoning socialists—the same socialists that Davis identified with.

In another sermon, written about a year earlier, Davis worried about the loss of freedom of expression:

> We are still freemen, at least in the world of the spirit. But the hounds of authority, power, and compulsion are at large in the world. Not since our ancestors fled their cruel exactions to lay the foundations of the New World in Freedom, have the forces of authority been so truculent and assertive, or so dangerous. We cannot escape the test.[23]

If we want good to overcome evil, if we want to preserve our freedom, if we want to resist authority—"compulsion at large in the world"—we have to work for that, "we cannot escape the test."

6. Authority Religion

We must, each of us, Davis argued, spend the time and effort to think through how to live moral and religious lives. We must bear our burdens. Our actions must follow. But this is difficult, time-consuming, error-prone, and anxiety-provoking work. We naturally seek "ready-mades," what Davis called "authority religion." This certainly has been true for me, although perhaps less in seeking a ready-made as in simply avoiding the question. But I begin to appreciate the pressing importance of Davis's injunction to bear our burden when I see these same "hounds of authority, power and compulsion" in 2024 that Davis worried about in 1918.

In a 2023 column David French speaks of the attraction and deep moral challenge of "authority religion." He describes the popular appeal, particularly among evangelical circles, of Bill Gothard's Institute in Basic

22. Hochschild, *American Midnight.*

23. Davis, "Great Tradition" (1918a), 8.

Life Principles. French writes, "The beating heart of Gothardism was a combination of authority and superstition."[24] I read this and immediately I was in mind of Davis's discovery, freedom, and consent versus revelation, authority, and obedience:

> The quest for certainty and control can tempt people of every faith and no faith. . . . Life is hard, and we want answers—even, perhaps especially, where answers are impossible to find. We crave control, even when attempts to establish control sow destruction in our loved ones' lives.[25]

Revelation, authority, and obedience are attractive. We want answers, and the more we experience bewildering change, change with "uncontrolled ferocity," the more we seek control—through revelation, authority, and obedience.

Change is not going away. It is in the nature of things. Life drives change. The question is, how can we best cope with change? Davis's answer was discovery, freedom, and consent. Central to discovery is humility. We are fallible. French concludes his editorial:

> The Apostle Paul stated a universal human truth when he declared that "we see through a glass, darkly." We can know things only "in part." The Gothard movement and movements like it reject that sense of doubt. They purport to reveal all the deepest truths and answer all our most difficult questions. Yet no person possesses such wisdom. And if there is one lesson we should take from "Shiny Happy People," it's this: When people claim to personally light the path and clear away the darkness, you know they are leading you astray.[26]

Or, to take a passage from the Bible, "What doth the Lord require of thee, but to do justly, and to love mercy, and to walk humbly with thy God."[27] We must bear our burden. Ready-mades, no matter how attractive, cannot substitute for the work we do when we bear our burden. In Davis's sermon just discussed, "The Great Tradition Becomes the Great Faith," Davis suggested that one of the important messages Jesus

24. French, "Shiny Happy People," 3. The "Shiny Happy People" of his title refers to an Amazon Prime documentary series of this title that follows the Duggar family, who subscribe to the teachings of Bill Gothard.

25. French, "Shiny Happy People," 6.

26. French, "Shiny Happy People," 6. French's biblical quote is from 1 Cor 13:12.

27. Mic 6:8.

preached was that "God's blessings come not as gifts, but as discoveries and achievements."[28]

It is *our* burden—not simply *my* burden or *your* burden, although it is that too. This burden demands individuals to think deeply about their moral and religious commitments, but it also demands sharing. We learn from each other, particularly from those who reach different conclusions. Remember Davis's response to cries of heresy:

> Let us widen the circle so that it will include the erstwhile heretic, and instead of trying to brand him as an outcast and person to be shunned, let us seek him out that we may learn what he has to tell us of life.[29]

Discovery, freedom, and consent should *open* a conversation. This is a conversation that Davis would seek to advance in a church, a "free church." In our more secular world, it is a conversation—or rather multiple conversations—that take place through many different channels: books, the academy, journals and magazines, entertainment, news media, social media, politics, "across the backyard fence," and, yes, places of worship. We cannot have all of discovery, freedom, and consent without these conversations, engaged with independence, courage, charity, benevolence, and humility.

7. Freedom and Responsibility

Sociologist Robert Putnam, in his 2020 book *The Upswing*, has characterized the century-plus from the early 1900s to our current day as an "I-we-I" phenomenon. He writes of an inverted U-shaped curve that represents

> a phenomenon we have come to call the "I-we-I" curve: a gradual climb into greater interdependence and cooperation, followed by a steep descent into greater independence and egoism. It has been reflected in our experience of equality, our expression of democracy, our stock of social capital, our cultural identity, and our shared understanding of what this nation is all about.[30]

28. Davis, "Great Tradition" (1918a), 3.
29. See ch. 2. Davis, "What Shall We Do" (1923a), 4.
30. Putnam, *Upswing*, 12–13.

In the subtitle to his book, "How American Came Together a Century Ago and How *We* Can Do It Again,"[31] Putnam is calling for action to reverse the recent sixty-year-long shift from "we" to "I" that Putnam sees plaguing our current culture. Putnam is optimistic. He believes we can reverse this trend. He says this because we have done it before. Over the first half of the twentieth century, we moved the needle from "I" to "we." This is our burden.

Putnam concludes his book with a chapter that recalls a 1914 book, *Drift and Mastery* by Walter Lippmann (1889–1974), an early twentieth-century progressive journalist.[32] Putnam writes of Lippmann's book,

> In the utterly new world of the early twentieth century—transformed by urbanization, industrialization, an increasing dependence on wage labor, the mushrooming of corporations and consolidations of every kind, the rewriting of social norms and customs, a rapidly growing and diversifying population, and raging debates about the role of individuals, institutions, and government in managing the challenges these conditions created—what was the democratic citizen to do?[33]

Lippmann's world was Davis's world, a world of rapid change with "uncontrolled ferocity."

Lippmann called for the members of the public, individually, but especially collectively, to bear the burden:

> At a time when American democracy suffered from the "drift" of overwhelming despair, Lippmann called for the "mastery" of history by an active, inventive, and disciplined citizenry. Of the prospect of engendering an upswing out of a downward drift, he contended, "it has to be done not by some wise and superior being but by the American people themselves. No one man, no one group can do it all. It is an immense collaboration." Americans, in other words, had to eschew the corrosive, cynical slide toward "I" and rediscover the latent power and promise of "we."[34]

Putnam then details the many various ways that the American public of the early twentieth century did bear their burden and initiate an upswing. And, he says, we can—we must—do it again.

31. Putnam, *Upswing* (emphasis in the original subtitle).

32. Putnam, *Upswing*, ch. 9, "Drift and Mastery." See also Lippmann, *Drift and Mastery*.

33. Putnam, *Upswing*, 317.

34. Putnam, *Upswing*, 317, quoting Lippmann, *Drift and Mastery*, 99.

Davis emphasized freedom and consent—as opposed to authority and obedience—and this could appear to run contrary to Putnam's prescriptions. Putnam's "steep descent," from 1970 to 2020, from "we" to "I," has emphasized individual free choice, "greater independence and egoism." One could conclude that Davis's freedom is the problem. We pursued freedom at the expense of efforts to find "our shared understanding." But for Davis, freedom is only free when everyone can share in its fruits, and this demands shared responsibilities. With freedom comes responsibility, burdens to bear.

The liberal republican principles on which the American democratic republic was founded, principles spelled out by John Locke,[35] attempt to square this circle of individual liberty with shared responsibility. This approach to governance is what philosophers call liberalism—not to be confused with the term "liberalism" used to describe left-wing politics.

8. Gifts-Based Liberalism

In an important article examining Canada's legalization of assisted suicide, David Brooks spells out two ways of understanding liberalism:

> Autonomy-based liberalism starts with one core conviction: I possess myself. I am a piece of property that I own. . . .
>
> The purpose of my life, in this version of liberalism, is to be happy—to live a life in which my pleasures, however I define them, exceed my pains. . . .
>
> But there is another version of liberalism. Let's call this gifts-based liberalism. It starts with a different core conviction: I am a receiver of gifts. I am part of a long procession of humanity. I have received many gifts from those who came before me, including the gift of life itself. The essential activity of life is not the pursuit of individual happiness. The essential activity of life is to realize the gifts I've been given by my ancestors, and to pass them along, suitably improved, to those who will come after.[36]

35. John Locke (1632–1704), English philosopher, is remembered for—among many contributions—his 1689/90 *Treatises of Government,* which significantly influenced the thinking that went into the development of the government of the United States.

36. Brooks, "Canadian Way of Death," 88.

Gift relationships are always about building and preserving community, the "shared understanding," or the "we" of Putnam's analysis.[37] Brooks's "gift-based liberalism" moves away from the pure individualism of "autonomy-based liberalism" and recognizes the relationships that we are born into—that are given to us at birth. Gifts-based liberalism recognizes the community-sustaining responsibilities that come with individual freedom.

Brooks notes that gifts-based liberalism gives "you membership in a procession that stretched back to your ancestors."

> It connects you to those who migrated to this place or that, married this person or that, raised their children this this way or that. What you are is an expression of history.[38]

Steven Cave, in a discussion of mortality (about which more in chapter 8) describes what he calls a "wisdom narrative" about mortality. An important element of this wisdom narrative is "gratitude," and, in particular, gratitude for all the things that had to happen in the long chain of events leading up to one's birth:

> An unbroken chain of many millions of ancestors over billions of years all managed to do their bit to bring us into existence, that is our blessing. . . .
>
> Complex life—and in particular—the life of any individual—is remarkable. Astonishing. Wondrous.[39]

In short, a gift. A gift we need to recognize.

But persons are not simply individual expressions of history. A person inherits a culture as well. In addition to the gift of life, Brooks emphasizes three other aspects of "gifts-based liberalism":

> You didn't create your dignity.
>
> You don't control your mind.
>
> You did not create your deepest bonds.[40]

All these aspects of one's core identity derive from the multiple communities one inherits at birth, or one joins through one's efforts. They are preexisting. Gifts, one must pay forward.

37. See Hyde, *Gift*. I have written about this aspect of gift relationships in scientific research, see my *Thing Knowledge*, ch. 10.

38. Brooks, "Canadian Way of Death," 92.

39. Cave, *Immortality*, 281.

40. Brooks, "Canadian Way of Death," 89–92.

While preexisting, they are not static. History is about change. Brooks describes the evolution—the "long procession"—of the culture and communities that are bequeathed to us in terms Davis would be very comfortable with:

> This long procession, though filled with struggles and hardship, has made life sweeter for us. Human beings once lived in societies in which slavery was a foundational fact of life, beheadings and animal torture were popular entertainments, raping and pillaging were routine. But gradually, with many setbacks, we've built a culture in which people are more likely to abhor cruelty, a culture that has as an ideal the notion that all people deserve fair treatment, not just our kind of people.
>
> This is progress. Thanks to this procession, each generation doesn't have to make the big decisions of life standing on naked ground. We have been bequeathed sets of values, institutions, cultural traditions that embody the accumulated wisdom of our kind. The purpose of life, in a gifts-based world, is to participate in this procession, to keep the march of progress going along its fitful course.[41]

Our burden is not to recreate all values "standing on naked ground," but to participate in an ongoing procession, learning from experience, our mistakes and our successes, and our powers of reasoning. But, most assuredly doing this in a social and cooperative manner, not as pure individuals. Pure "individual freedom" or "autonomy-based liberalism" ignores all the community ties that give our lives and our conceptions meaning, relevance, power.

> The good of humanity is not some abstraction—its grounded in the succession of intimates and institutions that we inherit, and that we reform, improve, and pass on.[42]

9. Our Culture, Our Inheritance

Davis's commitments were substantive. But there was support for them. Perhaps more to my current point, these commitments ground current culture. For those of us born in the second half of the twentieth century in the United States, we inherited these commitments. Philosophically and culturally, we have responded to this inheritance, struggled with it,

41. Brooks, "Canadian Way of Death," 92–93.

42. Brooks, "Canadian Way of Death," 93.

criticized it. Rejected it. We have created postmodernism out of modernism. This betrays our impatience.

Davis's transition from revelation, authority, and obedience to discovery, freedom, and consent was centuries in the making. It still is in the making. Davis likely would view "postmodernism" as a wobble, a moment of anxiety, a temporary loss of faith, in the centuries-long process away from ancient and medieval culture. He certainly was aware of such anxiety in his own day. Recall his discussion of the Epistle to the Hebrews from his 1947 sermon. Keep the faith, the epistle urged, even in the face of challenges and setbacks. This struggle is ongoing.

When I started my work on my grandfather's writings I expected to learn about his views on God, Jesus, the Bible, heaven, perhaps immortality. Along the way I found governance—discovery, freedom, and consent—I found modernism and change. I found the power of human ideals, truth, beauty, and goodness. I also found Davis's views on these more traditionally religious topics, and to these topics I now turn.

With a spirit of discovery, a spirit of freedom—and the responsibility it entails—I have felt better empowered to consider these questions that previously I have avoided. I do not expect revelation, but discovery—fallible discovery.

Where and how to begin? This would feel a very formidable task, a task I am likely not up to, were I to attempt this on my own. But my grandfather has been an admirable guide. And this betrays an important point.

No effort begins out of nothing. We learn from, start from, our culture and our inheritance—David Brooks's point. At a general level, for me, this has been American culture as it arrived and evolved during the second half of the twentieth century. At a more individual level, this has been my grandfather's thinking—influenced as it was, and as it had to be, by his own cultural inheritances. The views that I believe he worked out are certainly at the very liberal end of Christianity, if Christian at all—although he was a great admirer of Jesus Christ. Nonetheless, he started from a Christian tradition. He was particularly interested in the Calvinist, Reformation forms of Christianity that came to the "New World," and saw himself in line with this tradition, even while he disagreed with much of its orthodoxy.

A central feature of the Reformation was access to the Bible. Instead of a system where only special persons—bishops, priests—could read, interpret, and share the messages of the Bible with the rest of humanity, the Reformation ushered in a world where everyone was encouraged to read the Bible. Universal priesthood.

While this change was many years—centuries—in the making, it also was sudden. In 1536, William Tyndale was led to the scaffold, strangled, and burnt for the crime of translating the Bible into English. Two years later, 1538, Thomas Cromwell, chief minister to King Henry VIII, issued an injunction that a copy of the Bible in English be made available within every church available for anyone in the congregation to read. Davis wrote of this event,

> 1538, the year when the King's Secretary ordered Bibles chained in every church for public reading, was an epoch-making event in modern history. It is not stretching the imagination too much to say that it marks the beginning of modern liberal education.[43]

For Davis, here was a giant step forward towards discovery, freedom, and consent. This was the tradition Davis felt connected to, his culture, his inheritance. And so, my next step is to the Bible.

43. Davis, *Origins and History* (1916a), Lecture I, 4.

Chapter 4: **A Natural Book**

> Beginning in the faith that the Bible is a supernatural revelation, following in the fidelity to the belief, [searching] for all historic information about that revelation; the conclusion of it all has been to disprove the validity of their original assumption, and to place the Bible back into the realm of natural books, naturally produced and naturally transmitted.[1]

1. Each Individual's Responsibility

THE MANUSCRIPTS THAT I inherited from my grandfather came to me higgledy-piggledy in a trunk. There was no order, but neither complete randomness. Manuscripts were grouped in lumps, some with dates, some without, some typed, some handwritten. One of the first manuscripts that I worked on was his 1947 sermon discussed in chapters 1 and 2, "Not Revelation but Discovery, Not Forms but the Holy Spirit."[2] It was typed and easier to transcribe and edit. It turned out to be the last full text of a sermon manuscript he left.

One of the first handwritten sermons that I first worked on was from November 27, 1904. The Scripture text for this 1904 sermon, "Man's Responsibility," was Gal 6:5: "For every man shall bear his own burden." As already discussed in chapter 1, Davis's main target in the sermon was

1. Davis, "Results of Protestantism" (1931), 6. I slightly edited the language to make Davis's meaning clear. The full accurate quote is found below in section 3.

2. Davis, "Not Revelation" (1947a).

against authoritarian sources for religious and moral belief, and for the difficult, but he felt necessary, work that each individual should do to think through—and live—religious and moral lives. We must, each of us, bear our own burden. Davis argued,

> We can no longer hold to a conception of our relationship with God which will permit us to look to some agency outside our own person as a medium through which we are informed of God's will, and his moral purpose. The conception of a system by which the duty of discovering God's laws can be put upon the shoulder of some external agency, such as the Bible, the church, or Christ, is no longer tenable.[3]

Davis was a theist—and more on exactly what kind of a theist later—but a theist who did not accept on faith the teachings of "some agency outside"—the Bible, the church, even Jesus.

I was intrigued. Religion had always seemed to me a matter of relying on an external agency, some outside authority—the Bible, the Qur'an, a church's dictates, the pope, etc. These are exactly the authorities Davis excluded. For me, dependence on one or another of these authorities has been one point against established religion. I found no reason to believe that any of these sources were trustworthy. Apparently, Davis shared—at least some of—my skepticism.

2. Earl C. Davis and the Bible

I have always found the Bible largely impenetrable. The language is dated. The history is ancient, complicated, and seemingly remote from current concerns. The theism—to me anyway—unsupported, if not outright self-contradicting. Some of the moral prescriptions have resonated with me. Jesus' Sermon on the Mount—see Matt 5–7—makes some sense to me. But, for the most part, I have been deeply ignorant of the Bible. And it seemed that it would take a major effort to grasp the Bible's meaning(s), with limited payoff.

As I started the work on my grandfather's papers, this 1904 sermon gave me some solace. I didn't have to beat myself up over my ignorance of the Bible. I didn't need the Bible; indeed, *I shouldn't* rely on the Bible. It was just another "external agency," not to be trusted. My ignorance was excused.

3. Davis, "Man's Responsibility" (1904c), 5.

Working my way through my grandfather's manuscripts, I did find references to the Bible. There was the story from Heb 3:1–15, the Scripture reading for "Not Revelation but Discovery, Not Forms but the Holy Spirit." But many of the full text sermon manuscripts did not specify a Scripture reading. For the period of May 1908 through January 1911, a total of sixty-four full-text sermons, none identified a Scripture reading. I began to conclude that the Bible was not *that* important to my grandfather.

I could not have been more wrong. The last set of manuscripts that I transcribed and edited—still finishing as I began work on this chapter in February 2024—constitute a draft of a book on *The Origin and History of the Bible.*[4] Well over two-hundred single-spaced manuscript pages, these materials include seven chapters on the Old Testament, six on the New Testament, a chapter on the history of the English translations of the Bible, and fifty-eight distinct references to biblical scholarship. The individual manuscripts are titled "Lecture I, II, III, IV, V, etc.," from which I concluded that they were used in support of a program of religious education on the Bible—religious education aimed at adults, not children, and adults who are willing to navigate the archeological, historical, philological, and theological details of the complicated history of how this text—"the Bible"—came to be what it is.

Most of the Bible lecture manuscripts are not dated.[5] But internal evidence suggests that Davis wrote the manuscripts during 1916. One of the lectures *is* dated April 2, 1916.[6] The latest source he used was published in 1915.[7] And there also is a curious—tragically ironic—passage from one of his lectures where he argued that the writers of the Old Testament had no foreknowledge of the coming of Jesus Christ:

> There is the modern idea, which I may state that I hold, that the writers of the Old Testament had no more idea of the coming of Christ, or the significance of his life, than I have of the coming of the President of some republic in the year 2016. I believe that probably some country will have a ruler, or a chosen servant

4. Davis, *Origins and History* (1916a).

5. A couple of the manuscripts have notes attached, such as, "This was the material used Tuesday Jan. 9, 1951"; see Davis, *Origins and History* (1916a) Lecture XI.

6. Davis, *Origins and History* (1916a), Lecture XIII.

7. Hunting, *Story of Our Bible*. There is one exception, Montague Rhodes James's 1924 *Apocryphal New Testament*. But this exception was cited in some additional materials that were written later, not part of the original collection of lectures.

> to perform the general executive functions. I believe that such a president, ruler, or whatnot, will know more, be more just, more human, than the average public servant today. Quite likely, should there an especially strong and powerful, just and humane president appear that time, and should men look back into the literature of the generation that is now living, they would pick passages here and there from our attempts to describe a better state of society, and would say this president is just the sort of a man that we were looking for a hundred years ago.[8]

Obviously, Davis did not foresee the surprising election of Donald Trump in 2016. The fact that he chose 2016 as the future date about which he—and his contemporaries—could not predict "the coming of the President," suggests that he was writing in 1916—looking an even one hundred years into the future.

Davis's knowledge of the Bible was extensive, deep, and fully informed by the best scholarship available at the time he was writing.[9] In the outline for the penultimate lecture of his series, "Lecture XII: The Bible As a Whole" (there is no full text for this lecture) he summarizes the long, complicated history of the Bible shared in the previous twelve lectures. It is a history of the religious, ethical, social, and political—geopolitical—struggles of Judaism in Palestine from earliest records, ca. 2000 BCE, through the emergence of the early Christian church in the first centuries of the Common Era. As Judaism struggled to define itself through multiple devastating conflicts—with Egypt, Assyria, Babylonia, Persia, Greece, Rome, and other smaller powers—the Old Testament, emerged as a conceptual-ethical-political-cultural thread holding Judaism together. The New Testament developed out of the fracture of Christianity from Judaism. The last sentence of his outline for "The Bible as a Whole" gives Davis's overall assessment: "It is one of the greatest books in the world."[10]

As I learned reading Davis's lectures, the Bible provides a unique and valuable source of historical information about ethnology, ethics, philosophy, religious beliefs, and customs during this seminal period of history. Davis emphasized the breadth of biblical literature, covering

8. Davis, *Origins and History* (1916a), "Lecture V: Amos and the Prophets," 17.

9. Davis, *Origins and History* (1916a), "Lecture XV: Bibliography." Throughout my transcribed and edited versions of these lectures I have added footnotes that share some of the details about the scholars Davis was consulted.

10. Davis, *Origins and History* (1916a), "Lecture XII: The Bible as a Whole," 2.

history, law, religion, the prophets, poetry, etc. He clearly studied the Bible carefully and he thought highly of it indeed.

Davis used biblical stories and passages in his work as a minister. As I further worked my way through all the materials I inherited from him, it became clear that the Bible played a much more central role in his ministry than I initially thought. The materials he left for his later sermons—during the 1930s and 1940s—are (nearly) all outlines, not full texts. All of them include a biblical Scripture reading, among other non-biblical texts, tied to his sermons.[11] I came to realize that the lack of any identified biblical readings for his earlier full text sermons was an artifact of what he had written down in the manuscripts for his sermons. My early conclusion—supporting my own ignorance of the Bible—that the Bible was not important to Davis, was just wrong.

And yet, we have a puzzle. For Davis was clear in his 1904 sermon that we should not rely on the Bible to be "informed of God's will, and his moral purpose." But then he makes extensive use of the Bible to inform himself and his congregation of exactly that. What status did the Bible have for Davis? What status should it have?

3. The Bible and the Reformation

There are two answers to this puzzle. The first focuses on the Bible's role in the great historic transformation that Davis was very attentive to—the transformation from ancient/medieval views of revelation, authority, and obedience to modern views of discovery, freedom, and consent. The second focuses on the Bible's role in the Christian Protestant tradition Davis was part of.

The Bible was a critical part of the Reformation's transition from revelation, authority, and obedience to discovery, freedom, and consent. Instead of relying on the dictates of the pope and the Catholic Church—which reformers found to be hopelessly lost and corrupt—the early Reformation thinkers turned to the Bible.

In a talk Davis gave to ministers in 1931, "The Results of Protestantism," he sketched the story:

11. The materials for the sermons Davis gave while in Petersham can be found in the "Earl Clement Davis Papers" archive in a section entitled "Sermons, 1933–1953" (https://commons.clarku.edu/petersham_sermons/).

> We are not far from the truth in stating that Protestants started out on their historic career impressed by the profound conviction that they had been entrusted by Almighty God with the task of carrying to a lost world the only means of salvation, the Christian Religion, God's Will, as revealed in the Bible.[12]

The first step away from the authority of the pope was to the authority of the Bible. But this had an immediate consequence for the reformers:

> The Bible: being the channel through which God's will is revealed to man, the Protestant, in all good faith, must know all that there is to be known about the Bible.[13]

This need

> inaugurated that long, laborious, and heroic search for the will of God in the Bible. Textual criticism; historical criticism; and the mis-named higher criticism; it is the record of a sublime faith and disinterested loyalty. Whatever may be said of the failures of Protestantism, this story of the uncovering of the secrets is marvelously rich, both in the integrity of character, and in heroic fidelity.[14]

This centuries-long effort—which continues today[15]—reached a peak in the nineteenth century. The conclusion, according to Davis, was this:

> Beginning in the faith that the Bible is a supernatural revelation, following in the fidelity to the belief, that their search for all historic information about that revelation; the conclusion of it all has been to disprove the validity of their original assumption, and to place the Bible back into the realm of natural books, naturally produced and naturally transmitted.[16]

The task, then, moving forward:

> It remains for the churchman today to restore the Bible with its richness of material to a legitimate place in the religious life and

12. Davis, "Results of Protestantism" (1931), 5.

13. Davis, "Results of Protestantism" (1931), 5.

14. Davis, "Results of Protestantism" (1931), 6.

15. A very interesting current source that agrees with Davis on most particulars is Ehrman, *Misquoting Jesus*.

16. Davis, "Results of Protestantism" (1931), 6.

> free from the taint of magic and superstition with which it was colored during the medieval period.[17]

For Reformation Protestants, the Bible, the revelation of God's will, provided the lever to move religion—some religion anyway—away from trust in the authority of the pope to trust in the authority of the Bible. A first move away from authority towards discovery. But this, then, demanded increased scrutiny of the Bible itself. And this scrutiny revealed not a supernatural book of truth directly revealed by God, but a natural book—an important, informing, powerful book—but a natural book, written, copied, edited, translated, and published by individual humans over centuries.

4. The Texts of the Bible in History

Davis began his *Lectures on the Origin and History of the Bible* in a doubly surprising way. In the first place, the first lecture, "The English Bible," is about the various early efforts to translate the Bible into English, efforts that took place during the late medieval period, the 1300s through the King James edition of 1611, many centuries after the birth of Jesus, and more centuries still after early origins of the Old Testament. This first lecture started towards the end of a centuries' long history of the Bible.

In the second place, he opened the first lecture with a section titled, "Results." The text began at the end with the conclusions. Here are the first sentences:

> Ever since the opening of the Protestant Reformation this search for the Original Bible has been going on. What is the result? Thus far we may say this . . .[18]

He then provided what today would be called seven bullet points on the conclusions of efforts to reveal the origin and history of the Bible.

His first "bullet point" identified the dates when the New Testament (496 CE) and the Old Testament (ca. 180 CE) were established as the canonical texts that we know today. It took nearly five hundred years from the birth of Jesus to definitively settle on New Testament Scripture. A lot happens in five hundred years.

17. Davis, "Results of Protestantism" (1931), 6.

18. Davis, *Origins and History* (1916a), "Lecture I: The English Bible," 1.

The second and third "bullet points" spoke to the manuscript sources that archeologists, historians, and Bible scholars discovered in the Protestant effort to uncover the "true Bible":

> [Second.] We have discovered a few very old manuscripts, one that is a complete New Testament. This manuscript has been revised and corrected five times, and the last time in the 16th century. The second is a large fragment, very old. This also has been revised by later scribes.
>
> [Third.] We find that among the various manuscripts found there are several hundred thousand variations from a standard text, 200,000 at least.[19]

Davis noted that—at the time he was writing—the oldest known manuscript of the New Testament dated from approximately 331 CE. This manuscript included twenty-nine "books"—Gospels and Epistles—twenty-seven of which ultimately came to be regarded as Scripture. The manuscripts show significant amounts of editing—more than two hundred thousand variations on a "standard text." Clearly, a lot was happening to the manuscripts that ultimately made up the New Testament during these five hundred years.

His seventh bullet point:

> [Seventh.] Arguing from experience with all other [nonbiblical] manuscripts, and from known data, we know that, while they [the earliest biblical manuscripts] are doubtless substantially true to earlier documents, there is not a passage but that is open to a suspicion of textual error in them, but we have no means of knowing.[20]

He concluded his opening results:

> Unsatisfactory as this is to many minds, it is a fact, which we have to recognize, and take into consideration in measuring truly the origin and history of the Bible. If these conclusions seem to disturb your conception of the Bible, hold your judgement in abeyance until more evidence is in.[21]

The lecture—and indeed all the subsequent lectures—provided this evidence.

19. Davis, *Origins and History* (1916a), "Lecture I: The English Bible," 1.
20. Davis, *Origins and History* (1916a), "Lecture I: The English Bible," 2.
21. Davis, *Origins and History* (1916a), "Lecture I: The English Bible," 2.

Davis then moved on to the struggle to translate the Bible into English. Here he made a first essential—perhaps obvious—point to his English-speaking congregation. The Bible was not written in English. More important, translation provides an obvious point where meaning can slip. One of the early translations of the Bible into English that Davis discussed was prepared in the 1520s by William Tyndale (ca. 1494–1536). Of this translation, Davis wrote,

> The comparison of a few words will . . . throw a vast amount of light upon the entire problem of translating:

Traditional words in common use in the church	Tyndale's Substitution for same in his translation
"grace"	"favor"
"charity"	"love"
"confess"	"acknowledge"
"penance"	"repentance"
"priest"	"Elder"
"Church"	"congregation"
"Salvation"	"health"

> The rendering of Tyndale made the Bible conform to his ideas while the conventional rendering, the traditional one, made it conform to established practices.[22]

Who is right, Tyndale or "established practice?" Writing for his English-speaking congregation, Davis wanted to be clear at the outset that the English Bible—of whatever translation—involved a series of choices about words, choices that bring differences of meaning. Translation is not a simple conversion. So, understanding the meaning of the Bible must include attention to these choices and their implications.

Davis also wanted to emphasize the importance of the effort to provide a version of the Bible in "the vernacular," accessible to the lay person. Translated Bible in hand, people did not have to depend on priests to learn the word of God. Universal priesthood.

It would take me too far afield to go into the depth Davis provided in his lectures. The information is detailed and extensive, and concerns both Old and New Testaments. A couple of examples will suffice.

22. Davis, *Origins and History* (1916a), "Lecture I: The English Bible," 19–20.

With respect to the New Testament, for example, Davis discussed "rejected passages." Here one case:

> First, Mark 16:9–20. Omitted in the two oldest manuscripts. Although space is left for it in the Vatican manuscript. . . . Gregory, whose work on the New Testament is one of the best of the conservative sort, says, "Mark 16:9–20 is neither part nor parcel of that Gospel."[23]

Other "rejected passages" which he discussed include John 7:53–8:11 about the woman taken in adultery; also 1 John 5:7–8, Luke 22:43–44, Matt 16:2–3, John 5:3–4, and Rom 9:5, all passages that we have reason to conclude were not part of the "original text."[24]

Davis devoted a whole lecture to the matter of interpreting the Synoptic Gospels (Matthew, Mark, and Luke) where he argued that they cannot be understood as simple historical records, but must be understood as theological arguments, each creating their own story of Jesus' life to promote a particular strain of emerging Christianity.[25]

With respect to the Old Testament, he discussed several different and contradictory accounts of various significant Bible stories. For example the story of creation: According to Davis, Gen 1:1—2:4a provides one account of creation, the "seven days account" that begins with, "And God said, Let there be light."[26] Whereas Gen 2:4bff offers a different account, beginning with the creation of dry land: "These are the generations of the heavens and of the earth when they were created, in the day that the Lord God made the earth and the heavens, and every plant of the field."[27] Davis notes,

> The story of creation which begins with Genesis 2:4b is a primitive myth, and belongs to a document which they [biblical scholars] call "J" because it uses "Yahwey" or "Jehovah" for God. . . .
>
> Genesis 1:1–2:4b was written by a priest of the post-Exilic times. . . . He was interested in maintaining the orthodoxy of the Priestly practices and attempted to give a quasi-scientific explanation of the creation that would account for his festivals, and especially the sabbath as a day of rest.[28]

23. Davis, *Origins and History* (1916a), "Lecture II: History of Early Bible Manuscripts," 9–10. The quotation is from Gregory, *Canon and Text*, 511.

24. Davis, *Origins and History* (1916a), "Lecture II: History of Early Bible Manuscripts," 10–13.

25. Davis, *Origins and History* (1916a), "Lecture XI: The Words of Jesus," 9–10.

26. Gen 1:3.

27. Gen 2:4–5.

28. Davis, *Origins and History* (1916a), "Lecture III: The Origin of the Books of the

"Post-Exilic times" refers to the period during the sixth century BCE when the Jews were exiled from Jerusalem to Babylonia. Davis argued that the "seven days" story of creation (Gen 1:1—2:4a) was from this more recent—"post-Exilic"—tradition. Biblical scholars called this the "E" (for Elohistic) tradition. While the other story of creation (Genesis 2:4b and following) was from a different and older tradition, the "J" (for Jehovah) tradition. Davis argued, based on this scholarship, that Genesis as a whole is a mashup of these two different traditions.

Davis provided a kind of map of the various manuscript sources that came together over many centuries to become the Old Testament:[29]

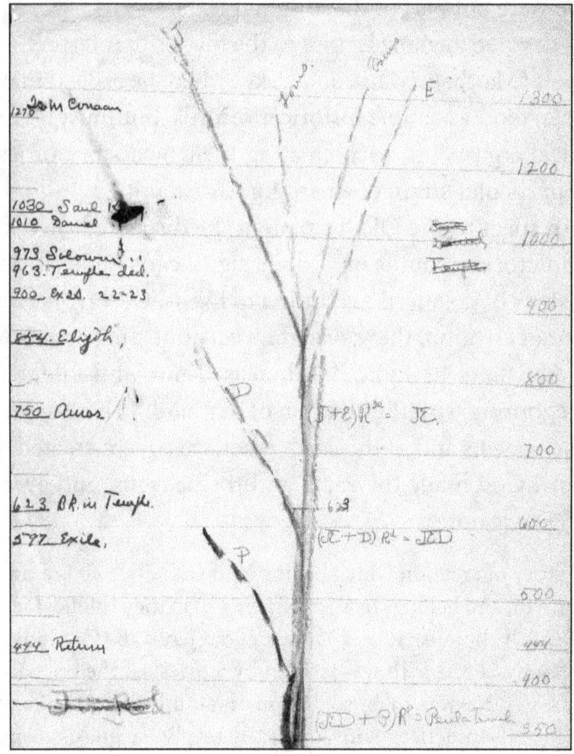

A hand-drawn diagram of the historical sources of Old Testament texts

Old Testament, Part 1," 16.

29. Davis, *Origins and History* (1916a), "Lecture IV: The Origin of the Books of the Old Testament, Part 2," Appendix 1, 22.

Putting aside all the many details here—and I have mentioned only few of a myriad number Davis presented—the point is that over the centuries of its creation, the texts of the Bible were modified and changed by multiple human hands for multiple—human—reasons. The Bible did not appear complete, "done and dusted," the word of God. Rather, it was shaped over centuries by innumerable persons unknown for many different reasons. This was what the Protestant reformers discovered when they sought the "original Bible." In their efforts to access the true revelations of God they found not a simple document of revelation, but a long process of creation by unnamed human contributors. In short, a natural book, "naturally produced and naturally transmitted."

5. Comparative Religion

This is the first answer to the puzzle: If Davis urged us not rely on the Bible to be informed of God's will, why then does Davis inform himself of the Bible, and use the Bible to share his thoughts about God's will? The answer is that the Bible played a central role in the great historic transformation into the modern age, from revelation, authority, and obedience to discovery, freedom, and consent. The authority of the Bible provided the first step away from the pope's authority. But ironically, this step resulted in the discovery of the Bible as a human document.

To appreciate the second answer this answer to the puzzle, we need to consider a second consequence of the Reformation: Protestant missionary zeal.

> Protestantism started on its mission with the conviction that the Bible was a revelation of the only plan of salvation offered to mankind and the only channel through which mankind, either in part or as a whole, might be saved. This attitude, of necessity, expressed itself in a missionary zeal.[30]

In addition to its unholy connections with colonialism, which Davis did not recognize or discuss, missionary zeal had unexpected consequences back upon Protestantism. As missionaries encountered other cultures they learned about other religions:

> Out of this tremendous experience of the Christian world in its foreign missionary enterprises there has come a vast increase on

30. Davis, "Results of Protestantism" (1931), 6.

> our part of our knowledge of other religions, their origin, their character, and their influence; out of it has evolved within the last century or less the comparative study of religions; the likenesses and differences that obtain between religions.[31]

From which Davis concluded that,

> while Christianity may be the best of religions, it is not different from other religions in its nature and its authority. To whatever extent it commends itself to us in our day, it commends itself by its intrinsic worth and truthfulness.[32]

In addition to dethroning the Bible as the revealed word of God, the Protestant revolution dethroned Christianity as the sole legitimate religion.

For Davis, Christianity *may* be the best, but it had legitimate competitors. More important, it had competitors from which we may learn: "Let us widen the circle . . . that we may learn."[33] In learning we strive for "intrinsic worth and truthfulness."

Davis did not write at length about other religions, Islam, Hinduism, Buddhism, Confucianism, among others. He was aware of other religious traditions, and he did mention them in his sermons and other writings.[34] But he also understood his lane, his culture, his cultural inheritance, *his tradition.* Unitarianism emerged as a liberal response to the Protestant Calvinism that came to the New World with the Pilgrims and the Puritans. So, while Davis was interested in and open to the religious lessons from other traditions and he was aware of and read the sacred books of other religions, he started from his own tradition with the Christian Bible, Old and New Testaments.

Still, a reasonable conclusion here would be that the Bible is—at best—only one of an extensive set of "sacred"—and yet natural—books. Why should we pay attention to any of them?

31. Davis, "Results of Protestantism" (1931), 7.

32. Davis, "Results of Protestantism" (1931), 7.

33. Davis, "What Shall We Do" (1923a), 4–5. And see my discussion of this sermon in ch. 2.

34. Davis suggests, for example, that the story of the birth of Jesus may have been borrowed from the birth of Buddha: "The story of the birth of Jesus as told by Luke is so closely like the story of the birth of Buddha as to compel one to believe that it was deliberately borrowed. The Buddhistic legend is older than the Gospel of Luke." See Davis, *Origins and History* (1916a), "Lecture XI: The Words of Jesus," 5.

6. *The Intrinsic Worth and Truthfulness of Religion*

Davis concluded his manuscript "The Results of Protestantism":

> If there is any validity at all to religion, it must rest upon a foundation which is valid, not only in our modern world of machines and science, but which was valid in the day of the Puritans and the Lollards; in the day of Gregory the Great, and the first missionaries among our barbaric forefathers in Europe. It must rest upon a foundation that was valid in the Roman Empire and in Egypt and will be valid a thousand years hence as well. Back of all the forms which, in the name of religion, mankind has ever created, there is the unconquerable faith and courage that has created them; faith that there are permanent values in human life and that courageous fidelity to those values has its root in the nature of things.[35]

For Davis, the validity of religion, the value of religion—value which has endured through the ages, and value which will continue to endure—was faith in permanent values in human life. The validity of religion was not found in any one religious institution or religious document. The validity of religion was not found in *the* Catholic Church, or *the* Old or *the* New Testament—or *the* Qur'an, or the sayings of Buddha, etc. For Davis, all these institutions and documents were reaching for these permanent values.

Insofar as an institution or a document—the Catholic Church, the Unitarian Church, the New Testament, the Qur'an, etc.—helps us to understand *and live* these permanent values, that institution or document contributes to the progress of humankind, the progress of the world. Therein is the validity of religion.

The converse here was also true for Davis. Insofar as an institution or document did not help—or no longer helped—us to understand and live these permanent values, that institution or document was no longer contributing to the progress of mankind. Churches and sacred books can

35. Davis, "Results of Protestantism" (1931), 8. The "Lollards" were followers of John Wyclif (ca. 1328–84), an English scholastic philosopher, perhaps the first to translate the Bible into English in the late fourteenth century, and the leader of a protest movement, "the Lollards," which questioned the legitimacy of the pope. Gregory the Great (ca. 540–604) was the sixty-fourth bishop of Rome—or pope—from 590 until his death. As pope he oversaw a significant expansion of papal authority, and the aligning of Roman worship with Christian practice.

lose their currency to help us forward, and Davis was quite ready to see them abandoned if this was the case.

When I came to understand Davis's view of the core to the validity of religion, I finally could understand a part of the title to Davis's 1947 sermon, "Not Revelation but Discovery, Not Forms but the Holy Spirit"[36] that confused me. I could understand, "Not Revelation but Discovery." But what did Davis mean by "Not Forms but the Holy Spirit?"

For Davis, "forms" referred to any specific religious institution—Baptist or Catholic or whatever—religious book—the Bible, the Qur'an, etc.—or religious practice—communion, etc. For Davis, a "form" had value—was useful—only insofar as it helped us understand and live by "permanent values." Davis, in this title, was claiming that the "Holy Spirit" was more important than any forms. But what, then, did he mean by the "Holy Spirit"? This is what Davis said about that term:

> There is a phrase that has had long usage in the Jewish and Christian tradition, The Holy Spirit. Its meaning has become narrowed by too technical use. The word Holy comes from the same root as our commonly used words whole, healthy. Spirit carries the meaning of the breath of life, life in you and in me, life in all about us, expression of all life existent in the nature of things. The Holy Spirit, the whole, healthy life, life with values and standards, life with purpose, life healthy and vigorous with its eye on some better tomorrow, some better age, some better world.[37]

As Davis used the term "Holy Spirit," he was speaking of "life with values and standards, life with purpose, life healthy and vigorous with its eye on some better tomorrow, some better age, some better world." He was speaking of life with faith in permanent values, life lived by these permanent values. The philosopher in me would say "objective values."

For Davis, the value of the Bible—or any religious "form"—lay in its ability to help us reach for, discover, *and live* lives with standards and purposes, lives aimed at a better tomorrow, a better age, a better world.

There is a short, handwritten note after the last typed paragraph of "The Results of Protestantism":

> 2 Qualities:
>
> 1. Integrity = Character
>
> 2. Courage[38]

36. Davis, "Not Revelation" (1947a). Discussed above in chs. 1, 2, and 3.
37. Davis, "Not Revelation" (1947a), 2.
38. Davis, "Results of Protestantism" (1931), 8.

This is where Davis believed permanent values resided, and from where they had impact on the world. They resided in the integrity or character of individual humans and in the courage of individual humans to live lives of integrity in the face of challenges and temptations. This was where progress towards a better age, a better world, came from. It came from the actions of humans with integrity, character, and courage. As we see repeatedly, what Davis called "human personality" played a central role in his thinking.

7. A Lesson from the Book of Amos

Among the last of Davis's full text sermons that I worked on was a bound set from 1910. His sermon from October 2, 1910, "The Democracy of the Bible," is instructive. He started by noting,

> The use and place of such books as the bible in human life has been so perverted and distorted by overzealous friends that we are not able to free ourselves from a certain prejudice against it. . . . The truth is that we have been bibled to a point of nausea by these pious ranters. In fact, many who have taken these people at their word concerning the Bible, in simple disgust have laid the book aside among the useless trash that humanity has outgrown.[39]

As I read this, I was both astonished by its blunt accusation, but also surprised by how well it captured some of my own feelings about religion today. Given my ignorance of the Bible, I have always felt at a disadvantage in responding to what has seemed to me to be today's pious ranting. And yet, it has still always felt to me like pious ranting.

Davis understood why people might respond to this situation by putting aside the Bible—and religion more generally. Pious ranting is a way to create *none* converts. But Davis thought this "a lamentable fact, for in so doing we are casting aside a great treasure."[40] Davis went on to argue that the Bible is a valuable document full of important lessons from history that bear on current—for him, 1910 current—problems.

He considered the drift away from religion that he observed underway in his time:

> We have before us today, in our own national life, a tremendous problem caused by the revolution in religious thought. On the

39. Davis, "Democracy of the Bible" (1910b), 1.
40. Davis, "Democracy of the Bible" (1910b), 1.

> one hand, we have the tremendous drift towards what some are pleased to call agnosticism, and away from the traditional forms and standards of religious thought and moral conduct.[41]

He easily might have been describing the ascendancy of the *nones*, had the concept then existed.

What was Davis's response? He turned to the Bible, thereby both responding to the perceived drift in religious commitment and to the idea that the Bible had little to offer the modern world. He found in the book of the prophet Amos a way to think about—to respond to—pious ranters, as opposed to what, for him, was the ethical demands of true religion:

> When Amos left the flocks of sheep in the fields of Tekoa, and came to the city of the king, with his stinging denunciations, declaring that their worship of God was the most obnoxious mockery, that their sacrifices, their solemn assemblies, and the noise of their songs God hated and despised, and he would not be satisfied until justice should roll down as waters and righteousness as a mighty stream.[42]

In the book of Amos, Amos condemns the then current religious standards and practices by speaking in the voice of God:

> Though ye offer me burnt offerings and your meat offerings, I will not accept them: neither will I regard the peace offerings of your fat beasts.
>
> Take thou away from me the noise of thy songs; for I will not hear the melody of thy viols.
>
> But let the judgement run down as waters, and righteousness as a mighty stream.[43]

Amos, a poor shepherd, but a powerful prophet, thought God sought righteousness. God did not seek offerings and sacrifices. Davis's interpretation of this bit of the Bible was that our religious priority should be on the pursuit of justice, not on policing of the observance of religious "forms."

Davis found a lesson in Amos for his day, a lesson we might find for our own day:

41. Davis, "Democracy of the Bible" (1910b), 3.
42. Davis, "Democracy of the Bible" (1910b), 4.
43. Amos 5:22–24.

> Then what happened? . . . The conservative element rallied to the old cry of the glory of God and the great work done in former times . . . and condemned the great Amos for his denunciations. . . . The logic of history has shown that justice and truth were speaking in the voice of Amos, and that iniquity and selfishness and greed were speaking in the voice of the pious priests and hunkers who condemned him.[44]

Righteousness is more important—more important to God, said Amos—than piety. Human justice is more important than religious forms: "Not Forms but the Holy Spirit."

The Bible had been a critical offensive weapon in the Reformation, challenging the authority of the pope. But, Davis lamented, the Bible had become a weapon of defense on the part of the pious ranters of his day: "Truth is not conservative, justice is not conservative. Greed is conservative, privilege is conservative."[45]

Davis found a lesson in the Bible, not a lesson of the revealed word of God, but a human lesson about justice and avarice.

> If you love humanity, if you are interested in justice, in truth, in progress, in humanitarian uplift, do not let a prejudice, brought about [by] superficial retailers of platitudes, deprive you of the use of a book that contains the records of one, two or more great historic struggles for freedom and justice, and was the arsenal of facts in a second great reformation. Do not be deceived by its accidental forms. . . . It is human. Its spirit is democratic, its real essence is humanitarian. Parts of it are worthless, but parts of it will survive on the merits of their intrinsic worth long after much of the up-to-date writings have disappeared.[46]

While little today is the same as was in Amos's time, certain human tendencies, human foibles, human weaknesses vex us today as they did in Amos's time. As a record of human history, human responses to these human weaknesses, the Bible, Davis argued, has something to teach us: Vested interests frequently will emphasize form over spirit. Speak truth to power. Justice trumps piety.

44. Davis, "Democracy of the Bible" (1910b), 4.
45. Davis, "Democracy of the Bible" (1910b), 5.
46. Davis, "Democracy of the Bible" (1910b), 5.

8. A Personal Bible

In addition to such human lessons from history, Davis argued for another important, more personal, use for the Bible—although not only *the* Bible, but any literature that helps: "Every man must have a Bible of his own, must have his literature to which he goes in different moods for help and uplift."[47] Life is not always easy—if it ever is—and everyone needs some help along the way. Davis found some of these helps in the Bible, among other books. Together these helpful bits of literature constitute what Davis called each person's "Personal Bible."

For Davis, the most important passage in his "Personal Bible" was the story of Jesus in the garden of Gethsemane.[48] Jesus went to the garden of Gethsemane after the Last Supper to gird himself for the trials he knew lay ahead. Davis:

> I do not know a more glorious passage in all literature as the expression of the desperate loneliness of the human soul in its loving service for humanity than the story of the Garden of Gethsemane.[49]

This was how Davis understood the story:

> Here is the lone man, whose life has been consecrated to the good of humanity, who has cast aside all considerations of wealth, of honor among his friends, of comfort, and ease, that he might drive home to a burdened nation the truth that in the secrets of his heart he felt that they must have. Now he had come to the critical time in his life, either all that he had said and done must go by default, and he must be branded merely as a demagogue, and openly deny the truth of his assertions, or he must pay the last penalty of his manhood demanded by the cruelty and injustice of [his] times. All his followers have deserted him, even the three most faithful disciples do not understand, and slept through his agony. Do you wonder that he alone with his convictions, facing the fact that all the world was against him, and clamoring for his life, broke forth into that natural human prayer, uttered alone in the silence of the nighttime, and in the agony of his soul. One of the great human moments of history. I love to read that when I hear of a man or a woman who has done

47. Davis, "Democracy of the Bible" (1910b), 5.
48. See Mark 14:32–42.
49. Davis, "Democracy of the Bible" (1910b), 6.

> the brave deed and faces the condemnation of the world alone. Its human. Its divine.[50]

It is human because we all face moments in our lives that demand courage, that demand integrity. It is easy enough to move ahead with the crowd or general opinion. But when you face a jeering crowd alone, that takes courage. It takes core values that one can uphold with integrity and rely on in the face of criticism. It is divine because this is how we can recognize the power of the force of good acting through courageous individuals. This was where Davis found the Holy Spirit, "the whole, healthy life, life with values and standards, life with purpose, life healthy and vigorous with its eye on some better tomorrow, some better age, some better world."[51]

The Bible may not be the revealed word of God, but for Davis, the Bible was an important, *useful,* piece of literature: "I have used the two illustrations [Amos and Gethsemane] at some length for the sake of pointing out the social and personal value of a great literature."[52]

Davis went on to observe that through history we have been modifying the Bible to suit current needs.

> To the Jews, it was the Law, the first five books of the Old Testament. To the early Christians it was the Old Testament as a whole, the Law and the Prophets. To the later Christians it was the Old Testament and part of the New Testament. For four hundred years after the time of Jesus, the Christian was adding and subtracting from its own contribution. In our own time, we are unconsciously doing the same thing. We are making our Bible of Democracy, from all the great writings of the past, we are selecting those choice bits that appeal to the depths of the human soul in all its varied moods.[53]

For Davis the Bible was important because it was a key document in the history of his Christian Protestant tradition. But more significantly, the Bible was important because it contained valuable insights, still does today. And not only Bible, but any such helpful literature. The "Scripture texts" which Davis used in his sermons include biblical passages and

50. Davis, "Democracy of the Bible" (1910b), 6.

51. Davis, "Not Revelation" (1947a), 2.

52. Davis, "Democracy of the Bible" (1910b), 7.

53. Davis, "Democracy of the Bible" (1910b), 7.

much else too. Emerson and Thoreau are frequently found, but many other writings as well.[54]

The ongoing adding and subtracting of all of these "holy texts," the continual recreation of "Scripture" to serve our deepest needs, tie us in the present to the past. The process reminds us that our trials and tribulations today are but a twinkle in a long human story, importantly *our twinkle*, but we are part of a long continuing human story:

> In this cumulative and selective process, we find our kinship to the past, and realize the true continuity of human history in the continuity of its great hopes, its great struggles for truth, and justice. Through the symbol of language expressing the hope, the thought, the aspiration, and the history of humanity through the centuries, we enter into that deeper and more wholesome idea that we are not merely the children of our time but of all time.[55]

So, for Davis the Bible was a natural human book, and a very important natural book, a book not to be discarded, but neither to be idolized.

The Bible was—and is—a primary source for information about Jesus and for information about the evolution of the Abrahamic God, two topics to which we now turn.

54. Ralph Waldo Emerson (1803–82) and Henry David Thoreau (1817–62) were friends and seminal figures in American Transcendentalism.

55. Davis, "Democracy of the Bible" (1910b), 7.

Chapter 5: **A Natural Man**

> If this legend [of Jesus] relates the events of a being other than a man, as we are men, it is as perfect a piece of cant and supercilious piety as one can find in the whole range of literature. But I will not rob myself of the honor and love which I bear to the man, Jesus of Nazareth, for his noble, heroic life, by transforming him into a supercilious nabob strutting about like a peacock among the people, displaying his gorgeous array of virtues and powers.[1]

1. A Natural Man

As I dug into Davis's thinking, I shared what I was learning with various friends, particularly my surprise at his focus on governance. This prompted a Christian friend to ask, "Does your grandfather have anything to say about Jesus?" I suspect that behind this question was a suspicion about the commitments of Unitarian Universalists—UUs—to Jesus and to Christianity.[2]

This suspicion—or fact(!)—is captured nicely in a passage from a recent novel about a search for a new UU minister for an imagined church, the Arroyo Unitarian Universalist Community Church, or AUUCC—pronounced *awk*. While the (imagined) search committee

1. Davis, "Temptation" (1906b), 2.

2. In 1961 the previously separate denominations, Unitarian and Universalist, merged to form the joint Unitarian Universalist, or "UU," denomination. Churches that had previously been identified as specifically "Unitarian" or "Universalist," in most cases became "Unitarian Universalist"—UU—churches.

brainstorms what they are looking for in their next minister, a member of the committee, Curtis—who recently joined the church from an evangelical church—says,

> "And don't you think there could be more, I don't know, religion?"
>
> We all stared at him.
>
> "What?" he said. "It is a church, and Rev Tom is a great guy. But I keep waiting to hear, you know, about God and Jesus and what we're supposed to believe in."
>
> "But Curtis, that's exactly what you'll never hear at the AUUCC" Charlotte said. "We don't push any dogma, doctrine, or creed. It's even fine that you're a Trinitarian."
>
> "I'm a what?"
>
> "A Trinitarian. You believe in the Trinity, the father, son, and holy spirit."
>
> "And you guys don't?"
>
> "We're *Uni*tarians. That means that we believe in one god."
>
> He looked around a little wildly. "So, you *do* believe in God?"
>
> He had us there.
>
> Jennie said, "Not me. But nobody's stopping you."
>
> Charlotte said, "At any rate, nobody will ever tell you what to believe."
>
> "Really?" said Curtis. "Huh. Okay, then. Never? What if I'd like to be told? I mean, isn't that why you go to church? To be told what to believe?"[3]

Of all the congregational churches that emerged from the Pilgrims and the Puritans, the Unitarians and the Universalists—now the UUs—have taken the greatest liberties with the congregational polity. There is no creed. Everyone has to figure it out for themselves—even if they want to be told what to believe—just as Davis urged. The result, in some cases, has been a distancing from Jesus and even God. Are UUs Christian? Hence, my friend's question.

To answer my Christian friend, my grandfather had a deep and abiding interest in Jesus. Many of his sermons concerned Jesus. Among other things, Jesus provided him with a classic instance of an individual defying religious authority. Jesus responded to the situation he found in Palestine and concluded that current Jewish religious belief and practice was not tending to the needs of the situation as he saw it. Consequently,

3. Huneven, *Search*, 79.

Jesus rejected the "authority religion" of his day. While this element of Jesus was clearly important to Davis, this was not the only interest Jesus held for Davis.

Of course, I knew something about Jesus, but I had never paid much attention to his story. The 1970 rock opera album, *Jesus Christ Superstar,* provided the greatest depth of my knowledge.[4] Should I have known more? Undoubtedly. But I grew up in a secular environment. Religion, Jesus included, did not play a role. Science and technology were more important. Certainly—perhaps ironically—my grandfather would have supported my interest in science and technology. Science was the route to discovery. But my grandfather still held deep respect for Jesus, and felt Jesus' story still resonated in his day, and I think he would say still in the twenty-first century as well. Reading Davis's writings has helped to fill this yawning gap in my understanding.[5] I can now appreciate the respect he had for Jesus, and how his story still has power.

In Davis's telling, Jesus was a remarkable, spectacular, heroic human individual. And that is the point. Davis was interested in Jesus the human being. Jesus certainly was an exceptional human being. But he was not—in Davis's view—a supernatural being, not, with God and the Holy Spirit, an element of the Trinity. Davis had no interest in taking literally miracles and other fables about a supernatural Jesus.

In Davis's view, the stories about Jesus lose their power if one thinks of him as a supernatural entity. In a 1906 sermon on the temptations of Jesus he wrote,

> If this legend [of Jesus] relates the events of a being other than a man, as we are men, it is as perfect a piece of cant and supercilious piety as one can find in the whole range of literature. But I will not rob myself of the honor and love which I bear to the man, Jesus of Nazareth, for his noble, heroic life, by transforming him into a supercilious nabob strutting about like a peacock among the people, displaying his gorgeous array of virtues and powers.[6]

4. *Jesus Christ Superstar,* music by Andrew Lloyd Webber and lyrics by Tim Rice, was first performed in 1971; unable initially to secure financing for the stage production, a wildly successful concept album of the music was released in 1970.

5. I have found other helpful, interesting, insightful, perhaps provocative sources to augment what I have learned from my grandfather. These include, Aslan, *Zealot*; Nolan, *Jesus Before Christianity*; Park, *Way of Jesus*; and Spong, *Jesus for the Non-Religious.*

6. Davis, "Temptation" (1906b), 2.

As a story about a human being, Jesus' story touches on the lived experience of all humans. We are all tempted. Sometimes we resist, sometimes not. The most fundamental temptations put our very integrity at risk. This was true for Jesus; it is true for each of us today. Standing firm in the face of temptation is not so impressive if one has supernatural powers. But standing firm when one has only human powers, *that* is something. The story of the temptations of Jesus—as a human being, not a supernatural deity—is a story that can speak to every human being. Jesus' story shows that we can resist temptation, we can—and should and must—protect our integrity. This was Davis's conclusion.

2. Jesus' Wisdom

In a 1923 sermon Davis directly took up the question of Jesus' Godly powers: "Did Christ Have the Power of God?"[7] He worked hard on this sermon; there are multiple drafts. The most important conclusion he argued for, again, is that the powers that Jesus had were purely human.

Davis saw Jesus as a man of knowledge that came from careful, insightful observations of the natural and human worlds around him. Davis backed this up with multiple biblical passages that demonstrate how keenly Jesus observed and understood the world he lived in.

> He had no secret mysterious sources of truth. He simply kept his eyes open, and his mind alert. He saw the sower in the field. He saw the widow giving her money in the temple. He saw the publican. He saw the pharisee. He saw the poor, the weak, . . . the blind. He saw the peace makers, and the persecutors; . . . the children in the market place; the merchants; the lepers; the outcasts and harlots. His teachings are a mirror of the life of Palestine in his day. He lived among living men, saw them, knew them. When he taught, he was dealing with real men and women, with all their noble qualities and their sins and limitations as well. He had no delusions. He knew.[8]

Jesus observed directly with empathy.

Davis illustrated empathic observation with the story of the Widow's Mite (Mark 12:41–44). Watching people passing in and out of the temple as they cast their donations to the treasury:

7. Davis, "Did Christ Have the Power" (1923b).
8. Davis, "Did Christ Have the Power" (1923b), 2–3.

> Here came the rich and haughty Sadducee; or perhaps the prosperous merchant, ostentatiously displaying his gift; or possibly a traveler, lately returned from a foreign country, stopping to greet his friends as he passes. Next comes one learned in the law swinging by among the more humble folk. Thus they pass: great and small; rich and poor; saint and sinner, while Jesus stands hard by, his keen searching eye following the passing show of Palestine.
>
> Suddenly his attention is arrested. Something important has happened, something worth calling to the attention of his disciples. You can almost hear his keen alert voice, "Peter, John, come here. I want to show you something." . . . "What is it?" you can imagine John asking. Then came the reply born of knowledge of human life, "Verily I say unto you, this poor widow cast in more than all they that cast into the treasury, for they all did cast in of their superfluity; but she of her want did cast in all that she had, even all her living."[9]

This is an interesting subtle observation about human nature, one that rings true for me today. People with less often can tend to be more generous—giving of "all their living"—than people with more—who give "only of their superfluity." Having possessions seems to drive a desire to cling to possessions.

Davis continued to share his picture of Jesus. Out of the understanding that came from Jesus' careful observation, Jesus created a new way of life, a philosophy of love of fellow human beings—and more on this in the chapters to follow. But why did people follow Jesus? Why might people today follow Jesus with this philosophy of love?

> Why should one follow this new way of life? Why should one love his neighbor as himself? Why should one forego the grosser purposes of life? Nay why do men and women love truth, honor, goodness? Why do they honor the hero, even if they themselves are cowards? Why do they honor the good in human life, even when they themselves have done evil?[10]

As I read these words by Davis, I was struck by the observation that cowards honor heroes, that those who have done bad things can still honor good. Certainly not universally true. But not unusual either. It is

9. Davis, "Did Christ Have the Power" (1923b), 3. The quoted material at the end is from Mark 12:43–44.

10. Davis, "Did Christ Have the Power" (1923b), 4.

an important fact about human beings, that we can admire those whose admirable traits exceed our own.

To return to Davis: Why do they honor the hero, even if they themselves are cowards? Jesus' answer to this conundrum, according to Davis:

> Life is an open secret. "Seek and ye shall find, ask and it shall be given you, knock and it shall be opened unto you." The world and life brings forth from its treasure that which you seek. What does life mean? What is the world like? What is God like? "What man is there of you, who, if his son shall ask him for a loaf, will give him a stone; or if he shall ask him for a fish, will give him a serpent? If ye then, being evil (being finite or human) know how to give good gifts unto your children, how much more shall your Father who is in heaven give good things to them that ask him?" God is at least as good as you are.[11]

The passage raises many questions. Certainly, I have questions about it. But for a moment, put aside these questions: Whether there is a God? Whether this God is at least as good as you are? Whether this God does provide as we would provide for our children? Whether life is an open secret? Whether it does make sense to forego the "grosser purposes of life" in favor of love for one's neighbor, in favor of truth, honor and goodness?

Important questions, all, but the point here is that, according to Davis, this is what Jesus believed. This was Jesus' faith, and he held to it with complete integrity, through the most challenging of tests, unto death. Jesus' faith was human. Jesus had no special access to the truth. Jesus' faith

> was not an infallible scheme presented to him for unquestioned acceptance. It was a living personal faith, born of his doubt, his questionings, his knowledge, his experience and his insight. . . . He had no magic knowledge about the meaning of life, or the nature of God, or God's purposes. He saw the choice of life. He saw the way of indulgence, lust, greed, leading to torment, remorse, and ashes. He saw the way of truth, love, and loyalty, leading to values that he believed to be imperishable and eternal. He made his choice. He staked his life on the higher values, love, honor, truth, on the faith that God exists, that life has eternal significance.[12]

11. Davis, "Did Christ Have the Power" (1923b), 4–5. The quoted biblical passages are from Matt 7:7–11.

12. Davis, "Did Christ Have the Power" (1923b), 5–6.

Seeing Jesus this way, putting aside the question of whether God does exist, or whether the God as Jesus imagined him does exist, was revelatory for me. The murky metaphysical questions about God recede, while the human questions, questions about character and integrity, about how to live, and live with moral integrity and courage, emerge.

It is a matter of human assessment of different ways to live, "the way of indulgence, lust and greed" or "the way of truth, love and loyalty." Put so, this seems simple, so obvious: truth, love, and loyalty clearly trump indulgence, lust, and greed. But put in the context of actual human life, it is not simple and obvious. We *do* respond to temptations, and our integrity *is* put at risk. It is the human question of one's willingness to believe in and work for a better life *for all* in the face of real challenges: in the face significant personal privations, even as we see others prosper at our expense. And all in the absence of certain knowledge about what is right. This is not easy; it is no simple matter. The vast majority of human beings do not bring Jesus' degree of integrity and faith to their lives. And yet we can admire him for his supreme degree of integrity and courage.

Jesus was hardly unique in holding to the integrity of his faith.

> It was not unique in him. There have been others along the way of human history who have had the moral courage to die for some great cause they have loved. To them we owe more than our poor lives can ever repay. For the sake of faith, in religion, in science and knowledge, in adventure and discovery, in the daily rounds of humble life, there have been those who have given their life for their faith, their loved ones, their duty, their God. It is a noble company, greater perhaps than we dream. "Greater love hath no man than this that he lay down his life for the brethren." We touch the garment hem of God's spirit when we come in touch with those who lay their own life upon the altar for the sake of truth and the brethren?[13]

In other writings, Davis spoke of other humans who, in his view, have led noble, courageous—heroic—lives. These included well-known religious leaders, Moses, Mohammed, Luther, Calvin, but also political leaders, Thomas Paine, John Brown, Abraham Lincoln; then-current social reformers, Jane Addams, Walter Rauschenbusch; authors, Heinrich Heine, and Leo Tolstoy.[14]

13. Davis, "Did Christ Have the Power" (1923b), 7–8. The quoted passage is from John 15:13.

14. Among other writings, see Davis, "Value and the Limitations of Allegiance"

There is more power in understanding Jesus as a mortal human being. We are human like Jesus. We have the same human powers as Jesus had. Jesus' courage and integrity are not beyond our reach in some supernatural realm. We too can change the world. Davis concluded his sermon, "Did Christ Have the Power of God?":

> That was the authority that Christ had and still has, the power of a faith tested in life, confirmed in death. Others have had it. Their gracious and holy lives have lighted the way of human history. They have kindled fires of noble purpose in thousands of souls. They have stimulated and confirmed that greatest of all human adventures, the faith that God is, and that life has eternal meaning. That is the power of God in the human soul. It was in Christ. It is in you.[15]

Faith in God—however one characterizes God, and more on this in the next chapter—is tantamount, for Davis, to faith in human beings as ethical beings.

Jesus was a remarkable individual, an individual whose life is worth our attention and study, whose life and ideals changed the course of history. But, for Davis, he was a natural human being, not a supernatural deity.

3. *What About the Resurrection?*

A human Jesus. But there is a long and deeply established tradition in Christianity that supports an alternative view of a Jesus as an element of the Trinity: God, the Son—Jesus—and the Holy Spirit. This view is closely tied to the story of the bodily resurrection of Jesus after his crucifixion. Multiple Christian holy days and traditions—Good Friday, Easter, the Pentecost—are tied to this story of Jesus. Davis took his insights on the wisdom of Jesus from biblical stories about Jesus. Doesn't the Bible also tell the story of the resurrection? And doesn't this then undermine Davis's conclusion—from the same biblical sources—that Jesus is "just" a man as all men are men?

(1909e); "Our Debt to Thomas Paine" (1909f); "John Brown and the Passion for Justice" (1909g); "Abraham Lincoln and the Needs of the Times" (1906c); "Social Unrest" (1910c); "Religion of Humanity" (1908a); "The Significance of Count Tolstoy" (1908b).

15. Davis, "Did Christ Have the Power" (1923b), 9.

There is a very long story here, one I cannot do full justice to. As the passage from the novel *Search*, quoted at the beginning of this chapter, implies, *Uni*tarians have always taken issue with the concept of the Trinity. Historically, for Unitarians there is just one God, and Jesus is a man, not an element of the Trinity. In this, Davis was following in the wake of long-held Unitarian beliefs.

The passage from *Search* also accurately presents the powerful importance of the congregational polity in the history of Unitarianism, with the result that there has been a large diversity of theological stances tied to Unitarianism through history, and there is an even larger diversity across the Unitarian Universalist congregations today. It would take me too far afield to delve into this history.

That said, Davis was himself quite cognizant of the claims made for Jesus' resurrection. The conclusion of his lectures on *The Origin and History of the Bible* addresses the story of the resurrection.[16] Davis recognized that this aspect of Christian belief—belief in the bodily resurrection of Jesus, and in his status as an element of the Trinity—was widespread, and that the Gospels could be read as supporting it. His Unitarian-inspired arguments that Jesus was "just" a man—and more compelling to us because of his pure humanity—challenged these interpretations of the Bible. Davis had to respond. This was the ultimate goal of his lectures on *The Origin and History of the Bible*—the final lecture, on the resurrection of Jesus.

Davis's lecture on the resurrection—against the historical accuracy of the resurrection as told in the Bible—proceeded by making three intertwined points. First, Davis noted that the earliest document arguing for the resurrection is 1 Corinthians (in chapter 15), written by the apostle Paul, perhaps about 55 CE. But Paul specifically does not argue for the *bodily* resurrection of Jesus, but rather for the *spiritual* resurrection of Jesus (see 1 Cor 15:45–52):

> Now this I say. Brethren, that flesh and blood cannot inherit the kingdom of God; neither doth corruption inherit incorruption. . . . In a moment, in the twinkling of an eye, at the last trump: for the trumpet shall sound, and the dead shall be raised incorruptible, and we shall be changed.[17]

16. Davis, *Origins and History* (1916a), "Lecture XIV: The New Testament Story of the Resurrection."

17. 1 Cor 15:50–52.

By contrast, the Gospels assert the *bodily* resurrection of Jesus. For example, in Luke:

> See my hands, and my feet, it is I myself: handle me and see; for a spirit hath not flesh and bones, as ye beheld me having.[18]

Davis also noted that the account Paul provided for the resurrection was not a historical relating of the facts, but rather a theological argument that it had to be so. Davis quoted Paul: "For as in Adam all die, even so in Christ shall all be made alive."[19] Davis continued by making this point:

> The question arises naturally at this point, why, if Paul knew of the events that are recorded in the Gospels, he did not refer to the records of the Resurrection of Jesus, and the resurrection of the saints at the time of Jesus' death.[20]

The conclusion Davis reached about Paul's account of the resurrection:

> Such then is the earliest record concerning the Resurrection. It is spiritual, demonstrated principally by argument, and, in so far as appeal is made to the experience at the tomb, the statement of fact varies from the statement of the Gospel.[21]

The second point Davis made is that there are multiple contradictions among the accounts of the resurrection provided in the four Gospels, Matthew, Mark, Luke, and John. All accounts agree that after the crucifixion Mary Magdalene went to the tomb where Jesus had been laid to rest only to find it empty. But who went with Mary Magdalene?

> Matthew has Mary Magdalene, and the other Mary go to the tomb. Mark has Mary Magdalene, Mary, mother of James and Salome; Luke has Mary Magdalene, Mary, mother of James and Joanna, while John has Mary Magdalene alone, but before she enters the tomb she runs after Simon Peter and John to come with her.[22]

18. Luke 24:39.

19. 1 Cor 15:22, quoted in Davis, *Origins and History* (1916a), "Lecture XIV: The New Testament Story of the Resurrection," 4.

20. Davis, *Origins and History* (1916a), "Lecture XIV: The New Testament Story of the Resurrection," 4.

21. Davis, *Origins and History* (1916a), "Lecture XIV: The New Testament Story of the Resurrection," 4.

22. Davis, *Origins and History* (1916a), "Lecture XIV: The New Testament Story of the Resurrection," 5.

The Gospels disagree on the timing of this:

> Matthew says that they went to the tomb as it began to dawn; Mark says, "Very early on the first day of the week, when the sun was risen"; Luke says that it was at early dawn, while John says that Mary went, "While it was yet dark."[23]

The Gospels disagree on other facts. Matthew speaks of a great earthquake that moved the stone blocking the entrance to the tomb, where Mark, Luke, and John don't mention an earthquake. Who entered the tomb—or did anyone enter the tomb? And so on. Davis:

> They are not differences in unimportant detail, but differences of important fact. If a witness on a stand should say that at a definite place at a definite time he saw one angel, and then later should, concerning the same time and place, [say] that he saw two angels, and again that he saw one man, and then two men, we would begin to question whether he had seen anything at all.[24]

The third point that Davis made addresses the reported fact that even after Jesus' appearance post-death, still some doubted: "And when they saw him, some worshiped him; but some doubted" (Matt 28:17). This is—in part—why the bodily resurrection of Jesus is important; doubts were overcome by physical touch and a shared meal (see, e.g., Luke 24:39–43). But, according to the Gospels, before the crucifixion, before entering Jerusalem, Jesus had already told the twelve what to expect—that he would be raised up on the third day (see Matt 20:17–19, Mark 10:32–34, Luke 18:31–33). And yet they still doubted. Davis: "It sounds absurd to read in the accounts of the Resurrection of their terror and surprise at seeing him risen, or their stubborn unbelief."[25]

Davis concluded that the Gospel stories were not—and should not be taken to be—historical accounts of the resurrection:

> What it all means is that these records are not historical, nor are they possible sources of historical facts. They are legends, or myths, which, for dogmatic reasons in part . . . have been

23. Davis, *Origins and History* (1916a), "Lecture XIV: The New Testament Story of the Resurrection," 5. The accounts Davis quotes are from Matt 28:1, Mark 16:2, Luke 24:1, and John 20:1.

24. Davis, *Origins and History* (1916a), "Lecture XIV: The New Testament Story of the Resurrection," 6–7.

25. Davis, *Origins and History* (1916a), "Lecture XIV: The New Testament Story of the Resurrection," 11.

> associated with the person of Jesus. That the events as described in the Gospels, the physical resurrection with the flesh and blood, the wounds, the eating of fish, etc., did not take place at all we have two good witnesses. The first is the Gospel records themselves, for they say so many things unintentionally that their intentional story is spoiled. The second witness is the witness of Paul. The Gospels bear witness to a physical resurrection. Paul, to a spiritual resurrection, declaring flatly that flesh and blood cannot inherit the kingdom of God.[26]

So, Davis argued, we may learn much about the life and times of Jesus from the Gospels, but we should not take them as historical documents. They have other purposes.

Which then raises the question: Where do the stories of the resurrection come from and what is their purpose? Davis answered this question by discussing various early and traditional spring festivals, festivals that celebrate rebirth—or "resurrection"—as a new growing season emerges from winter. The Easter story of the resurrection of Jesus, in addition to elevating Jesus' status to that of God, also provided a Christian version for—or cover for—these traditional "pagan" spring rebirth celebrations.

Davis concluded his lecture—and the set of all fourteen lectures—as follows:

> What then is the relation between these two lines of facts that I have developed? On the one hand, the very confused and uncertain and contradictory accounts of this alleged resurrection; on the other, this wide spring festival during which the death and resurrection of gods was celebrated under varying forms, many of them so closely suggestive of the accounts concerning the death and resurrection of Christ.
>
> We know by deliberate confession of a contemporary Church Father that the Christmas celebration, and the Christmas legends were of pagan origin, and that in the fourth century, the Christians, being unable to stamp out the pagan winter solstice festival, with which the birth of their God Mithra was celebrated, deliberately took over the whole ceremony, myth and all, and substituted Jesus. We have every reason in the world, except a direct statement for believing, that this is what was done with the spring festival of Easter, when in various

26. Davis, *Origins and History* (1916a), "Lecture XIV: The New Testament Story of the Resurrection," 11.

> parts of the Roman Empire, the death and resurrection of the God of vegetation was celebrated.[27]

The resurrection is not—argued Davis—historic fact, but a useful fiction, a way to enroll and incorporate traditional practices and beliefs into Christianity, and thereby to further empower Christianity.

4. Modernity and Materialism

If Christianity does not rest upon a foundation of a supernatural Jesus Christ, wherein is the power behind a human Jesus Christ to support Christianity? Davis offered what was to me a surprising answer to this question. But to get to the meat of his answer I need to take a brief detour into one of the critical challenges that modernity placed upon religion.

Shortly after he took up his first ministry, Davis spent considerable time working over and thinking through the 1906 book by University of Chicago theologian, George Burman Foster, *The Finality of the Christian Religion.*[28] The book sets up—and proposes a solution to—the conflict between scientific materialism and religion deprived of supernatural resources. This is how Davis put the problem:

> Supernaturalism . . . is gone. But in the great humanistic movement of which this overthrow of authority-religion is one result, and the re-establishment of man in the world is another, the prime question before the world today is whether this re-established man shall be merely a man of sense or shall he be a man of spiritual power. Here we come to face the great problem of materialistic naturalism, wherein the high spiritual developments of man are reduced to the level of natural causes alone.[29]

27. Davis, *Origins and History* (1916a), "Lecture XIV: The New Testament Story of the Resurrection," 16–17.

28. George Burman Foster (1858–1918) was a theologian and faculty member of the (Baptist) Divinity School at the University of Chicago, and author of the 1906 book *The Finality of the Christian Religion*. Among the manuscripts Davis left were two handwritten manuscripts focused on Foster's *Finality of the Christian Religion*; one reads like a lengthy book review and the other reads as Davis's considered conclusions from Foster's book. Both versions can be found at Davis, "Finality of Christianity" (1906d). It is also worth noting that Davis's teacher at the Harvard Divinity School, William Wallace Fenn (1862–1932), developed a close friendship with Foster while he was in Chicago (1890–1901). No doubt this relationship prompted Davis to take Foster's 1906 book seriously.

29. Davis, "Finality of Christianity" (1906d), 3–4.

In the scientific worldview that took off during the nineteenth and twentieth centuries, we explain all that happens with natural causes. "Modern physics" explains the motions of the "heavenly" and terrestrial bodies. Darwin and his successors explain the plant and animal worlds—particularly human beings—with evolution by natural selection. No mention of God, or special supernatural interventions, is needed.

There was considerable push back against this materialist scientific worldview. Think of the 1925 Scopes Monkey Trial, when John Scopes was accused of illegally teaching evolution. For Davis, this was pushing back against discovery in favor of revelation, an "atavistic response" to modernity. Certainly not the road Davis supported.

But if we accept the modern, materialist, scientific story of the world, what is the point of religion? Davis fully recognized this dilemma. Continuing the passage just quoted:

> The disintegrating, demoralizing effect of the system of thought which declares that we are what we are as a result of the sole action of mechanical laws which have produced us, without giving place for the spontaneous action of a free personality, is as much to be feared as the equally demoralizing supernaturalism.[30]

Twentieth-century scholars have called this "the disenchantment of the world." It's all "just" scientifically explicable cause and effect. Nothing special with human beings—even special human beings like Jesus. We are "just" more complicated billiard balls bouncing against each other in dizzying patterns of cause and effect.

The solution that Davis and Foster found to this demoralizing situation is located in the phrase just quoted, "without giving place for the spontaneous action of a free personality." The solution is free will.

For a philosopher—for me—this is not so much a solution as a different statement of the problem. Davis and Foster speak of the "spontaneous action of a free personality." But is it spontaneous? Beyond the fact that it *feels* spontaneous, what evidence is there that we have free will? William James, cofounder of American Pragmatism (see chapter 2), struggled mightily with this aspect of modernism. According to John Kaag, James was dangerously—today, we would say "clinically"—depressed because he thought he lacked free will—that is, because of the implications of the rising tide of modernism. James resolved his

30. Davis, "Finality of Christianity" (1906d), 4.

depression by choosing—freely (!)—to believe in free will.[31] This became an important element of James's pragmatism, also an element in James's approach to religion, initially spelled out in his essay, "The Will to Believe."[32]

I won't here argue for free will beyond noting that this was Foster's and Davis's position, "the spontaneous action of a free personality." In addressing the problem of change—see chapter 2—Davis depended on free will. It is through free will that humans, with their fears and hopes for the future, their aspirations, and their actions in effort to realize these aspirations, add direction to pure materialism. It is this avenue that provides Davis room for the possible influence of human ideals of truth, goodness, and beauty in history, how the arc of history can bend towards justice.[33]

5. What Is the Essence of Christianity?

To return then to Jesus. With Foster, Davis asked, what is "the essence of *Christianity?*"[34] What is the essence of a religion based on the life of Jesus *Christ?* He ruled out the teachings of Jesus: "If we seek to affiliate ourselves to him [Jesus] on the basis of the acceptance of his teaching, we shall find that we have to part company with him at once. He believed in angels and demons, which we do not."[35] He ruled out the morality of Jesus: "Should we seek a common moral ground with him, it would be difficult. Many of the moral problems of today receive no treatment at his hands."[36] It is not the specifics of what Jesus said, for he lived in a different time: "The things that he said, the thoughts that he expressed, the doctrines that he preached, these are not the abiding, but the transient, in his life."[37] What then?

> The foundation of Christianity is Jesus, but the essence of the life of Jesus is not in words or deeds, as such, not in alleged miracles,

31. Kaag, *Sick Souls.*

32. James, "Will to Believe"; see also James, *Varieties of Religious Experience* and *Pluralistic Universe* (1909).

33. As mentioned in ch. 2, philosopher Philip Goff, in his book *Why?*, also attends to this question, and among other things argues for a space for free will within a scientific worldview.

34. Davis, "Finality of Christianity" (1906d), 4.

35. Davis, "Finality of Christianity" (1906d), 5.

36. Davis, "Finality of Christianity" (1906d), 5.

37. Davis, "Finality of Christianity" (1906d), 5.

> or claims to messiahship, but in the personality of the man who said the things and did the deeds, and about whom the myths and legends collected. . . .
>
> Here he [Foster] finds, and we find, the basis of our faith. Not in word, not in deed, not in doctrine, not in any external objective of faith, but in the welling up within us of the spontaneous power of personality, that power, which is the culmination of our life, that expresses itself in the ceaseless activities of man. Jesus' significance as a religious leader is found in this, that those powers of love, those deep human sympathies, those eternal hopes, the great expounding power of love and human fellowship, these inner things of the spiritual personality he made the basis of his regulating principle of life.[38]

This passage stopped me in my tracks. Davis and Foster ruled out all the obvious reasons to revere Jesus: It is not what Jesus believed—for he believed in stuff we do not, "angels and demons." It is not his morality—for he barely touches on current knotty moral problems. It is not what he said—for the specifics were pertinent to his time, not ours. "Not in word, not in deed, not in doctrine, not in any external objective of faith." It is Jesus' personality that is key. But what does this mean?

Personality is tricky because Foster and Davis were writing before "personality" had become a specific topic of psychological study—thanks in part to William James. Psychology now largely owns the word, and its usage and meaning have shifted from when Davis and Foster focused on the personality of Jesus.

Davis and Foster elaborate on Jesus' personality as "those powers of love, those deep human sympathies, those eternal hopes, the great expounding power of love and human fellowship, these inner things of the spiritual personality." Still—for me anyway—this remains opaque.

Personality, as they are using the term, is related to what we today might call "character." Personality is tied to "commitments"—to love and human fellowship—commitments to the possibility of a better world, commitments to action—with integrity and strength of purpose—to steadfastly take steps to achieve a better world. Personality is tied to faith in this: the possibility that we can—and should—make a better world.

Equally important, for Foster and Davis, personality is the seat of a human being's free will. Personality is where humans interrupt the "demoralizing effect" that human action can be explained solely "as

38. Davis, "Finality of Christianity" (1906d), 5–6.

a result of the sole action of mechanical laws." It is "the spontaneous power of personality" that demonstrates both what was most significant and enduring from the life of Jesus, and how the world is not merely a world of mechanical causation.

Combine human free will with the ideals of truth, goodness, and beauty that come from within the personality of Jesus—but also from within the personalities of other human beings—and we have religion without supernatural sources, religion that is part of our modern, scientific world. But a religion that provides a place for what might be called spiritual values, or perhaps more in keeping with a scientific worldview, human ideals, aspirations, and choices:

> Thus we arrive at the essential power of the son of Joseph and Mary who has left such an imprint upon the history of the world. Christianity, the religion of which he is the founder, becomes not a religion of a book, not a religion of a creed, not a religion of doctrine, not a religion of texts, and sayings of Jesus, but a religion of personality. . . . So Christianity is a religion in which we are religious, not because we read a bible, but we write a bible because of the inner power of our personality. We are not the doers of good deeds, and the livers of the noble life, not because some book or clericus or whatnot tell us to, but because we are dominated by the power of some ideal.[39]

It is Jesus' personality that matters. But not just Jesus. As Foster and Davis are using the term, personality is what matters for *all* human beings, for each of us: "So Christianity is a religion in which we are religious, not because we read a bible, but *we write a bible* because of the inner power of our personality." We express our personalities, we "write a bible," each of us, every day. Foster and Davis, among others I have no doubt, inverted of the source of morality, the source of divinity. God is not "out there," God is "in here," in aspects of our personalities, in each of us.[40]

As will become obvious in subsequent chapters, human personality emerges as the essential element of Davis's approach to religion: human personality, the key locus of the divine.

39. Davis, "Finality of Christianity" (1906d), 6–7.

40. See Davis, "Idea of God" (1908c); this sermon is discussed in more detail in ch. 6.

6. The Deification of Jesus

Jesus was a remarkable human being. But he was also a man of his times. In his 1909 sermon, "The Value and the Limitations of Allegiance to Religious Leaders," Davis was clear that inspirational leaders are effective because they capture the concerns, the hopes and fears, the aspirations of their times. Jesus arrived on the scene as Palestine was undergoing rapid change. Jewish traditions were interacting with Greek and Roman influences.

> Jesus felt the pulse of this new universalizing process, he gave expression to it, and became the leader of its first great outward manifestation. He was not the cause, but the product of the movement, making his own large contribution to it.
>
> If we could get back into the atmosphere of the time in which he lived, we should come upon men, in whose minds there were strange wild thoughts, high ideals which ravished their very beings.[41]

Jesus was sensitive to these changes. He took them in, clarified them and reflected them back to the people. In doing so he provided them a more coherent and moving version of their aspirations.

According to Davis, Jesus was a leader because he responded to the spirit of his times:

> Do you imagine for one moment that the men who became the disciples of Jesus simply left their work to follow blindly the chance dreamer that came along and told them to follow him? Things do not happen that way. Back of it all is the setting of unrest, and longing idealism. He spoke to them as one having authority, not because he spoke of something new to them, but because he was speaking to them of, and clarifying for them, thoughts and ideals that were not foreign to them. The shepherd had come, and the sheep knew his voice.[42]

Jesus responded to the changed feelings of the people, changed in response to the new influences of Greek and Roman cultures. The people of Palestine responded to Jesus because he powerfully captured these changes, and he was able to articulate for them their new ideals of life.

41. Davis, "Value and the Limitation" (1909e), 3–4.

42. Davis, "Value and the Limitation" (1909e), 4. See also Matt 7:29, "For he taught them as one having authority, and not as the scribes."

Jesus was a remarkably effective leader with an amazing ability to articulate new ideals of God—as I discuss in the next chapter—and of the role of love for one's fellow man. New ideals, as Davis had it. His early disciples responded to him because of these abilities:

> Once, with a spontaneous enthusiasm, men rallied around the leadership of Christ, recognizing in him the embodiment, and the effective agent of their idealism.[43]

But it was the deification of Jesus that Davis was most anxious to address in this sermon. Later, and no doubt as part of the effort to establish a new powerful religious institution—Christianity—Jesus was reconceptualized. Davis was not surprised, although clearly disappointed:

> A cult of hero-worshippers, not entirely devoid of a sickly sentimentalism, have usurped the place of those who accorded him, in the early days, their spontaneous loyalty. To them, among whom he moved, he was the beloved leader. To their followers, he became the supernatural agent of God. As days passed by and hero-worship took the place of honest loyalty, more and more he became removed from the life of men, becoming in turn a demigod, and then very God himself, until at last, like the disciples of old, they knew only that he had been taken from them, but they did not know where he was laid.[44]

This reconceptualization took hold. Some—many or most?—religious leaders might say, the revealed truth of Jesus as God became the core of Christianity. It has been passed down as a foundation of Christianity.

> Such [is] the situation today in the great body of the Christian church. We still accept the name that is connected with Jesus, many still pay him a formal worship as to a God, or a hero, but the vital influence of him as a help in common everyday human life is gone.[45]

For Davis this reconceptualized Jesus was a huge loss. A loss both because of the loss of his "vital influence" in everyday life, but more importantly because it creates a chasm between Jesus—God—and the rest

43. Davis, "Value and the Limitation" (1909e), 5.

44. Davis, "Value and the Limitation" (1909e), 5.

45. Davis, "Value and the Limitation" (1909e), 5–6. Here is a different expression of Davis's concern expressed in the second half of the title to his 1947 sermon, "Not Revelation but Discovery, Not Forms but the Holy Spirit." See ch. 4, section 6.

of us mortals. On the other hand, from Jesus the human, mortal human as all of us are, we can receive

> wisdom, inspiration, uplift, vision, even consecration itself. . . . Wherever we get that help, whether in the man who lives today, or in the man who lived hundreds of years ago, it is a help not because the person who gives was removed from us by some great unhuman power, but because he is akin to us and has touched the simple true chords of the symphony of human life. Those who have lived, received and they gave. It is for us to receive and to give.[46]

Davis urged his congregation to put aside ideas of a supernatural Jesus. Jesus the natural man has more moral power than a supernatural Jesus. But what about God? Here too, Davis urged a natural interpretation, one to which I now turn.

46. Davis, "Value and the Limitation" (1909e), 6.

Chapter 6: **Natural Deity**

> It is the "Master Presence" that holds us in its all-absorbing Grip. The living God, the God that is Life, that is Human Life, that dwells in the individual men and women, with all their noble hopes, all their achievements, all their defeats and their limitations, all their mistakes, and selfish, cruel sins, the God that is all this and more, infinitely more, that is the totality of life, that God grips our souls.[1]

1. Religion Without the Supernatural

STARTING FROM THE BAREST elements of religious education, I had now learned from my grandfather's writings about an approach to the Bible and to Jesus that did not need supernatural trappings. This seemed to me both unusual and appealing—insofar as it agreed with my own prior leanings against the supernatural. Davis's arguments for the Bible being a natural book, created—and re-created and re-re-created, etc.—by human beings over centuries struck me as quite convincing. I similarly found convincing his arguments that Jesus was a man as all men—and women—as all humans are human. I found the moral implications of a human Jesus powerful and surprising. How very valuable Jesus is as a model of a moral *human* life, a *human* life of moral courage and integrity.

And yet I am fully aware that these views are controversial. I write these words on the Monday after Easter, the holiday that traditional Christianity celebrates Jesus' resurrection. For my grandfather, it was the

1. Davis, "Thirst for a *Living* God" (191Xa), 3.

holiday celebrating seasonal rebirth—a different kind of resurrection. While Davis's approach makes sense to me, I know there are many who would take serious issue with it. Paul wrote in 1 Corinthians:

> Now if Christ be preached that he rose from the dead, how say some among you that there is no resurrection of the dead?
>
> But if there be no resurrection of the dead, then is Christ not risen?
>
> And if Christ be not risen, then *is* our preaching vain, and your faith *is* also vain.[2]

This is a powerful element to the founding of Christianity. It would be the height of my arrogance to dismiss this after the limited religious education provided by my grandfather's writings.

At the same time, Davis's arguments opened an avenue into religion for me, where previously I had simply ignored the whole thing. It is an avenue that could appeal to those who, like me, have little to no willingness to accept a supernatural story on faith alone, particularly when a natural story is available. Perhaps Paul was wrong, there could be religious faith without a supernatural Jesus. Such a faith would not be in vain. This does seem worth pursuing, worth consideration.

These are deep and difficult matters, matters that people have fought over for centuries. One of the most important lessons I learned reading Davis's writings is just how important these matters have been through history. Matters of life and death. Nation making and destroying. Prior to reading through all these materials, I was aware of religious conflicts—hard to miss—but I had not appreciated the human mindset that drove these conflicts: deeply felt commitments to doctrines for which we have no proof and little evidence in the modern sense of the word. But people believed; they had a certain kind of faith. This faith drove great accomplishments including succor for the poor and downtrodden. But it also drove incessant conflict, for we did not have a better way to sort out disagreements.

Davis's picture of the transition away from revelation, authority, and obedience to discovery, freedom, and consent—toward a different kind of mindset, a new different kind of faith, with a different way to sort out disagreements—does seem a step forward to me, if one yet incompletely taken.

2. 1 Cor 15:12–14.

Part of what comes with this new kind of faith, as Davis saw it, is each person's responsibility to think these matters through—to bear their burden. And so, with a great deal of humility, I continue forward. A natural book and a natural man, what about the most central—seemingly—supernatural element of religion, God? Davis landed, again, with nature. But the pathway and the nuance are interesting and important.

2. God as an Occasional Visitor

On June 14, 1908, Davis preached a sermon with the lengthy title, "The Moral Significance of the Evolution of Religious Faith: From the Idea of God As an Occasional Visitor, to the Idea of God As the Indwelling Goodwill."[3] He opened the sermon reminding his congregation of the vast change in the picture of the universe that had taken place in the previous few hundred years.

> Looking at the universe as we now do, in light of what the astronomers and scientists have taught us, it is almost impossible for us to realize that the time ever was when men could think that the earth was a flat surface surrounded by a great flowing ocean. Still more surprising does it seem when we learn that the heavens were something like an inverted bowl, on the inner surface of which were attached the stars and the planets. That idea of the world has become for us now only a kind of intellectual antique, which interests as a curiosity of cosmic philosophies to be put away in our museums of intellectual relics.[4]

Change—again—an underlying theme of nearly everything Davis wrote. However, his focus in this sermon was not change in our scientific picture of the world, but change in our conception of God, for this too had changed—and continues to change.

It is to Jesus that Davis attributed an important element of change in our conception of God. In Davis's telling, the God that Jesus inherited from his Jewish culture, the God that appears in the Old Testament, was best regarded as a person—a special person—but akin to a person in many respects:

> He was a big man. . . . God was a person, similar to them in all ways, subject to fits of anger, jealous of the honor paid to him,

3. Davis, "Idea of God" (1908c).
4. Davis, "Idea of God" (1908c), 1.

> punishing his enemies, rewarding his friends, entering into conspiracies, leading the armies of the children of Israel, winning victories for them. In short, this person, Jehovah, was just like any of the leaders of the tribes of Israel, differing only in this, that he was more powerful, greater, and had powers and capacities so great that he could accomplish things that the leaders of the tribes were helpless to bring about.[5]

This anthropomorphized picture of God is reinforced by the behaviors of his Jewish subjects, by how they interacted with and treated their God.

> Their God came to earth occasionally. Moses went to see him on Mt. Horeb. He met Moses and delivered to him the ten commandments. He appeared to Moses and told him to go down into Egypt to free the children of Israel.
>
> But in no place does the nature of God appear more clearly than in the religious services, of the feasts and the sacrifices. . . . Their God was a man, like themselves. When they had a big celebration over some victory, or some important event, they desired their God to be present with them and enjoy their feast. So, they brought to the feast not only the food and the oil and the wine, necessary to satisfy their own appetites, but they brought their choicest breads and grain and burned them on the altar. They killed [the] best and most perfect beasts and burned them on the altar. . . . Then the best of their feast wines were poured out on the ground to satisfy the thirst of Yahweh. By this method his presence was assured, and his good fellowship in their pleasures added to the merriment and the fun of their great festival days.[6]

Here is a picture of God, more or less human, but of course more than human, who would visit occasionally.

I admit that, while my grandfather went on to argue that Jesus changed this picture of God, and while we no longer feed him at feasts, it remains a pretty common picture even today. Certainly, the most famous God imagery—I think of Michelangelo's *Creation of Adam* on the ceiling of the Sistine Chapel—shows a man with a white beard reaching out an arm and touching the hand of Adam. While we know that Michelangelo's imagery is metaphor, still, what is the alternative?

5. Davis, "Idea of God" (1908c), 2.

6. Davis, "Idea of God" (1908c), 2.

3. God as Spirit

Davis found Jesus' alternative conception of God in John's Gospel, specifically in Jesus' interaction with a woman from Samaria (John 4). The woman says to Jesus, "Our fathers worshipped in this mountain; and ye say, that in Jerusalem is the place where men ought to worship" (John 4:20). But Jesus replies, "Woman, believe me, the hour cometh when ye shall neither in this mountain, nor yet at Jerusalem, worship the Father" (John 4:21):

> But the hour cometh, and now is, when the true worshippers shall worship the Father in spirit and in truth: for the Father seeketh such to worship him. God is a Spirit: and they that worship him must worship him in spirit and in truth.[7]

After sharing this passage from John, Davis went on to say,

> Considering the circumstances under which this is said . . . the idea which he intends to convey to her is plain. You still worship a god who is a big person, to be found on some mountain, or in some temple. But that is not the true worship; God is not a person to be worshipped in the temple or on the mountain. But God is a spirit to be worshipped as a spirit and in truth. This, I say, is the new turn given to the idea of God in the time of Jesus. God is not a person but a spirit.[8]

This idea of God as spirit may be as much a creation of John, as of Jesus, for John is the writer who focused not on Jesus' bodily resurrection, but his resurrection as spirit (see chapter 5). For John, "In the beginning was the Word, and the Word was with God, and the Word was God."[9]

God is not a "big person," but a spirit. But what kind of spirit? Here I find myself plunged into deep and cold waters. Davis had some ideas of the kind of spirit Jesus had in mind, which I shall share momentarily. And Davis also had his own take on this notion of God as spirit, which I shall also share shortly. But I must admit I find all of these specifics challenging, and as I have learned dipping slightly into the vast literature of our changing conceptions of God, there are nuances upon nuances here.

7. John 4:23–24.
8. Davis, "Idea of God" (1908c), 4.
9. John 1:1.

I have found what little I've read of this history fascinating, but still, these are difficult metaphysically murky waters—at least for me.[10]

4. God, the Father

While these are deep and cold waters, the move from conceptualizing God as a "big man," an "occasional visitor," to something more abstract, "God, in spirit and in Truth," makes sense to me. Certainly, if there is a God, this God is not a big man. This God must be something quite different, less corporeal, more spiritual. So, bracketing my general skepticism here, the move to God, in spirit and in truth, seems right.

But what kind of spirit? This is how Davis described the spirit Jesus—as portrayed by John—had in mind:

> God is a spirit, but he is that spirit who could teach Jesus the meaning and the depth of life, not alone through the law and the prophets, but as well through all the manifold wonders and beauties of the luxuriant life of nature which he saw about him, and from which he drew one of his choicest truths. The lilies of the field, the birds of the air, the cornfields, the life of the sea of Galilee, all spoke to him of the spirit whom he worshipped in spirit and in truth.[11]

So, God is connected to the lessons we can take from the natural world: the beauty and abundance of the living natural world around us. Not only the natural world, but also the human world,

> the manifold interests of human life, the same spirit spoke to him, opening to him the secrets of the human soul, and through the secrets of the human soul, the secrets of the great spirit whom he worshipped in spirit and in truth.[12]

The spirit that Jesus worshiped was, according to Davis, the spirit from which Jesus gained his understanding of the truths of the natural and the human worlds around him.

This spirit spoke to Jesus through Jesus' ability to understand the common people around him:

10. The book that I have found most interesting on this topic is Aslan's *God*. Karen Armstrong's *History of God* also is very good.

11. Davis, "Idea of God" (1908c), 4. On God and the luxuriant life, see Matt 6:28–30.

12. Davis, "Idea of God" (1908c), 4–5.

> In the life and the experience of the common people of Palestine, shot through and through with thoughts, feelings and aspirations, in which Jesus saw disclosed the nature of the spirit, did he find the faith that made his life sublime.[13]

And it is this understanding the led Jesus to a conception of God as the spirit of love and care.

Of the many parables that Jesus used to share this insight, the story of the prodigal son (Luke 15:11–32) heavily leans the spirit of love and care.

> Like unto this father of the prodigal son, was the spirit whom Jesus worshipped in spirit and in truth. Because he saw here in this human spirit of parental love and care, the highest and the deepest feelings of human life, childless though he was, he turned to the great spirit with whose power he saw that the whole earth and all life was saturated, and uttered the simple word, so full of the deepest of human feelings, Father.[14]

Here we get the concept of "God, the Father." But not the "big man father," rather a more "abstract father," the father of infinite love and compassion: God the father as an extension of—an abstraction of—the relations that a human father has for his children. God, the Father is the metaphor Jesus used to describe his conception of a God-spirit of love and compassion.

5. God, the Indwelling Goodwill

God, in spirit and in truth, and God, the Father—for me, anyway—push against each other. God, the Father, is easily tied back to God, the big man, the occasional visitor. It makes sense to me that Jesus might have used this metaphor. It called to mind what evidently was a widely held picture of God—as a big man—and moved this picture forward to a God-spirit of love and compassion. In moving to a new conception of God—God in spirit and in truth—Jesus used a metaphor that tied this new conception of God back to a conception of God with more currency at the time. But the metaphor still carries "big man elements."

Davis took the message of the metaphor but dropped the metaphorical scaffolding. God is the spirit we understand from our deepest insights into nature and human nature:

13. Davis, "Idea of God" (1908c), 5.
14. Davis, "Idea of God" (1908c), 5.

> Thus did Jesus speak to the inquiring men and women of his time. You want to know about God? God is a spirit; and we must worship him in spirit and in truth. He is in the life of nature, in the life of man, in your life. Through your experiences as men and as women, you, as children playing in the fields, as lovers tender and true, as fathers and mothers, as workers in the world, you come to understand the great truth and meaning of human life, disclosed in you and through you by the spirit of the infinite goodwill.[15]

God "is in the life of nature, in the life of man, in your life." This is where Davis found God the spirit, in each of our human experiences of nature and of human nature.

Jesus' parables and metaphors work, according to Davis, because they call on common human experience. Experiences as parents—as in the story of the prodigal son—experiences of nature—the luxuriant abundance of nature:

> And why take ye thought for raiment? Consider the lilies of the field, how they grow; they toil not, neither do they spin:
>
> And yet I say unto you, That even Solomon in all his glory was not arrayed like one of these.
>
> Wherefore, if God so clothe the grass of the field, which today is, and tomorrow is cast into the oven, shall he not much more clothe you, O ye of little faith?[16]

Speaking to his congregation, Davis urged them, if they but look to their own experience—of nature, of humans, of themselves—they will, each of them, find God. And the God that their experience will reveal, the God in spirit and in truth, the God that Jesus worshipped, is a God "of the infinite goodwill."

Once so understood—that the universe is ordered by "the infinite goodwill"—Davis argued that life's beauty and abundance emerge like the transition from black-and-white to technicolor:

> It is like the combined effects of the rain and the sun upon the vegetation, making them to grow and unfold the full capacity of their nature with such leaps and bounds and to make one fear that he may hear their triumphant shout of joy, as leaf after leaf unfolds itself to make beautiful the world, as tiny bud burst

15. Davis, "Idea of God" (1908c), 6.

16. Matt 6:28–30.

> forth into the full beauty, sending forth its fragrance broadcast over the earth; as the flower fades way and gives place to the fruit, and then best of all comes the rich and bounding harvest. So also is he who knows the meaning of the life ordered in the great good will. Every act is full of bounding joy, every thought teams with goodwill and noble purpose. Selfishness and cruelty become impossible. . . . Once get a glimpse of the meaning of the meaning of life, as it really is, and all the relationships of life change, and life itself becomes a new thing.[17]

I admit this is a lovely, beautiful picture of a world ordered in the infinite goodwill. But this picture struggles with other experiences, experiences of hunger and want, of brutality and hate, of the despoiling of the natural world. I do not think we can say that lived human experience speaks univocally of the infinite goodwill.

6. Overcoming Evil

Davis was not oblivious to the hardships, the ugliness, the awfulness, the evil in the world. His vision of the infinite goodwill, while drawn from (selected) experiences is better understood as an ideal, an aspiration for the world, not simply as a picture of the world as it is. The world as it is, is change, constant change.

Human aspiration, human ideals, human visions provide direction to change. He opened his June 13, 1909, sermon, "The Making of Reality," as follows:

> The function of human personality, which gives to human life its most profound significance, is that of making reality. Whether we so wish it or not, the fact remains that the thoughts we think, and the conduct that expresses those thoughts goes to constitute the reality in the midst of which we live.[18]

He continued by contrasting the story of King Herod, as presented in the 1901 play, *Herod: A Tragedy*, by Stephen Phillips,[19] with the story of Herod's contemporary, Jesus. He concluded this comparison as follows:

17. Davis, "Idea of God" (1908c), 7.

18. Davis, "Making of Reality" (1909h), 1.

19. Stephen Phillips (1864–1915) was an English poet and dramatist, author of *Herod: A Tragedy*.

> Both Jesus and Herod are dead. The one is remembered simply because he happened to be a king of Judea, while the other was dreaming of the ideals of his youth, and dared to think that justice is more powerful than the sword. The one crushed from his life the only bright spot in trying to achieve through injustice. The other, always true to his ideals even to the point of complete renunciation, is still one of the men, perhaps the one man above all others, whom the world honors, loves and cherishes, because he loved his fellow man, and saw in him the spirit of the living God, whom he worshipped in spirit and in truth, because he dedicated his life to the making of that reality which makes for righteousness and peace and happiness in human life.[20]

It is through our ideals, and the actions we take in accordance with our ideals, that the world is made. Jesus "dedicated is life to the making of that reality."

We have choice here. Human free will was a critical part of Davis's picture of the world. As Davis saw the matter, Jesus articulated a sharp contrast:

> He saw the choice of life. He saws the way of indulgence, lust, greed, leading to torment, remorse, and ashes. He saw the way of truth, love and loyalty, leading to the values that he believed to be imperishable and eternal. He made his choice.[21]

Davis was urging the same choice to the members of his congregation. If we make such a choice, if we consecrate our lives to this vision, we take critical steps in its realization. We make the world and can make the world better.

As Davis saw the situation, working towards this vision, this vision of a way of life Jesus modeled, this vision that Jesus took from his God-spirit of infinite love and care, has been, and will always be, an ongoing process. The world is change, not completion. Working towards this vision has been a process that has required—and will continue to require—the participation of individual human beings, exercising their free will toward the realization of their ideals:

> We cannot over-estimate the tremendous obstacles to be overcome. . . . The task calls for noble men and women, inspired by the highest religious and moral aims of which the human soul is capable, men and women who have a righteous hatred of all

20. Davis, "Making of Reality" (1909h), 7–8.
21. Davis, "Did Christ Have the Power" (1923b), 6.

> sin, all error, but who have a deep sincere love for the sinner, and the erring. The task calls for men and women who in their homes, in their churches, in the towns in which they live, may, by the very simplicity and consecration of their lives, become a powerful force in doing this great work of man, of growing up into the truth of God. . . . It cannot come to us as Divine Fiat.[22]

It is the fact that these ideals—truth, goodness, and beauty—somehow are "in human beings," and that human beings can pursue them of their free will, that leads to human progress. It will not come by "Divine Fiat," but only through ongoing—difficult, burdensome—labor and toil.

As I read these words that my grandfather wrote over one hundred years ago, I have strangely mixed feelings. Yes, I can see the power of the idea. But the moral burden—being "inspired by the highest religious and moral aims, having a righteous hatred of all sin, all error"—catches my breath. This level of moral perfection feels very much out of reach, beyond—at least my—human imperfection. Even while Davis urged his congregation to have "sincere love for the sinner and the erring," we are still establishing a high moral bar, a bar that can feel impossible. At the same time, I am put in mind of the strong moral compass that my mother brought to her children. "Mary morals," my brother called it. No wonder. My mother imbibed at her father's table—and her children sat at her table. But still a high bar.

7. Thirst for a Living God

Another sermon from the 1910s, "The Thirst for a *Living* God,"[23] offers a different angle on Davis's view of God. When I first read the sermon, I had little sense of what my grandfather might have meant by the phrase "a living God." My untutored idea—clearly not knowing Davis's work—was that "a living God" was some kind of existing supernatural being, a being that was—is—alive, alive and engaged with this world. I also thought that human faith was connected to this, that the living God was "living" in part because of a person's active—living—faith in him/her; and that this faith would drive actual—living—behavior. The Living God. Lacking this faith myself, and having a more skeptical attitude about God generally, I was curious what my grandfather had in mind.

22. Davis, "Growth and Salvation" (1906e), 6.

23. Davis, "Thirst for a *Living* God" (191Xa).

Davis opened the sermon noting the "attitude of indifference" that "people today" (1910s) had towards religion.[24] If anything, this attitude of indifference has increased into the twenty-first century. In Davis's day, he noted that even where there was church attendance,

> there is a sort of a dry rot permeating it all, so that it fails to hold the devoted, spontaneous consecration that has marked the great religious movements of the past.[25]

Davis described the situation as akin to a deserted village. The buildings are there, but the people are gone, "the master spirit that made the place alive has gone."[26] This was the situation he saw with organized religion in his day:

> Much that same feeling has come into the formal village of organized religion. From all sides come the complaints that the zeal, the vitality, the whole souled interest has fled. A spirit of ennui has crept over the body. All the furnishings of doctrine, or sacrament, all the customs and formalities are the same. Pious exhortation, appeal for consecration, appeal for loyalty fail to overcome the dismal feeling, for many at least, that no longer does "the Real Presence," dominate the ancient village, where God once was.[27]

Davis's diagnosis of this situation was that we confuse religious forms with genuine religious faith—"Not Forms But the Holy Spirit"[28]—that we confuse the living with the dead:

> We are forever confusing the permanent spirit with the accidental manifestation. We look for the living among the dead. We seek for spiritual warmth before the dead embers of the past. To be sure they once glowed, but they glow no more. No dead God can satisfy our living souls and only a living God can rekindle the fires in our dead hearts.[29]

As Davis saw things, organized religion—religion dependent on creeds—invoked notions of a God of past times. This God may have been powerful

24. Davis's concern about the increased apathy towards religion that he observed in the 1910s was a frequent topic of his sermons from the 1910s.

25. Davis, "Thirst for a *Living* God" (191Xa), 1.

26. Davis, "Thirst for a *Living* God" (191Xa), 1.

27. Davis, "Thirst for a *Living* God" (191Xa), 2.

28. Davis, "Not Revelation" (1947a).

29. Davis, "Thirst for a *Living* God" (191Xa), 2.

and consequential in its time, but things change. Everything changes, and a "living God" must be continually remade to be pertinent, powerful, persuasive in contemporary life:

> For God is not static, God is life. While we are worshiping the deserted village, that we once built, the life spirit has passed on and is building elsewhere. The God that we made was vital and interesting while we were making him. But when we had finished and put a fence about him, he was dead. Life flows on.[30]

What is this living God, this God that is life?

> The word "God" is a word which we use in a symbolic manner to express our conception of the totality and essence of things. God is spirit, God is life, said Jesus. Even so it is. In the face of the tremendous fact and challenging mystery of natural and human life, we feel the over-powering grandeur of it all, and with that strange, subtle heroism which makes even the least of mankind wonderful, and we cast forth onto the unexplored seas of effort, and truth. To the best of our experience, and wisdom we explain that Great Mystery of Life, and call it God, an imperfect symbol of our imperfect insight into the reality and possibility of Life.[31]

In keeping with Davis's attention to ongoing change, with the idea of our ongoing, ever-reaching efforts to find knowledge—truth—as we learn more "our imperfect symbol of our imperfect insight" must grow, must change. What stays constant here is "the tremendous fact and challenging mystery of natural and human life."

For Davis, it was through the living God that we stand in awe of the world we inhabit:

> It is the "Master Presence" that holds us in its all-absorbing Grip. The living God, the God that is Life, that is Human Life, that dwells in the individual men and women, with all their noble hopes, all their achievements, all their defeats and their limitations, all their mistakes, and selfish, cruel sins, the God that is all this and more, infinitely more, that is the totality of life, that God grips our souls.[32]

This "living God," this human sense of awe, grandeur, and yet of order and of infinite possibility for change, growth, positive growth, this

30. Davis, "Thirst for a *Living* God" (191Xa), 3.
31. Davis, "Thirst for a *Living* God" (191Xa), 2–3.
32. Davis, "Thirst for a *Living* God" (191Xa), 3.

God—and not some God from an ancient fable—this God has the power to change how we think:

> When we look at life that way, we no longer feel the haunting fear of vacuum, of absence. Every being, everything, every life, every shrub, is pulsating with such tremendous vitality, such wonderful hope, insuppressible purpose, that we are fairly carried off out feet, by the infinite sweep of life, which like a mighty river carries us past the present of today towards the infinite possibilities of to-morrow. Villages may be deserted, ancient creeds may become void of life, but the streaming, surging, flow of life goes on, building, creating, dreaming, loving, and living. There is the Living God, for which we hunger and Thirst.[33]

As he said in his 1908 sermon, God "is in the life of nature, in the life of man, in your life." Or, as he concludes "Thirst," God is "Life, Life and evermore Life."[34] Life, with its "depth and its power, irresistible in its uncontrolled ferocity, or magnificent and majestic in its disciplined and intelligent best."[35] This, for Davis, was the living God.

8. Pantheism and Two Principles of the Modern World

God—"in the life of nature, in the life of man, in your life"—is a long way from God the occasional visitor. This comes very close to pantheism, where the universe in its entirety is a manifestation of God, is God. Reza Aslan, in his 2017 book *God: A Human History*, arrives at a similar place, pantheism:

> I arrived at this epiphany through my own long, and admittedly circuitous, spiritual journey—both as a scholar of religions and as a person of faith. Indeed, the history of human spirituality that I outline in this book closely mirrors my own faith journey from a spiritually inclined child who thought of God as an old man with magical powers, to a devout Christian who imagined God as the perfect human being; from a scholastic Muslim who rejected Christianity in favor of the purer monotheism of Islam, to a Sufi forced to admit that the only way to accept the

33. Davis, "Thirst for a *Living* God" (191Xa), 3.
34. Davis, "Thirst for a *Living* God" (191Xa), 3.
35. Davis, "Not Revelation" (1947a), 1.

> proposition of a singular, eternal and indivisible God was to obliterate any distinction between Creator and creation.[36]

Later, Aslan writes,

> As a believer and a pantheist, I worship God not through fear and trembling but through awe and wonder at the workings of the universe—for the universe is God. . . . I recognize that the knowledge of good and evil that the God of Genesis so feared humans might attain begins with the knowledge that good and evil are not metaphysical things but moral choices.[37]

Here Aslan speaks to two elements of God: outer—awe and wonder at the workings of the universe—and inner—the origins of good and evil in our moral choices, the action of personality of free will. These are the same two elements, outer and inner, that Davis focused on with his Living God.

Pantheism can sound like a kind of cheat—at least to me. Define God as all of the universe and, by definition, God exists. God is what is. But does such a God mean anything?

For Davis—and I think for Aslan—the answer was yes. This affirmative answer comes from reflections on these two elements, outer and inner—the workings of the universe, and the origins of good and evil.

Davis's pantheistic God was more than a definition. It was a commitment to a meaningful universe, and a commitment to the power of the ideals of humans to work themselves into reality. This was Davis's new kind of faith, not faith in a revelation, but faith in the order of the Universe and the power of humans to make progress toward their ideals.

In his September 19, 1909, sermon, "Two Great Principles of the Modern World," Davis aimed to clarify how our modern conceptions differ from those of the ancient world, specifically including our modern conception of God. Here Davis set out his new kind of faith.

For Davis, the first great principle of the modern world, the principle that distinguished the God of the living from the God of the dead, was "faith in the substantial integrity of the universe."[38] This is the faith that we can and should be in awe of the universe, but furthermore, that we also can and should make rational sense of the universe. The universe is amazing. Equally amazing is the fact that through our efforts

36. Aslan, *God*, 166.

37. Aslan, *God*, 169.

38. Davis, "Two Great Principles" (1909b), 2.

at discovery—through our experience and through science—we can make rational sense of it. We can and should have awe and wonder in the universe's ongoing kaleidoscopic change—sometimes beautiful, sometimes terrifying—but *not* just chaos. This is the faith that the scientist must bring to scientific investigation: It is possible to gain in our understanding the world.

By contrast, distrust in the integrity of the universe

> is part and parcel of the old world ideal. . . . Upon it, as a foundation, rests the ancient doctrines of depravity of man, the ideals of class rule, and the notion that religion is some kind of supernatural vaccination, which will prevent those upon whom the vaccine acts favorably, from suffering the disease of sin, and assuring them immunity from eternal damnation.[39]

Distrust in the integrity of the universe was—for Davis—part and parcel of the ancient world's revelation, authority, and obedience.

The modern world, instead, opts for discovery, freedom, and consent:

> When the modern man goes about among men, he does not hold his nose in the air, condemning man for his depravity, and withdrawing from contact. In spite of the fact [that] the conditions of the laboratory of human life do not come up to his notions, he keeps on working, confident [that] if he seeks in all honesty, he will find the truth, confident that the appalling conditions are not the evidence of a blunder, but the evidence of immaturity, and that as humanity goes on honestly seeking for the truth that shall make men free, it shall find the truth. Faith in the substantial integrity of the universe means above all else, a faith in the substantial integrity of men, and the possibilities of human life.[40]

The modern world is a world of change. Appalling conditions are evidence of the unfinished nature of the world—not a blunder in its making.

This led Davis to his second principle of the modern world, *progress*, that ongoing human work can make things better:

> This is the second article in the faith of the modern man, growth, development, progress, in truth, in the power to appreciate the beauty, and in goodness and righteousness. The moral vigor of

39. Davis, "Two Great Principles" (1909b), 3.
40. Davis, "Two Great Principles" (1909b), 3.

> our time is consecrating itself to the work that grows out of the conviction that human life is not entirely what it ought to be.[41]

In addition to faith that the universe is orderly—understandable—Davis's new kind of faith included faith that human efforts to improve things are not purely in vain. Progress is possible.

As I have already argued (chapter 2) progress is a tricky business. But the fact that progress is tricky—hard to define—demonstrates that Davis's pantheistic God means something. Davis's pantheistic God underlies the integrity of the universe and the possibility of progress. Davis's "modern faith," faith in a pantheistic God, lies behind his consecration to act to improve the universe, to create the garden of "Eden in our future."[42]

Davis's pantheism rested on the law-like or understandable—and yet ever-changing—universe, and on the human drive to imagine this universe—particularly the human part of it—better and take to steps to improve it. I am reminded of Immanuel Kant's widely quoted remark, "Two things awe me most, the starry sky above me and the moral law within me."[43] Davis took it as a fact—not of definition or philosophical argument—that human experience, not revelation, shows us these "outer" and "inner" processes at work as we go about our lives.

10. Humans Are Part of the World

In another sermon, from January 9, 1910, "Is There Any Sense in Praying?,"[44] Davis connected "outer and inner." He reminded his congregation of the "outer" part of God:

> We go out into the winter night, and amid the silence, look into the heavens. We see the little dots of radiating light shining out from the black background of space. We try to imagine the extent and the meaning of it all. . . . We know that they [the stars] move in such complete harmony, and in such accurate paths, that we, men so small in comparison with them . . . know enough of their movements to be able to predict to

41. Davis, "Two Great Principles" (1909b), 3.

42. Davis, "Two Great Principles" (1909b), 3.

43. Immanuel Kant (1724–1804) was a German philosopher and central Enlightenment thinker. This quotation is from the conclusion to his 1788 *Critique of Practical Reason*.

44. Davis, "Is There Any Sense" (1910d).

> the minutest fraction of a second. . . . We stand transfixed by the very stupendousness of what we see.
>
> Overcome we cast our eyes to the ground, and behold, it is covered with the tiny particles of snow that have fallen from the atmosphere above. The same force that brought them floating softly, gently to the ground, and holds them there as we stand, and holds us there also, is the force that marked the pathway of the stars and fixes the rising and the setting of the sun. . . .
>
> But the inquiring spirit is aroused in us now. Our searching eye penetrates the cold lifeless snow, that lies at our feet, and sees hidden there seeds and germs of that force which we call life. We know that the days are fast coming, when the rain, and the sun will melt the snow, warm the earth, and draw from beneath its surface, the life of vegetation. Then our imagination, fed by the treasures of memory, carries us forward to the luxuriant days in June, when all the earth is alive with the evidences of that strange mystery of life.[45]

He then moved to "inner":

> So much for the outer world. But not less strange and marvelous is the inner world of man, where are thoughts, hopes, aspirations, loves and hates, dreams and visions, longings for truth and adventure, ideals, and purposes. . . . Is it not wonderful that we should have the desire to know about the laws of life, and seek to penetrate the vast seas of the unknown? Is it not wonderful, that we, men and women, infinitely small particles, should control the very powers amid which we live, and make them serve our ends? Is it not wonderful that we should have dreams and visions of life that go far beyond all that we hope to see in reality, and is it not wonderful that we should pin our faith upon those ideals, and let them take command of us and guide our action? Is it not wonderful that a man will take an idea, which seems to defy all the reality about him, and alone stake all on the truth of that unseen ideal?[46]

Here we have the outer and inner elements Davis's modern pantheistic God.

But they are connected.

> What is the meaning of this inner wonder at the outward reality that we see? Is there any relationship between the two? Does the

45. Davis, "Is There Any Sense" (1910d), 2–3.

46. Davis, "Is There Any Sense" (1910d), 3.

> world within bear witness to the great universe without? Does the world of thought and personality within derive its being and existence from the very forces of the universe that we see without? Is there any connection?[47]

We are part of the universe, not apart from it:

> We are at this moment, with all our limitations, and all our possibilities, with all our achievements, and all our failures, just the product that these great universal laws and forces have made us, and that we and humanity after us shall become what these real ideals of ours hope for. The ideals are indeed the germs of life implanted in us by the universal life that has been operating through all the ages, and that they are the prophecy of things that shall be, that they evolve, develop, come into being in human life, not through chance and caprice, but through law and order, that they are of the very nature of the universe and the universal life.[48]

Davis's faith in the "integrity of the universe" and in "progress," come to the same thing: A faith that the universe is so constructed that human moral progress is part of the integrity of the universe. The possibility of progress is built into the universe through the reality of human ideals and actions, which are also part of the universe.

The integrity of the universe includes human ideals. They were not put there by an external God—although I suppose that is a possibility, it is not a necessity. The universe just is as it is, and what the universe is includes the seeds of life, and these seeds include a form of life that has the capacity to think of ideals and the capacity to work towards these ideals:

> Just as they have come into being in human life, in the form of an ideal, so will they, responding to the very laws which have produced them, both laws of matter and of mind, become established in reality. The ideals of today are the seeds that we plant for the harvest of reality tomorrow.[49]

Davis's pantheism, his faith in the integrity of the universe and in progress, is substantial. It goes beyond a mere definition. And yet it is not a matter of argument either. One either acts to improve the world—action

47. Davis, "Is There Any Sense" (1910d), 3–4.
48. Davis, "Is There Any Sense" (1910d), 4.
49. Davis, "Is There Any Sense" (1910d), 4.

that reveals this faith—or not. Davis's theism is a question of fact, of how one acts in fact.

11. Transcendent and Immanent

All these fancy ideas. Writing about God almost of necessity elevates the language to a highly abstract and insubstantial feeling realm. Integrity of the universe. The human potential to realize our ideals. It all sounds fine but removed. The language lives in the upper atmosphere of limited oxygen. Humans—most humans anyway—don't live in this atmosphere. In the next chapter I will bring some of this down to earth with a discussion of Davis's idea of heaven—heaven on earth. How we create the garden of Eden in our future. But I don't want to leave this discussion of God quite yet.

In an interesting paper Davis wrote while a student in Divinity School—"Sermons I: The Leadership of Jesus"—he described what struck me as a not-uncommon scene where God or Jesus might be evoked:

> A few months ago, at the funeral service of a very dear friend, the opportunity came for seeing from another's point of view the conception of Christ. . . . I found myself in the room where the casket still remained. . . . The mother knelt before the casket and in a simple prayer, addressed in part to God and in part to Jesus the Christ, besought Jesus to come for her only son upon whom she was looking for the last time. To her, Jesus was the nearby friend who would help her and sustain her in trouble, who would care for her son. God was far away, [a] transcendent God, but I could almost see Jesus standing opposite her looking upon the sorrowing mother with compassion and love in his face. He was the friend and source of strength.[50]

This struck Davis—and strikes me—as human: Seeking solace from a "nearby friend," a powerful friend who could and would care for her deceased son. Whatever one may think about immortality—and more on this in chapter 8—the scene is human. Wherever that mother's son was—if anywhere—she would no longer be able to look out for him. A human-deity-Jesus fit the bill. Davis called this need, "the Christ Idea":

50. Davis, "Leadership of Jesus" (1903a), 1.

> I would call this inherent sense of the nearness of God and man, the *Christ Idea*. Either in thought or in symbol this idea must be satisfied.[51]

This set up the problem to which Davis's paper is addressed: How can *Uni*tarians, who deny the Trinity, who deny a human-deity-Jesus, respond to this need? How can Unitarians include the Christ Idea in their conception of God with only a human Jesus? Davis developed a response by distinguishing a "transcendent God" from an "immanent God." A transcendent God is aloof, far way, abstract, anything but human. An immanent God is caring, nearby concrete, human. The Jesus of the Trinity is an ideal immanent God. As Davis saw the situation, the Christ Idea is one reason for the power and persuasiveness of the Trinity. What could the Unitarians offer instead?

As a Divinity School student Davis expressed the problem in denominational or quasi-creedal terms: What can the *Unitarians* offer instead? But the question remained for Davis's more mature ideas of a pantheistic God, God that is "Life, Life and evermore Life." How can this very abstract idea of God accommodate the Christ Idea? How can a pantheistic God, God that is "Life, Life and evermore Life," feel caring, nearby concrete, human—"immanent"?

12. Prayer

One way to approach this question is to ask what would it mean to pray to a pantheistic God? In the sermon on prayer already mentioned in section 10, Davis spoke to this question. He began by acknowledging and dismissing the idea that we pray to a big man God or a human-deity-Jesus.

> Prayer was a petition or a request asked of God as a special favor. It rested upon the basis that God was a person who could listen to the petition of each one, decide upon its merits, and give or reject, just as the king might decide upon the merits of a petition from one or a group of his subjects. Now it is evident that such an idea of prayer is impossible according to the modern ideas of God.[52]

As Davis understood the modern world, there is no big man occasional visitor to whom one could appeal in prayer.

51. Davis, "Leadership of Jesus" (1903a), 2 (emphasis in the original).
52. Davis, "Is There Any Sense" (1910d), 1.

There is no big man out there to come to one's rescue. But for Davis, real prayer should look inward:

> But the wish, the longing for that which is of value, of real value, in human life, expressed in words or left in the secret chambers of the mind, is a real prayer. . . . And I believe that wishing, longing for truth, for justice, for goodness and beauty, for the realization of the ideal, is just a true natural function of human life, and that the efficiency of human life in realizing that ideal, and coming to know that truth, depends largely on the intensity and the frequency of wishing, and the longing of the true prayer.[53]

Real prayer, as Davis understood the term, is spelling out to oneself—for oneself—those ideals one holds deep. It is a cry for the strength to live up to these ideals and for the strength to take steps to see them realized in the world.

We might pray to win the lottery or for the exam we are not prepared for to be postponed. But, as I understand Davis, this is just so much wishing upon a star, an expression of a trivial kind of hope for oneself, but not a real prayer. A colleague of mine once shared with me his argument that prayer does not work. If it did work, he said, he would surely be dead, for he knew that many of his students prayed for his demise ahead of an exam. For Davis, this is not a real prayer.

Real prayer, for Davis, had to connect to those deep ideals, ideals for a better world. It is a "longing for truth, for justice, for goodness and beauty." And real prayer, for Davis, was part of how humans came to understand these ideals and how humans came to consecrate themselves to their realization.

> Prayer is that comparison of the things as they are with the things as they ought to be, when the comparison is accompanied with the conviction that the universe makes for things as they ought to be, and we become its agents.[54]

Real prayer is part of how we make the world a better place.

What then of Davis's Christ Idea? Davis did not care if one had a "big man" in mind while in prayer—although only the right kind of "big man." It came to the same thing:

53. Davis, "Is There Any Sense" (1910d), 7.

54. Davis, "Is There Any Sense" (1910d), 8.

> So, the fact of prayer, being a human function, is not affected by whether or not one happens to believe in a big man god as the concentrated personality of the universal powers that make ideals legitimate things, or whether or not one believe that the powers that men at one time believed were concentrated in a personality, are now believed to be diffused through all the universe, and everything is pulsating with them.[55]

A "big man God," for Davis, was fine insofar as that "big man" was a way of conceptualizing "the concentrated personality of the universal powers that make ideals legitimate."

Davis thought of God as "the integrity of the universe," outer and inner. Human personality, for Davis, was the conduit through which progress became possible in our universe. Human personality is part of the universe—not apart from it—and so the fact that humans do have ideals, and the fact that humans have taken successful steps to realize these ideals means that the integrity of the universe includes progress "for truth, for justice, for goodness, and beauty." Davis called this God.

And what of the woman praying for Jesus to protect her deceased son? As I understand Davis, this is entirely appropriate, meaningful. For her, as Davis would reframe how to understand her prayer, "Jesus" names "the concentrated personality of the universal powers that make ideals legitimate things." She prays for the ongoing support of her son's personality in whatever form it takes post-death. She prays for the support of her son's personality as it merges with "the concentrated personality of the universal powers." The name, "Jesus," makes this highly abstract—and indeed hugely speculative—prayer concrete, intimate, immanent, and not simply transcendent. "Jesus" does not name a person, but a personification of an abstraction. And, as for the speculative nature of this suggestion of the immortality of the son's personality, more in chapter 8.

55. Davis, "Is There Any Sense" (1910d), 8.

Chapter 7: **Heaven on Earth**

> But to think that Christ paid the price that is required of you and me for entry into the kingdom of heaven, is to misapprehend the first simple principles of his life. The kingdom of which he taught is not a place to which we may or may not go, but it is a spirit which enters into you and me and transforms the essential purpose of life and creates a condition of life.[1]

1. A Spirit Which Enters into You and Me

DAVIS LIVED IN A world of constant change, and yet a world where the life of Jesus—the human personality of Jesus—still retained power to command our attention, admiration, study, and emulation. Davis's God was a far remove from a "big man," an "occasional visitor." Instead, God, for Davis, was present in all of the world and in each and every human being. Davis jettisoned the—for me—dubious epistemological religious claims to supernatural revelation. His pantheistic God cleared away the—for me—murky metaphysics of a separate spiritual God. And yet, his natural liberal religion carried significant meaningful commitments, including the possibility to understand of the universe, and the power to improve the course of the changing world through human ideals and aspirations.

For Davis, the changing world was intelligible and capable of human-directed progress. Exactly what constitutes this progress remains difficult to spell out in a world of constant conceptual flux. But, for

1. Davis, "Bearing of Burdens" (1908d), 2–3.

Davis, it had something to do with ideals of truth, beauty, goodness, and justice for all.

Davis's religious focus was very much on the here and now, and not on some possible redemption in an afterlife in heaven. His focus was on heaven on earth.

> But to think that Christ paid the price that is required of you and me for entry into the kingdom of heaven, is to misapprehend the first simple principles of his life. The kingdom of which he taught is not a place to which we may or may not go, but it is a spirit which enters into you and me and transforms the essential purpose of life and creates a condition of life.[2]

Heaven is not a place, but an attitude. It is an attitude spelled out in the purposes of living, in the ideals and aspirations for a better world. It is an approach to living where human effort works for a better world. Whatever may be achieved by these efforts is not the ultimate reward, but merely a waystation in an ongoing—centuries ongoing, millennia ongoing—human-directed effort to improve the human condition. For Davis, this work was the reward. It was joyful. It was our participation in the evolution of life, in the evolution of the universe.

Which brings us down from the challenging theological heights, where we have concerned ourselves with the nature of God, the possible divinity of Jesus—or of human beings generally—and the ramifications of a world of constant change, down to the here and now, and our participation in the here and now. One of the more surprising essays he wrote while a Divinity School student concerned housing for the poor; it included blueprints.[3] On October 25, 1908, he preached a sermon, "The Need for Extending More Rational Methods in Dealing with the Small Offenders Against the Social Order."[4] A week later his November 1, 1908, sermon was titled, "Practical Politics and Civic Righteousness."[5]

The sermon preached the week following his "high principle" sermon, "Two Great Principles of the Modern World"[6] (see chapter 6), was titled "What to Do."[7] It was very specific. In his view, the point of the

2. Davis, "Bearing of Burdens" (1908d), 2–3.
3. Davis, "Housing the Poor" (1903b).
4. Davis, "Dealing with Small Offenders" (1908e).
5. Davis, "Practical Politics" (1908f).
6. Davis, "Two Great Principles" (1909b).
7. Davis, "What to Do" (1909i).

Pittsfield Unity church where he was minister was to make a difference in the here and now:

> We are here in this fellowship of men and women for a purpose. We believe that through the channels of this group, we are going to make a direct and valuable contribution to the life and growth of men. We stake our faith on the conviction that we can do something here that must be done for mankind, something that can be done here, can be done by us and those who shall join us. . . . In doing this, we rely, not upon the magnitude of our institution, not upon the scope of our claims, but upon the unconquered and unconquerable courage of the human will, dominated by the overlordship of a great conviction and purpose.[8]

Taking on and working toward the ideals of truth, beauty, and justice, with courage, conviction, and purpose, was Davis's heaven on earth. Here he found the "spirit that enters into you and me."

2. The God of Democracy

Davis always tied his concerns for improving things back to his religious principles and his deep commitment to discovery, freedom, and consent. So, while he had very specific ideas about necessary improvements—for example, with respect to housing—ultimately his focus was tied to governance. Democracy—a government of the people, by the people, and for the people, a phrase he frequently quoted from Lincoln's Gettysburg Address—was primary.

For Davis, democracy was the civil-secular instantiation of discovery, freedom, and consent. As Davis viewed history, it was the prior move in religion, through the Reformation, that set the stage for American democracy. He wrote of "the God of Democracy" as the spirit of his age—the aspirations of modern humans for discovery, freedom, and consent:

> When I see humanity looking up from its toil, it's want, its misery, its evil, and, with a look of hope on its face and the ring of faith in its voice, send out its challenging call to the building of the God of democracy according to the principles of the democracy of God, I feel as if I must take the shoes from

8. Davis, "What to Do" (1909i), 2.

> off my feet for I know that the place whereon I am standing is holy ground.[9]

With American democracy Davis saw discovery, freedom, and consent, certainly by contrast with the monarchy it replaced, with its divine right of kings underwritten by revelation, authority, and obedience.

Davis had no illusions about American democracy. It was not perfect and needed attention and improvement. In his sermon, "What to Do," he wrote, "Now the field of our work is, first of all, the city of Pittsfield," and in Pittsfield, among other things, he discussed the state of housing—not good—public transportation—in need of improvement—public schools—not stimulating enough—civic engagement—woefully lacking.[10] For Davis—and still today—civic engagement was—and is—our shared commitment to making American democracy work. His assessment strikes me as true today, woefully lacking.

As mentioned in chapter 2, from Davis's point of view it was the congregational polity of the Pilgrims and the Puritans that set the stage for American democracy. This view was picked up by Forrest Church in his 2003 book *The American Creed: A Spiritual and Patriotic Primer*:

> From hard acquaintance with the tyranny of state-sponsored religion, in establishing their "civic politic" the Pilgrims were motivated by a desire to separate their church from England's state. The Puritans . . . felt no such compunction. Yet they too laid the foundation for the American Creed. Congregational polity—a priesthood of all believers—leads directly to the idea of democratic government. And the practice of religious liberty naturally suggests (and, to a degree, mandates) its correlate, civil liberty. If the Puritans failed to make these connections themselves, their primary commitments to congregational polity and their own religious liberty certainly facilitated the speed and manner in which they were later made.[11]

A priesthood of all believers—universal priesthood (see chapter 2)—presupposes free inquiry, for if inquiry is not free some authority is constraining it.

And yet Church writes of "a priesthood of all *believers*. "Believers" would seem to constrain, to exclude atheists and likely others whose

9. Davis, "Democracy of God" (1910e), 5.
10. Davis, "What to Do" (1909i), 4–8.
11. Church, *American Creed*, 5.

beliefs were "outside accepted limits." Part of the history of the New England theocracy during the seventeenth century and the early eighteenth century revolved around efforts to establish these boundaries. Very strict rules were adopted on what was acceptable—religiously and civilly. The Salem witch trials are notable historical markers of this boundary setting and the cruelty of the theocracy.

In the later part of the seventeenth century and the early part of the eighteenth century, as more people of more diverse backgrounds and views came to New England huge stress was put on the theocracy. The Pilgrims and the Puritans came to New England to free themselves from oppressive authoritarian limitations on their religious practice and belief. In their early largely homogeneous population, a New England theocracy could function without coming into conflict with the principles of free inquiry and universal priesthood. But this homogeneity was lost over time. Problems emerged.

Davis wrote of three problems:

> There were three considerations, one from within the Church, and two without, that began to undermine the Theocracy as soon as it was established. These are, 1st the question of Church membership centering about the idea of Baptism and communion; (2) The question of suffrage; (3) The treatment of heretics.[12]

The rules for church membership were very narrow and burdensome: "None were admitted to the adult membership who could not relate some instances of the transforming operation of God in their own lives."[13] As for suffrage, only adult—male—members of the church were allowed to vote: "In 1643, out of 15,000 inhabitants only 1,800 were voters. In 1646, the petition to extend the suffrage was presented to the General Court."[14] Finally, the matter of heretics, especially Quakers and the "Salem witches," the harsh judgements against these "heretics," banishment and burning, were deeply unpopular:

> Charles II issued a Decree of Toleration, known in New England history as the "King's Missive," ordering the officials in New

12. Davis, "Rise and Development" (1906a), "Lecture VII: The Forces Without the Theocracy," 1.

13. Davis, "Rise and Development" (1906a), "Lecture VII: The Forces Without the Theocracy," 1–2.

14. Davis, "Rise and Development" (1906a), "Lecture VII: The Forces Without the Theocracy," 4.

> England to suspend proceedings against the Quakers, and if any were then in prison, to send them to England for trial. To send anyone to England for trial was too much for any New Englander to do, so all the Quaker prisoners were released. This was a decisive victory for the Quakers, and a blow at the Theocracy.
>
> In the witchcraft persecutions in the 1690s we find the final effort of the Theocracy to sit in judgement and condemn heretics. The popular feeling against this final attempt of the Theocracy became so great that it had not a little to do with its downfall.[15]

Ultimately the pressures were too great to contain. The theocracy fell.

Universal priesthood and freedom of inquiry doomed efforts to put boundaries around "believers." As Peirce later put it, "the social impulse is against it" (see chapter 2):

> The man who adopts it will find that other men think differently from him, and it will be apt to occur to him, in some saner moment, that their opinions are quite as good as his own, and this will shake his confidence in his belief.[16]

Similarly, Davis concluded that creeds—attempts to establish the boundaries of "believers"—were "intellectually impossible."

In matters of civil governance the modern world of discovery, freedom, and consent was, for Davis, the world of democracy. It was a historic moment when American democracy emerged to put these pillars of modernity into place in civil government. But no human creation is perfect. And while the advent of American democracy was a watershed moment for Davis, he was clear there was ongoing work to do.

In the early years of the twentieth century, Davis was concerned the decline of civic engagement. In his sermon, "What to Do," he complained about the apathy of his fellow residents of Pittsfield:

> We have recently held caucuses for the nomination of men for various political offices. The town, as well as the state, and the nation, are facing large and serious problems. The men whom we shall send to these various bodies are to act in ways that influence us and our posterity. Yet how many of us know what these men believe about the questions which they have to decide? . . .

15. Davis, "Rise and Development" (1906a), "Lecture VII: The Forces Without the Theocracy," 6–7. The "King's Missive" was issued in 1662 and was concerned specifically with the persecution of Quakers by the New England theocracy.

16. See Peirce, "Fixation of Belief," in Menand, *Pragmatism*, 16.

> We are sending men to the general court. They are likely to be called upon to act on the proposition of a federal income tax. How many men in the city of Pittsfield know how our representatives are likely to vote? In fact, how many men know how we want them to vote? A measure of the utmost importance, and yet not a word has been said about it.[17]

Davis walked the walk here and ran for office as Alderman of Pittsfield in 1911. And lost. He was committed to taking steps in the here and now to improve things.

3. A Rich Abundant Life

In a 1910 sermon, "The Social Ideal of the Modern World,"[18] Davis discussed three great achievements of the modern world. The first was public education and the second was the extension of suffrage. Democracy needed—and needs—both. Intelligent civic engagement depended on an educated public. Education may not be sufficient—as we can see in our own times—but it is necessary. Davis was writing at a time of rapid expansion of public education.

Suffrage is perhaps the more obvious need for democracy. The Fifteenth Amendment to the Constitution, ratified on February 26, 1869, gave male African Americans the right to vote. This did not solve the suffrage question for male African Americans, as the painful story of Jim Crow attests. But it did establish the core right. When Davis wrote this sermon in 1910, suffrage had not yet been extended to women, but that was on the way—the Nineteenth Amendment, granting the right to vote to women, would be ratified on August 18, 1920—and, as Davis put it, conceptually already we were a long way from the divine right of kings.

Davis continued his sermon, "The third great achievement of the modern world is the industrial development." Davis was a great admirer of the accomplishments of the industrial revolution:

> We have made great strides, at the cost of great suffering to be sure, towards a system of production and distribution that shall enable men to supply the physical necessities at a cost of labor which is well within the possibilities of our capacities and needs. The development of this great industrial system, aside from its

17. Davis, "What to Do" (1909i), 5–6.
18. Davis, "Social Ideal" (1910f).

> financial aspects, is of the very bone and fiber of the modern world. Each combination, each merger is an achievement of progress. We are learning how to produce and distribute the necessities of life.[19]

The advances of the industrial revolution—if we took appropriate advantage of them—should lead to greater individual freedom.

In another manuscript, "The Dream of a Christmas Shopper," about which more below, he calculated:

> We have discovered that with all able bodied people working five hours each day, we can easily satisfy all the needs that we have. You will now have time to read, to play, to enjoy your children, to do something for the community.[20]

A five-hour workday! Whether or not this calculation was correct, it was clear that the industrial revolution did radically increase productivity.

Davis saw the productivity gains from the industrial revolution as a huge benefit, progress realized. It was enough of a benefit that we could recognize the "cost of great suffering," and still see a net gain. Particularly important to Davis was the greater freedom that would be afforded to people to attend to and support the growth, development, and education of their children.[21] This was the message of hope and progress that Davis took from the industrial revolution. As Davis saw it, the industrial revolution promised more opportunities for a "rich abundant life" for all.

Davis's interest in the industrial revolution went deeper than the material benefits it afforded us. For Davis life was about exploration and discovery. Science and technology had vastly expanded our view of, and understanding of—and indeed appreciation of—the Universe we inhabit:

> Food, shelter and raiment of some kind are essential. Whether we like it or not, we must keep up this pace of labor: it is part of the structural relationship that we bear towards the whole of things.
>
> But beyond this primitive necessity of labor comes another factor, the constant urge of our creative and adventurous search into the mysteries of the universe; the scientist, the inventor, the discoverer of new things and ways; here we share in the creative

19. Davis, "Social Ideal" (1910f), 13.

20. Davis, "Dream of a Christmas Shopper" (1916c), 5.

21. At the time Davis wrote "The Dream of a Christmas Shopper" he and his wife Annie had four children, ages ten, eight, four, and one.

> process that is constantly alluring us on into the undiscovered wilderness upon the edge of which we live.[22]

Industrial innovation sat side by side with discovery in revealing to us more about the mysteries of the universe we inhabit. It demonstrated our powers of intervention and control. We are not simply mere particles driven here and there by forces beyond our control. We have some ability to control these forces, to implement our hopes and aspirations for a better world, to direct the unstoppable onrushing change. For Davis, scientific discovery and industrial innovation have deep spiritual connections to our appreciation of—to our living in—the universe.

Still there were problems that needed to be addressed. We needed to find ways to help those who have been "knocked into the ditch of poverty and unemployment and despair":

> Out of the ditch they must come, and in part by the helping hand of those on relatively safe ground. That is emergency work.[23]

Then there was laissez faire capitalism:

> In viewing and criticizing the industrial conditions of today, we must distinguish between the great constructive work of developing a system of production and distribution, and the entirely incidental element, the development of the capitalistic class. This latter is a mushroom growth and will bide its day.[24]

While the increases in the efficiencies of production and distribution were great, they were accompanied by problems. The task ahead—the critical task for Davis's here and now—was to ameliorate the suffering and to excise "that mushroom growth," the "capitalistic class," that had hitched a ride with the industrial revolution.

Equally important—and a "long-range task"—was to "coordinate labor with thought,"

> not for the primary purpose that we may have wealth and goods and activity in abundance, however essential these are as means to life, but primarily that we may have life, rich and abundant, intelligent, creative, decent, and purposeful.[25]

22. Davis, "Sermon on Labor" (191Xb), 2.
23. Davis, "Sermon on Labor" (191Xb), 4.
24. Davis, "Social Ideal" (1910f), 13–14.
25. Davis, "Sermon on Labor" (191Xb), 4.

A rich abundant life—not so much materially abundant as intellectually, morally, and spiritually abundant—that for Davis was the great long-range opportunity provided by the industrial revolution. And the great task ahead was fixing labor relations.

4. Democratic Socialism

For Davis, democratic socialism was the answer. He was an active and committed socialist, certainly through the first two decades of the twentieth century. He wrote multiple essays and sermons devoted to this subject.[26] From his socialist lens, he was convinced that democratic socialism should be, and would be, the outcome of World War I. In a manuscript that dates from the period after the United States entered the war but before the Armistice, "Democracy and Socialism," he wrote,

> In whatever direction we may turn we come upon the idea, if not the words, "After the war, Socialism." Sometimes this idea is expressed in the language of the conservative who fears; again, in the language of the student who tries to preserve a scientific poise of impartiality; and sometimes it comes from the hopeful believer; but everywhere the result is the same, the growing realization that "after the war, Socialism."[27]

History did not develop as Davis imagined—at least not on the timeline he had in mind. Furthermore, socialism became intertwined with and confused with communism, particularly central state communism of the Soviet Union and later the People's Republic of China. After World War II the "communist menace" became the major element defining the Cold War. Perhaps now—post-Cold War—a new and different assessment of democratic socialism is possible. But clearly it is an uphill battle

26. Of the documents that have survived at least sixteen directly concern socialism and five have "Socialism" in their titles: "Churches and Socialism" (1910g); "Socialism: A Reply to The Common Assertion That the Socialist Movement Is Atheistic, Irreligious, and a Menace to the Family" (1910a); "Socialism" (1912); "Ethical Aspect of Socialism" (No Date-b); "Democracy and Socialism" (1918b). Other essays or sermons directly concerned with socialism: "Industrial Cooperation" (1906f); "Sermon on Labor" (191Xb); "Social Unrest" (1908g); "Class Struggle" (1910h); "Social Ideal of the Modern World" (1910f); "Churches for Truth and Justice" (1910i); "New Era" (1914); "Dream of a Christmas Shopper" (1916c); "Peace Service Sermon" (1918c); "Significance of Labor Strikes" (1918d); "Strike of the General Electric Company Employees" (1919c).

27. Davis, "Democracy and Socialism" (1918b), 1.

against entrenched prejudices and anxieties—if not some clear problems with the implementation of any "socialist utopia."

As I have been working through my grandfather's writings, I have found my own concerns and prejudices about socialism confronted by his many confident and explicit supports for socialism. While I am the grandson of a socialist, I am also the son of an entrepreneur who founded a company that invented, manufactured, and sold innovative new scientific instruments.[28] My father would not have supported his father-in-law's socialism—although my father was drawn to and loved his father-in-law. And conversely, my grandfather was excited by the kind of work my father was doing—scientific and industrial innovation. Just as much as he was a socialist, Davis also was completely in thrall with the results of science and technology, to the possibilities that our techno-scientific "modern world" was opening up. Discovery, not revelation.

Davis was a socialist. But he also was deeply and completely committed to American democracy; he was a fan of scientific discovery and the possibilities for positive change afforded by technology. And he was a liberal Christian. As I began to read through his writings in the summer of 2021, these four simultaneous commitments—socialism, democracy, science and technology, liberal Christianity—did not easily square with each other, at least not with my naïve conceptions of them. Obviously, Davis thought about these things differently than I have done. This space that he found for socialism *and* democracy *and* science and technology, *and* Christianity is a space I find worth examining.

In Davis's view of history, the rise of the industrial system was leading towards—not away from—democratic socialism:

> This great industrial system has created the machinery that has made necessary, rational, and valid the thoughts of a social democracy. In other words, this industrial system has been, and is today, the legal parentage of the social democratic movement. The system, with its byproducts of greed, lust for power and dominion that have crumbled in the great war, has directly produced the thought, the development of democratic tendencies. Socialism, or social democracy, is not the idle dream of a visionary soul, not the vision of an idealistic society, it is the logical, and essential development, the next step in social evolution.[29]

28. I have written about the history of my father's company, Baird Associates. See my *Thing Knowledge* and "Histories of Baird Associates."

29. Davis, "Democracy and Socialism" (1918b), 4.

Davis held the view that the "Great War" was the result of capitalistic excess, that the horrors of the war would demonstrate to the world the advantages of global cooperation—not competition. Global trade supported peace. And finally, Davis argued, democratic socialism would support this cooperative stance.

While Davis recognized capitalism's role in providing the resources behind the industrial revolution, he did not think capitalism was an essential part.

> Capitalism has produced this great international system of production and distribution. This great international system has given rise to the principles and the programs of a social democratic order of society. Social democracy came not to destroy but to fulfill the creative genius of capitalism. The evils of capitalism will be left behind. "After the war, socialism."[30]

Davis pictured the excesses of capitalism "with its byproducts of greed, lust for power and dominion" leading to their logical terminus in the horrors of the Great War. And so, "after the war, socialism."

5. Labor Problems

Davis was deeply attentive to—and deeply involved in—labor problems that had arisen with the industrial revolution. Shortly after the Armistice ending World War I, employees of several General Electric plants—including a large operation in Davis's hometown of Pittsfield, Massachusetts—went on strike. Davis wrote of the details in "The Strike of the General Electric Company Employees."[31] After the strike was resolved, with the approval of management, the employees, and the War Labor Board, Davis was appointed to administer the resolution of the strike. He was viewed as a fair broker by all parties.[32]

30. Davis, "Democracy and Socialism" (1918b), 4.

31. Davis, "Strike of the General Electric Company" (1919c).

32. Davis never wrote at length about this work, and I have wondered if it was not an element of his decision to leave Pittsfield for his next ministry at the Church of Our Father in Lancaster, Pennsylvania. In a review of a book by Everett Dean Martin he wrote, "Twice I have had to face the task of de-mobbing a crowd. On one occasion it consisted of about 2,000 angry strikers, bent on riot." See Davis, "Notes on Everett Dean Martin" (1920), 9.

Early in his career, in 1906, Davis wrote an essay, "Industrial Cooperation,"[33] which provided an analysis of one of the sources of labor problems along with a possible solution, not a panacea, but "worthy of much more consideration than has hitherto been accorded it, not only because of its moral [value] but also because of its economic worth."[34] Conceptually, the idea of "industrial cooperation" is straightforward:

> Industrial cooperation in a general way includes within its scope all tendencies in industrial life which have as an end the closer organic relationship of the factors of production. In any business enterprise, whatever may be its size or nature, there are three essential elements involved, viz, labor, capital, and managing ability.[35]

Industrial cooperation is about encouraging a "closer organic relationship" between the three factors of business: labor, capital, and management.

Davis spelled out these three factors in the simple case of a family farm run by "Mr. Jones":

> If we analyze this simple situation into its component parts, we discover that Mr. Jones Capitalist, and owner of the farm and tools, hires Mr. Jones as manager to run the farm, and again Mr. Jones, manager hires Mr. Jones, laborer, to do the work.
>
> In varying proportions these three elements are present in every productive industry, and each is an absolute necessity.[36]

The idea of "industrial cooperation" is to bring these three elements into a more "organic relationship"—closer to what Davis saw in the family farm—than had become typical in large national or multi-national industrial organizations.

The bulk of "Industrial Cooperation" was concerned with two examples from the nineteenth century. The first example was a printing house in Paris founded by Edme-Jean Leclaire (1802–72) where the profits were shared with the workers. The second example was N. O. Nelson Manufacturing Company in St. Louis, Missouri—ultimately expanding to Edwardsville, Illinois—founded by Nils Olas Nelson (1844–1922). Nelson Manufacturing had a somewhat complicated method of profit sharing and—perhaps more important—employee participation

33. Davis, "Industrial Cooperation" (1906f).
34. Davis, "Industrial Cooperation" (1906f), 4.
35. Davis, "Industrial Cooperation" (1906f), 4.
36. Davis, "Industrial Cooperation" (1906f), 4.

in ownership of the firm. More details can be found in Davis's essay, but both concerns were financially successful and successful in improving the conditions and prospects for labor.

Davis analyzed the labor and financial efforts as follows:

> From the point of view of the employer of labor, if one may judge from present conditions, there are three pressing problems. 1st is the problem of securing good workmen. 2nd to arouse their interest in the welfare of the firm, and last, but not least to retain them in one's employ.[37]

The approach to industrial cooperation led to satisfactory results with respect to all three pressing problems. With respect to the problem of retaining good employees, Davis wrote,

> The final cause of the dissatisfaction and unrest of the workman is not that he does not receive enough, but that he has no prospects ahead of him. . . . Many, if not most, reach the high-water mark of attainment in a few years. . . . At best it is not inspiring. Sometimes it is hopeless.
>
> Now here is a plan which offers the workman the possibility of looking forward to, and actually realizing the fact of an increasing income, depending upon his own thrift and faithfulness. Give most workmen that opportunity and little will be heard of strikes, lock-outs or labor troubles.[38]

Davis concluded his essay:

> In short this one tale seems to say that the organic relationship of the factors of production, and a frank recognition of their interdependence, not only avails for the increase of wealth-producing efficiency, but also for life-producing efficiency. To be sure it has limitations, but it also has possibilities.[39]

By developing a closer "organic relationship" between labor, management and capital, the friction of dissatisfied labor—"strikes, lock-outs or labor troubles"—are avoided. The workmen—and women, as the shirtwaist strike of twenty to thirty thousand women in 1909–10 demonstrated[40]—would be motivated to help their firms succeed

37. Davis, "Industrial Cooperation" (1906f), 11.

38. Davis, "Industrial Cooperation" (1906f), 12.

39. Davis, "Industrial Cooperation" (1906f), 16.

40. The shirtwaist strike of 1909 was the largest strike by female American workers to its date, involving twenty to thirty thousand workers. The strike began on November

because they would share financially in their firms' successes. Better, this led to financial success for the firms involved.

Twelve years after writing "Industrial Cooperation," Davis was in the thick of the labor problem in Pittsfield. Early on, as the 1918 General Electric Pittsfield strike evolved, Davis wrote an essay, "The Significance of Labor Strikes from the Point of View of Evolution of Religion."[41] The essay covers a lot of ground. He placed the 1918 GE strike in context with other strikes during the 1910s, some shockingly violent.[42]

Davis tied the situation in part to the "industrial change from the home industry to the factory."[43] He referenced a short, twenty-two-page pamphlet, *Recollections of a Mill Worker,* written by a Pittsfield woman who had worked in Pittsfield's textile industry throughout her life, watching the change from home industry to factory:

> In a very simple straightforward way she tells the story of this change, and without being conscious of what she is saying, she pictures the transformation in the Pittsfield textile industry from the neighborly, friendly relationships of the employer and the worker, to the cash-nexus basis of labor and capital.[44]

The change from friendly neighborly relationships to pure "employer-employee" relationships was, as Davis thought about these matters, a critical causal factor behind the GE strike.

By 1918, the organic relationship between capital, management and labor was missing:

> To bring it down to the concrete situation here in Pittsfield, we have a large industrial plant. . . . It is managed by a man who may or may not own any stock in the company. . . . The controlling part of ownership is located outside of the city. Not only because of the fact of numbers of both employees and owners, but also because of the fact of absentee ownership, the personal human relationships that once obtained on the small factory are gone.

23, 1909, and lasted until February 1910, when many of the demands of the workers had been met, including better pay, shorter working hours, and equal treatment of workers in and outside of the union. Davis mentioned this strike in his January 9, 1910, sermon "Is There Any Sense" (1910d), 6.

41. Davis, "Significance of Labor Strikes" (1918d).

42. Twenty-one people, including strikers' wives and children, were killed in a clash during the 1914 Ludlow, Colorado, miners' strike.

43. Davis, "Significance of Labor Strikes" (1918d), 3.

44. Davis, "Significance of Labor Strikes" (1918d), 4.

> With it too is gone the possibility of that ameliorative oversight which existed when the owner knew and shared largely in the interests of life, the joys and sorrows, of the workers.[45]

The first issue, then, behind "the labor problem," as Davis saw it, was the distancing—is "alienation" too strong a word?—between the owners and the workers.

The second issue, for Davis, tied back to discovery, freedom, and consent. The workers needed to have a voice in the conditions under which they were employed.

> The essential issue between them is not one of wages, although that is a factor. Nor is it indeed, the technical [matter] of the recognition of the labor union, although that is a factor. But it is the right of the men who work for wages in a factory . . . to have a collective word in determining the conditions under which they shall work, as against the right of the owners of the factory, who do not use it, to dictate through their representatives the terms of employment, with no ultimate appeal.[46]

This is a matter of freedom and consent:

> As you easily see this is no superficial disagreement. It involved the very foundations of our industrial life, and there are at stake those principles of democracy about which we seem to be so much concerned.[47]

The principles of democracy—discovery, freedom, and consent—were challenged by this kind of industrial growth.

Davis concluded his essay with an appeal:

> One aspect of the change of men's ideas in the world of religion has been to [de-]emphasize the glories of a heaven beyond death, and to emphasize more the necessity and the desirability of a more tolerable and a more just and a more Christ-like world here. . . . To this great task, then, of applying the principles of democracy to the industrial life of tomorrow, in the interest of all men without distinction of class, I make my appeal.[48]

45. Davis, "Significance of Labor Strikes" (1918d), 4–5.
46. Davis, "Significance of Labor Strikes" (1918d), 6.
47. Davis, "Significance of Labor Strikes" (1918d), 6.
48. Davis, "Significance of Labor Strikes" (1918d), 8–9.

Davis wanted us to focus on improving conditions in life, not on "the glories of a heaven beyond death." This meant applying "the principles of democracy to the industrial life of tomorrow." Faith in discovery, freedom, and consent, required addressing the relations between capital and labor.

Davis believed that socialism—giving the workers voice in, and in some cases ownership of, the means of production—could square modern industry with freedom and consent. Obviously, he did not see socialism as a threat to democracy, quite the contrary.

Davis was aware that we had to work to preserve our democracy while embracing socialism:

> I said a moment ago that by many it seems to be taken for granted that after the war comes socialism. But whether that development will be in the direction of a bureaucratic Socialism, or will preserve and establish the spirit of democracy, will depend upon the zeal and intelligence, the sound statesmanship of those who have a real faith in the soundness and validity of democratic principles.[49]

What Davis had in mind with democratic socialism was that the workers would have a voice in, an interest in—and in some cases, ownership of—the means of production. He sought to diminish or collapse the class distinction between capitalists and workers. All, together, share in the efforts and the fruits—and risks—of industrial affairs.

6. Socialism and Christianity

Davis appealed for a more "Christ-like world" at the end of his essay on the General Electric strike.[50] Clearly, he saw a connection between his conception of Christianity and the kind of democratic socialism he favored.

In his 1910 essay, "The Churches and Socialism," Davis described the social, political and ethical problem of the day as follows:

> It is an irrepressible conflict between the rights of personality and the rights of wealth. Shall the industrial system be the servant of human life contributing to its growth and development, and to the emancipation of personality? Or shall it remain the

49. Davis, "Democracy and Socialism" (1918b), 1.

50. Davis, "Significance of Labor Strikes" (1918d), 8–9.

> lord and master to whose command we must submit and upon whose altar we must place our sacrifices of degradation, poverty, debauchery, corruption, and even life itself. . . . Is society to remain plutocratic or shall it become democratic? Shall wealth remain monarchical, or shall it become socialized? That is the essence of the social question today.[51]

Opening pathways for the development of each individual's "personality," Davis's sine qua non of an abundant human life, had to be the goal. Not profit. The question, then, was does the "industrial system" work in service of "the emancipation of personality," or do human personalities work in service of the industrial system, with "sacrifices of degradation, poverty, debauchery, corruption, and even life itself." Fundamentally it was a question of priorities: human personalities or the industrial system.

For Davis, the answer was obvious:

> If churches really were what they pretend to be, there would be no question as to the attitude. Especially Christian churches, whose followers have read the sermon on the mount, must understand that men cannot worship God and Mammon. . . . Churches, if they are true to the pretentions with which they present themselves before men, they must insist upon the supremacy of the human soul, and the principles of freedom, and justice, and life in the struggle of men against a life-destroying institution.[52]

And, indeed, in Jesus' Sermon on the Mount we have, "No man can serve two masters: for either he will hate the one and love the other; or else he will hold to the one and despise the other. Ye cannot serve God and mammon."[53]

This does seem simple—and yet it is complex. Matthew 6:24 is clear that one "cannot serve God and mammon." But this does not in itself provide a positive argument for democratic socialism. One way of reading Jesus' message—that Davis would also recognize and support—focuses on *individual* devotion to God, and not *collective* devotion to some specific economic/political brand of justice.

One of Davis's closest friends, and the long-serving minister of the First Church of Boston, Charles Edward Park,[54] wrote about one's individual devotion to God:

51. Davis, "Churches and Socialism" (1910g), 7.

52. Davis, "Churches and Socialism" (1910g), 7.

53. Matt 6:24.

54. Charles Edward Park (1873–1962) was minister of the First Church in Boston

> The thought of God is the most private of a man's private possessions. . . . For in his thought of God a man betrays his innermost being, the very formula on which his individuality is compounded. . . . Since individualities, like autumn leaves, are never exactly duplicated, it follows that there are as many thoughts of God as there are individual souls to form them.[55]

As Park had it, each person develops their individual conception of and relationship with God. Jesus' emphasis on each person's individual relationship with God was one element of the striking prophetic break of Jesus' message to his Jewish tradition which instead emphasized God's relationship to the Jewish state.[56] Davis would have agreed with all this.

But for Jesus there are two great commandments. The first emphasizes each person's individual devotion to God, "thou shalt love the Lord thy God with all thy heart, and with all thy soul, and with all thy mind, and with all thy strength."[57] The second emphasizes each person's responsibility to each other person, "Thou shalt love thy neighbor as thyself."[58]

In addition to one's individual relation with God, Jesus was clear about a shared—a collective—project. Park wrote,

> Remembering this, we must be careful how we say that Jesus tried his best to share with others his own special concept of God. We nowhere find such a desire explicitly stated. . . . He urges them to love God with all their heart and soul and mind, as the first commandment in their Law bids them do. He charges them to discover in God every right quality that they can discover in the best of men. . . . He teaches them, at least by implication, that God has a purpose, a Kingdom of Heaven to establish on earth; and is waiting for them to undertake this enterprise with him as his junior partners. . . . He speaks of God as My Father in Heaven; but he is very definite that the relationship is not exclusive. He nowhere tells them that his is the "only begotten Son of God." They are his sons as well as he.[59]

(Unitarian) from 1906 until he retired in 1946. See his "Eulogy for Earl Davis."

55. Park, *Way of Jesus*, 21–22.
56. Park, *Way of Jesus*, 20.
57. Mark 12:30.
58. Mark 12:31.
59. Park, *Way of Jesus*, 21–22.

Park's "way of Jesus" is first to develop a personal relationship with God, and second to be a "junior partner" with God in his purpose to establish a kingdom of heaven on earth.

These two central commandments from Jesus begin to define God's purpose—as Jesus understood God—to establish a kingdom of heaven on earth. Insofar as socialism supports care for one's fellow human being, supports individual personality over Mammon, supports an "abundant life" over "simple abundance," insofar as socialism supports Jesus' kingdom of heaven on earth, a Christian case can be made for democratic socialism.

But there remains an unresolved tension between the emphasis on individuality and on collectivity. This is perhaps particularly evident in American culture. Park reflected on this:

> For still another thing, individual opportunity is sure to awaken violent competition; and, say what you will to the effect that industry is the life-blood in America's veins, and that competition is the soul of industry, you cannot deny that competition is an obstacle to the Second Great Commandment. You can no more raise a crop of brotherly love in the soil of competition than you can raise a crop of potatoes in a swamp.[60]

Park shared Davis's enthusiasm for industry, but, also with Davis, Park was interested in industry for the benefit of all:

> For there is such a thing as industry for the benefit of all the parties concerned: management, labor, and consumer. And there is such a thing as mutually advantageous competition.[61]

Park did not conclude that democratic socialism is the correct resolution to this tension between individuality and collectivity, that democratic socialism is the correct route to the kingdom of heaven on earth. Park instead focused on etiquette and ethics:

> Nowhere is the need of a proper code of etiquette and ethics more evident than in this detail of our modern activity.[62]

Park looked to the work of "Chambers of Commerce and Rotary Clubs," and he urged, "More power to their elbow." Still, he was clear that until we find the solution to bitter competition between companies and between

60. Park, *Way of Jesus*, 46.
61. Park, *Way of Jesus*, 46.
62. Park, *Way of Jesus*, 46.

management and labor the second commandment and the kingdom of heaven on earth will remain elusive:

> But until they succeed, the spirit of modern industry, with its competition, and all the intensity of feeling and bitterness, and all the unprincipled tricks and devices that competition still connotes will remain essentially incompatible with the Second Great Commandment, and a formidable obstacle to its obedience.[63]

Adopting a politically more radical position, Davis thought that democratic socialism provided the way forward, a way that, as he saw it, supported the dynamic processes of industrial modernization, while prioritizing human souls over mammon.[64]

7. Socialism, Democracy, Science and Industry, Christianity

At this point we can see the space that Davis found for his simultaneous commitments to socialism, democracy, science and industry, and Christianity. It is the space that his view of "the modern world" points to. It is the space characterized by freedom, discovery, and consent.

For Davis, democracy provided the means to ensure freedom and consent within the constraints of a large multiplicity of individually different conceptions of freedom. While capital might be the financial muscle of industry, discovery is the heart and soul of science and industry. As we learn more about the world—and more through our interventions in the world—we gain in terms of material abundance. But, more importantly for Davis, we gain in terms of spiritual abundance. Democratic socialism would provide one means to prevent a capitalist authoritarian plutocratic monarchy of wealth, and to bring industry into the modern world of freedom, discovery, and consent. Whereas, for most working

63. Park, *Way of Jesus*, 46–47.

64. It is entirely possible that this apparent disagreement between Davis and Park is more a function of time and age. Davis was an active socialist, advocating for democratic socialism, as a young man in his thirties and forties during the 1910s. This was a high watermark for democratic socialism in the United States. I have not found any discussion of socialism by Davis after 1920. Park's remarks above were written in the 1950s, when both Park and Davis were in their seventies. Moreover, by the 1950s socialism had gotten confused with Soviet communism and the Cold War.

people, a capitalist-based plutocracy is just another form of authority and obedience. Democratic socialism supports freedom and consent.

Democratic socialism also provides a way to reconcile Jesus' two great commandments. Each individual can enjoy personal freedom to love *their* "Lord thy God with all thy heart, and with all thy soul, and with all thy mind, and with all thy strength," while also loving each of their neighbors "as thyself."

This space that Davis found for his simultaneous commitments to socialism, democracy, science and industry, and Christianity is neither uncontested nor unproblematic. I have already suggested that Davis did not sufficiently appreciate the role of capitalism in motivating entrepreneurial spirit. This pursuit of wealth—worshiping of Mammon—may not be reconcilable with worshiping God, or perhaps in more secular terms, worshiping full human flourishing. But it is a real human fact. Worshiping Mammon may be spiritually empty. Literature frequently attests to the hollowness of such worship. Money can't buy you love, we're told. But, particularly in a competitive and financially precarious world, for many worshiping Mammon is more about seeking security. Yes, for some capitalists it may be about "greed, lust for power and dominion," which, also—alas—did not crumble in the Great War. Jesus' second commandment is a surprisingly high bar to reach in an insecure world.

We can—and we have—blunted some of the excesses of capitalism through various governmental actions. In Davis's time there was the Sherman Anti-Trust Act of 1890. We did create a federal income tax—with or without the knowledge and support of Davis's Pittsfield's citizens—and we now have various levels of progressive taxation. We now have the National Labor Relations Board, and the right of workers to organize. The Occupational Safety and Health Act of 1970 created the Occupational Safety and Health Administration (OSHA). Despite all this—and many other governmental efforts—our situation today is stubbornly similar to that in Davis's time, with grotesque income inequality, autocratic challenges to democracy—both governmental and industrial—and labor problems, etc.

8. Dreams of a Christmas Shopper

In late December 1916, sometime after the World War I battle of Verdun concluded on December 18, Davis wrote a short essay, "The Dream of a Christmas Shopper."[65] This does not read like a sermon, and so it is not entirely clear what audience he had in mind, perhaps a Christmas-time newspaper editorial, never published to my knowledge. Here we see in some detail Davis's idealistic picture of his democratic socialist heaven on earth.

The piece starts with Davis relating his cheerful Christmas thoughts as he walked home from an evening reception. He saw happiness and optimism among the crowd of shoppers; as he put it, "Glory shines around."[66] After getting home his mood was shattered by the day's headlines:

> "Rumanian Army No Longer in Action." "French take 11,387 prisoners at Verdun Fighting." "United States needs a larger standing army." "Sylvia Pankhurst arrested for holding a 'peace meeting.'" "Strike to continue." "United States needs a million rifles."
>
> What a fool I had been to allow myself to forget that this is a "practical age," that we are reasonable men, and reason rules. What an idiot I had been to imagine that those people . . . were happy in buying things to give away. . . . We are out for the almighty dollar. That is the only thing that counts. "Giving" is folly.[67]

He then nodded off by the fire and had his "Dream of a Christmas Shopper." In his dream he awoke on December 26 to find a changed world. People seemed happy, upbeat as they went to work. He followed a group of workers to their factory where "Mr. Manager" made the following announcement:

> I have some important news to tell you this morning. I have just been talking with the people who own this factory. They tell me that in as much as we here who do the work, and manage this factory, and make so many valuable things for the lives of the people, and really know how to make them, they have decided to give over to us this great machine that we use together to be used by us to make more and better things for all the people. We are to manage and operate it ourselves. . . . So, from now on these machines that we manage and use are ours. Can we do it?[68]

65. Davis, "Dream of a Christmas Shopper" (1916c).
66. Davis, "Dream of a Christmas Shopper" (1916c), 1.
67. Davis, "Dream of a Christmas Shopper" (1916c), 2–3.
68. Davis, "Dream of a Christmas Shopper" (1916c), 4.

As the dream developed, it turns out that in factories all over the world the owners were handing over to the workers the "means of production."

> So the changes came thick and fast. By this magic spirit the whole nation had been transformed into a great family, making things, ideas, and ideals for each other. Each was doing his part, according to his ability, and each was receiving his compensation according to his product.[69]

Not just things, but "things, ideas and ideals": Davis's abundant life.

The war ceased and the antagonists began to work together to rebuild the damage done. Indeed, "negotiations were underway for a federation of the world."[70] Closer to home, Davis dreamed of big changes for Pittsfield, Massachusetts. Gone were the "three-deckers, and the tenement houses"; in their place, "cottages, plain, beautiful and home-like, grace the large lots on our new boulevards."[71]

> Best of all, as the years passed by, I saw being built . . . a great municipal building. Slowly and irresistibly, it was rising upon solid foundations, a thing of beauty and use. No ordinary building, but the product of the love labor of all the citizens, of all of us. Not one cent of labor paid for, but every bit contributed out of the leisure, and the devotion of free citizens to the symbol of the community life, a great cathedral of our common aims, the gift of our free spirit.[72]

And among the many people bustling about working on this municipal building, Davis dreamt "of a strong majestic figure clad in the garb of an Oriental Carpenter":

> After long minutes of gripping silence, I saw him move, gaze around the building, look into the faces of the throng that was going in-and-out of the temple. I think I saw lips quiver, and his body tremble, and he said half to himself and half to those nearby, "This day is my dream fulfilled. Thy kingdom come."[73]

69. Davis, "Dream of a Christmas Shopper" (1916c), 5.
70. Davis, "Dream of a Christmas Shopper" (1916c), 5.
71. Davis, "Dream of a Christmas Shopper" (1916c), 6.
72. Davis, "Dream of a Christmas Shopper" (1916c), 6.
73. Davis, "Dream of a Christmas Shopper" (1916c), 6.

"Daggie the dog" woke Davis up, and he slowly came back to the reality of the headlines, the "reality of this 'practical, business world.'"[74] But, evidently still under the spell of his dream, he wondered,

> Was my dream so foolish after all? Was it not just a little rapid journey into the Christmas of tomorrow, and the life of tomorrow? So it seemed to me, and I went to bed to sleep on the thought that to the realization of my dream world, I give myself so far as in me lies. That is my Christmas gift to my children, my children's children and yours.[75]

Davis dreamed of a socialist world utopia where the workers owned the means of production, there was no "capitalist class," and communities worked together for the common good, building their great municipal government buildings together as the cathedrals were built in the Middle Ages. This was his ideal, his gift to his children and his children's children, his heaven on earth.

"His children's children"; although he never knew of my existence, he referred to me here—along with his sixteen other grandchildren.[76] The world that his grandchildren now inhabit is a far cry from the ideal he expressed in his "Dream." Still his thinking, his aspirations for an abundant life for all—including things, ideas, and ideals—his heaven on earth, remain a gift to his grandchildren and to all of us.

9. The Individual and the Collective

Park, writing in 1956, at a time when there was significantly more belief in the possibility of shared commitments and collective action, was clear about the deep strain of individualism that runs through American culture:

> Remember that our Founding Fathers were hungry for individual opportunity. . . . They got off on the wrong foot, with a robust gigantic idea of the value of individual opportunity, and a frail anemic idea of the value of individual responsibility, to

74. Davis, "Dream of a Christmas Shopper" (1916c), 7.

75. Davis, "Dream of a Christmas Shopper" (1916c), 7.

76. Earl and Annie Davis's four children—John, Foster, Byron, and Mary—produced seventeen grandchildren, of whom ten are still alive, mid-2025, and now there are great-grandchildren, great-great grandchildren, and even two great-great-great grandchildren.

> the state and to the rights of others. And it is just that distorted perception of values that we have not relinquished.[77]

Davis too valued individuality. And he was also clear about individual responsibility, and the importance of joining together in collective action.

Davis and Park had different ideas about how to reconcile individualism with collective responsibility and action. Davis thought individuality and individual responsibility could brought into alignment through shared socialist democratic action. Park focused on less radical actions, on various forms of public and private community development.

Whatever the solution, here is the core problem: the vigorously contested space of individualism versus collective action. For most of the last half-century we have been fed a robust diet of Ronald Reagan's "government is not the solution to our problem, government is the problem."[78] There well may have been government overreach and certainly there have been—and are—government inefficiencies and corruption. Still, this stance—that government is the problem—has eroded our ability to conceptualize, let alone execute, effective collective action towards realizing shared social goals, common goods. Jesus' second commandment remains as elusive as ever.

This attitude is part of the picture Robert Putnam provides in his "I—We—I" story.[79] As discussed in chapter 3, Putnam details the change from a focus on collective action, which reached a peak in the 1960s, to a focus on individual freedom—now approximately where it was when Davis was writing in the 1910s. Putnam argues for a return to "We" from our current "I:" *The Upswing: How America Came Together a Century Ago and How We Can Do It Again*. Whether Davis's democratic socialism is the best solution for our current situation I do not know. But I do know that Davis spoke to the same problem we struggle with today: a need for finding a space for shared ideas and ideals, and for shared collective action.

We will find this space when we allow a spirit of our shared humanity to enter our souls. A spirit that "transforms the essential purpose of life and creates a condition of life." Here is the path to heaven on earth.

77. Park, *Way of Jesus*, 44–45.

78. Reagan, "Inaugural Address 1981," para 9.

79. Putnam, *Upswing*.

Chapter 8: **Immortality Here and Now**

> We are not playing a game but living the life of an immortal being, through whose soul shoots the shaft of life of a living god. That is the big thought, the big transcendent faith that through the ages man has gleaned by the travail of his soul in the midst of the mystery of life. Whatever language he uses, whatever symbol he speaks with, that is the song that he sings this day, the triumphant song of an unconquerable faith in the imperishable worth of his own soul.[1]

1. Another World?

DAVIS FOCUSED ON LIVING, on the amazing and wonderful—sometimes deeply painful, sometimes joyful, always pregnant with wonder—fact of being alive, alive to the rich beauty of the natural world, alive to the opportunities afforded us to have what he called an abundant life. He was not blind to the manifest suffering in the world. But, as he saw it, this suffering showed that there is work to be done, that reality did not measure up to our ideals. Doing this work, consecrating our thought, time, effort, and action to improving the world, to bringing reality closer to our ideals, was part of the joy of living. As Davis saw history, the heroes that we remember are all people who have advanced the ideals

1. Davis, "Church as a Fellowship" (1917a), 5.

of truth, beauty, and justice in the world of the living.[2] It was heaven *on earth* that interested Davis.

Davis opened 1911 with a New Year's Day sermon, "The Demands of the New Year."[3] He started with a kind of potted history of heaven. The history was structured around the problem posed by the distance between reality—actual lived experience—and "ideality"—how we think things should be: the problem that reality falls far short of ideality.

According to Davis, the "primitive Christians," in the first years after the crucifixion, looked

> for the coming of the Lord down out of heaven in a supernatural manner. The kingdom of God should come on earth as it was in heaven. They took no thought for the morrow, they discouraged marriage, they cast aside their property, they considered not the questions of slavery, or poverty, but only this, that they should prepare as many as possible for the second coming of the Messiah. This second coming they believed would take place immediately, within the generation of those living. . . . They could look into the heavens, and almost see the full, completed kingdom coming to them out of the deep blue.[4]

It didn't happen.

How, then, to reconcile the fact that their living reality fell far short of their ideals? As Davis told the story, the institutional emergence of the Christian Church created a kind of structured transition between lived reality and ideality—heaven in "another world":

> The monk and the nun gave themselves up wholly to the religious life. They broke all the ties of human allurements and lived the life of the spirit apart from the world. The priest came inbetween, having partly severed himself from the worldly and partly allied himself with the heavenly. He lived in the world but not of it. He consoled those who lived in it and pointed them to the other world. Next comes the laity living in the world and of it but hoping that through the aid of the priest and the influence of the monk, not to become entirely emmeshed in its entanglements.[5]

Davis thought that this approach was "the answer of despair."

2. Davis, "Essence of Manhood" (1911b).
3. Davis, "Demands of the New Year" (1911a).
4. Davis, "Demands of the New Year" (1911a), 1–2.
5. Davis, "Demands of the New Year" (1911a), 2–3.

The subsequent Protestant alternative was equally—if not more so—an answer of despair:

> The kingdom of heaven could not come down to earth, as primitive Christianity believed, nor could the earth, even by the devise of the monastic, attain to the ideal. To the protestant this reality was a vale of tears, but by the grace of God we might go to the ideal in another world. Having survived this life for a period, and endured its hardships, death might bring us to the perfect and the holy in a life beyond death. . . . Heaven cannot be here, nor can it come down to us, but we will go to it after we have passed through this vale of tears. But the protestant view of life was so gloomy that he did not expect that the achievement of heaven for all, but only for a few. Each one thought that by the grace of God, he himself and a few others would get in. The rest would enjoy eternal reality.[6]

Eternal reality—hell—was the view that the "real world"—the here and now—would forever be foreclosed from the ideals of truth, beauty, and justice. For the strict Calvinist only the elect few—whose election was preordained by God—would gain entry into this other world in a life after death. A different kind of despair.

As Davis told the story, both Catholic and Protestant focused on the afterlife where one might—if one was particularly virtuous and/or fortunate—experience heaven. Davis did not buy this picture because it gave up on living. Focusing on heaven in another world foreclosed on efforts to create heaven on earth. In this sense, it represented a deeply pessimistic view of the world. The world of the living is just a vale of tears.

By contrast with all these approaches, Davis's approach to religion, what I call his "natural religion," focused on creating heaven on earth, heaven in the here and now, heaven for the living:

> We do not ask that the kingdom of righteousness shall come down out of heaven, but that it shall and will grow and develop in our very midst. The very forces that make reality also make ideality. The ideality of today becomes the reality of tomorrow. God is present in the world working through reality to the achievement and conservation of those life values that are worthwhile. . . . We do not ask to be transported to another world in which the whole thing shall be perfect, and our only task shall be to sit about the throne and sing in the heavenly choir and live a life

6. Davis, "Demands of the New Year" (1911a), 3.

> of idle purity. The answer which our time is giving to that old question [the distance between reality and ideality] is that we shall share in the work, in the zeal, in the tempered enthusiasm, in the glorious life of achieving for and with humanity the ideal which is the child of reality, and the fulfillment thereof.[7]

Instead of a vale of tears, as Davis understood things, the modern world was a world of promise. By our efforts we can make genuine progress towards a better world of—and by, and for—the living. It would take effort—every person had to bear their burden. But Davis's modern picture of the world was fundamentally optimistic in outlook.

Looking to the past we can see that things have gotten better; looking to the future we can have faith that they will get better still—if we put in the necessary work.

Davis's picture had the virtue of giving hope for the living and providing avenues for concrete action to improve the world. Don't simply endure life to—possibly—achieve something good in an afterlife. Recognize the beauty and possibilities of lived experience. Build on this. Commit to a better future, while recognizing the elements of truth, beauty, and goodness that are present in current lived experience.

What then to think about death? There is remarkably little in Davis's writings that speaks to this question. Shortly I will discuss a sermon he gave in the early 1920s, "Will a Belief in Immortality Survive?"[8] But the very framing of this sermon is instructive. He didn't ask what the afterlife is, or what we should or should not do to prepare for it. He asked whether belief in immortality will survive. Survive what? Survive modernity with its focus on "materialistic naturalism," or a "reduction" of the world to "the level of natural causes alone," with no room for any kind of a spiritual understanding of humankind—or of the natural world more broadly.[9]

Davis's commitment to discovery—not revelation—came with a commitment to evidence and experience, and modernity. We must seek and find truth through our efforts; it is not supernaturally revealed to us. And what evidence do we have about a possible afterlife or immortality, about another world? Precious little, if any. And so, with his modern focus on discovery, Davis had little to say about death, the afterlife, or any kind of immortality.

7. Davis, "Demands of the New Year" (1911a), 4.
8. Davis, "Belief in Immortality" (192X).
9. Davis, "Finality of Christianity" (1906d), 4. See also ch. 5.

He offered hints that I will follow up on shortly. First, however, I will leave Davis's writing, to discuss a more recent interaction of my own with thoughts about immortality. This will help put into perspective what Davis did say about life after death.

2. Nanotechnology Immortality

During much of the first decade of the twenty-first century I was involved in research on the philosophical and social implications of a hot new field, nanoscience, and nanotechnology. The prefix, "nano," refers to a unit of measurement, a nanometer, one billionth of a meter. This is very small, for most people, unimaginably small. A human hair is approximately 90,000 nanometers wide. A red blood cell is about 10,000 nanometers. A typical virus is about 100 nanometers. Things that are "nano-sized," perhaps 1–100 nanometers, are atomic-molecular. Nanotechnology refers to our abilities to manipulate reliably, accurately, and precisely nano-sized objects—basically move individual atoms and molecules around, precisely, reliably—and in doing so achieve desirable ends. A variety of advances in scientific instrumentation that occurred in the last decades of the twentieth century opened the world of nano-level manipulation.[10]

The advent of nanotechnology also opened the floodgates to various kinds of "nano hype." Nanotechnology would solve all the pressing problems of the world: cancer, environmental degradation, climate change, energy production, storage, and distribution, you name it. Undoubtably much good has come, and will come, from this work. But the nano hype world that I found doing this research was breathtaking. A science fiction world—and better than the Jetsons'.[11] Within a generation a nano-heaven was about to emerge from our laboratories. For me, as a somewhat skeptical philosopher, the uncritical embrace of this utopian "nano-future" was more than a little disorienting, disturbing.

I realized something genuinely weird was going on when, in 2002, during a coffee break at a nano-focused conference, a perfectly serious and seemingly sane fellow conferee came up to me and commented, "It is really sad and distressing to know that ours will be the last generation

10. See, for example, my 2004 paper, written with Ashley Shew, "Probing the History"

11. *The Jetsons* was an animated futurist sitcom that ran from September 1962 until March 1963, and later reruns were broadcast through syndication. New episodes were produced between 1985 and 1987. See "Jetsons."

to die." Nanotechnology would "cure mortality." I was astonished, and on multiple levels. Could we really "conquer death" through various nanotechnological efforts? Would it even be a good thing? Mortality is such a central fact of human existence. All our individual, social, cultural lives carry forward with the fact of our mortality in the background—if not the foreground. "Death and taxes" as the saying goes.

On April 9, 2003, in oral testimony given to the US House of Representatives Committee on Science, noted entrepreneur and futurist Ray Kurzweil shared the following with the committee:

> Nanotechnology and related advanced technologies of the 2020s will bring us the opportunity to overcome age-old problems, including pollution, poverty, disease, and aging."[12]

According to Kurzweil, speaking in 2003, by the 2020s—now!—we will "overcome aging."

Shortly after this, Kurzweil co-authored a book, *Fantastic Voyage: Live Long Enough to Live Forever.*[13] He did not intend the title to be hyperbole. Kurzweil and his coauthor, Terry Grossman, acknowledge that we do not *now*—that is in 2004—have "all the techniques we need to indefinitely extend human life," but we are acquiring these techniques, and we are doing so quickly enough that, with some attention to staying healthy, "immortality is within our grasp." They write,

> Our paradigm-shift-rate—the rate of technical progress—is doubling every decade. . . . So . . . the knowledge exists, if aggressively applied, for you to slow aging and disease processes to such a degree that you can be in good health and good spirits when the more radical life-extending and life-enhancing technologies become available.[14]

Science and technology are progressing so fast that—some—people alive today (that is, in 2004) would have a shot at immortality by availing themselves of technologies that are sure to emerge soon.

Kurzweil and Grossman saw three bridges to immortality. The first bridge was to live healthy, so that one would be alive when new biotechnology cures for the standard killer diseases—cancer, heart disease, others—became available. Living healthy certainly includes diet and

12. *Societal Implications*, 3.
13. Kurzweil and Grossman, *Fantastic Voyage.*
14. Kurzweil and Grossman, *Fantastic Voyage*, 3.

exercise, but they took this to a significantly more intensive level. Much of *Fantastic Voyage* is about the detailed regiment of diet, vitamins, and exercise that they argued could keep one alive until we have cures for killer diseases.

The second bridge will be provided by biotech cures for these killer diseases. These cures will allow us to live even longer, long enough to arrive . . .

At the third bridge: genuine nanotechnology-artificial intelligence inspired immortality. This might come from some kind of radical transplantation—replacing aging bodies or parts of bodies with better longer-lasting bodies or parts—or from some kind of ongoing body upkeep by tiny "nanobots" added to our bloodstream.[15]

For Kurzweil, born in 1948, this seemed a possible—and desirable—recipe for action. By taking good care of his body, he would be in his eighties or perhaps nineties when he believed he would be able to avail himself of "more radical life-extending and life-enhancing technologies." He could live long enough to live forever. Of course, the recipe wouldn't work for older people, for people who succumb to killer diseases before cures arrive, to people who die from COVID, etc.

Kurzweil was not—and is not—alone. Several Silicon Valley moguls have pursued the science and technology of immortality. Google launched Calico in 2013 to "better understand the biology that controls aging and lifespan. . . . We want to use the knowledge we gain to discover and develop interventions that enable people to live longer and healthier lives."[16] According to the *Washington Post,* Jeff Bezos has invested in Altos Labs, whose "mission is to restore cell health and resilience through cellular rejuvenation programming to reverse disease, injury and the disabilities that can occur throughout life."[17] This same *Washington Post* article notes that "immortality—or anti-aging, as researchers soberly call it—is the next big thing. Estimates put the industry's worth at a staggering $610 billion by 2025."[18]

These efforts are ongoing and are yielding remarkable progress in our understanding of human biology—the biology of life more

15. Recent developments in artificial intelligence—e.g., ChatGPT—which Kurzweil both predicted and played a role in bringing about, have only deepened his confidence that we are on the verge of conquering death. See Kurzweil, *Singularity Is Nearer*.

16. https://www.calicolabs.com/.

17. https://www.altoslabs.com/.

18. Zenou, "Long and Gruesome."

generally—and, in particular, in our understanding of aging. Venki Ramakrishnan's recent book, *Why We Die: The New Science of Aging and the Quest for Immortality,*[19] is a good, readable, and thoughtful statement of the 2024-current state of the art.

At the radical end of the "transhumanist movement"[20] the idea of finding a better more durable "substrate" for our human selves, has been pursued, perhaps by "uploading" our brains into some kind of silicon-based computer "cloud." The Borg on the horizon.

3. Immortality: Four Ways

In his 2012 book *Immortality,* Stephen Cave argues that the human drive for immortality "is embedded in our very nature, and its result is what we know as civilization."[21] Cave considers four fundamental ways—four "immortality narratives"—through which humans have tried to achieve immortality:

1. Simply staying alive.
2. Returning to life after death through resurrection—where we physically regain bodily life after death.
3. Surviving after death as a spiritual entity.
4. Living on through our legacy—including our children, the people we influence, the works we leave behind, etc.

The bulk of Cave's book examines each of these approaches to immortality, showing how each has fundamentally directed human behavior through history. And yet, in Cave's view, each approach has failed to deliver immortality. Nanotechnological immortality is just the most recent attempt at immortality, also doomed to fail.

Cave opens the book discussing what he calls the "mortality paradox." The paradox lies in the fact that we know that, like all living beings we observe, we too are living beings with finite lives; we will die. And yet, we cannot conceive of our own individual death.

19. Ramakrishnan, *Why We Die*. For an update on the work of Calico Life Sciences and Altos Labs, see *Why We Die*, 115.

20. See "Transhumanism."

21. Cave, *Immortality*, 2.

> Death therefore presents itself as both inevitable and impossible. This I will call the *Mortality Paradox*, and its resolution is what gives shape to the immortality narratives, and therefore to civilization.[22]

On a first examination the paradox has some currency. We are most certainly aware of the fact that all living beings we know of—including humans—have finite lifespans. Mortality is a central fact of human existence. At the same time, it is very difficult—if not impossible—to conceptualize one's non-existence. This is because in the act of trying to conceptualize one's non-existence, one must employ one's point of view, a point of view that requires that one exists.

While Cave concludes that none of the four "immortality strategies" works, that we are stuck with our mortality, he also argues that this not a bad thing. Our

> mortality imparts to our existence an urgency and allows us to give it shape and meaning—we have a reason to get up in the morning and engage with the world while we can; we have reason to make this the best of all worlds, because we know there is no other.[23]

This resonates with Davis's focus on living. If one thinks of the afterlife as the site for heaven, one has less motivation to make the world of the living the best world it can be.

Cave resolves the mortality paradox by arguing that it is indeed true, we cannot conceptualize our non-existence. He draws on an argument from the Stoics. In 300 BCE Epicurus wrote,

> While we are, death is not; when death is come, we are not. Death is thus of no concern either to the living or to the dead. For it is not with the living, and the dead do not exist.[24]

Cave also quotes twentieth-century philosopher Ludwig Wittgenstein making a similar point in his book, the *Tractatus:* "Death is not an event of life. Death is not lived through."[25]

22. Cave, *Immortality*, 16.

23. Cave, *Immortality*, 286.

24. Epicurus (341 BCE–270 BCE) is quoted in Cave, *Immortality*, 274.

25. Ludwig Wittgenstein (1889–1951) is perhaps the greatest twentieth-century philosopher. This quotation is from his 1922 book, *Tractatus Logico Philosophicus*, passage 6.4311. This passage is quoted in Cave, *Immortality*, 275.

After discussing the four "immortality narratives," Cave considers a fifth narrative, "the wisdom narrative," which, Cave argues, presents positive way to acknowledge and live with our mortality. He identifies three elements to the wisdom narrative, elements that help put the thought of—the fear of—non-existence at bay, while also making living a finite life worthwhile: (1) cultivating selflessness, (2) learning to live in the present, and (3) gratitude. He writes,

> So: awareness of self might be important, but excessive concern with the self only exacerbates the fear of death, or loss of self, and leads one to a life of self-absorption. In order to combat this, we should cultivate selflessness, or identifying with others. Similarly, picturing the future helps us to plan a successful life, but excessive concern with the future causes us to focus on the tribulations that lie ahead of us—and forget to live now. Therefore we should learn to live more in the present moment. And third, imagining all the things that could threaten our existence might help us avoid them, but in excess it leads us only to worry about what we might lose rather than appreciate what we have. Therefore we should cultivate gratitude.[26]

Echoing some of the language in Davis's writing, Cave notes about gratitude in particular that

> an unbroken chain of many millions of ancestors over billions of years all managed to do their bit to bring us into existence, that is our blessing. And it is an extraordinary one, involving more strokes of luck and cosmic coincidences than are possibly countable. . . .
>
> Complex life—and in particular—the life of any individual—is remarkable. Astonishing. Wondrous.[27]

Davis would agree. The life of any individual is remarkable, astonishing, wondrous.

4. Davis and Cave

Davis would also have been moved by some of Cave's arguments. Cave suggests, for example, that "many commentators have recognized the correlation between a focus on an eternal afterlife and a willingness to

26. Cave, *Immortality*, 277.

27. Cave, *Immortality*, 281.

unquestioningly accept injustice and deprivation in the world."[28] This is exactly Davis's conclusion about the pessimistic outlook that the Catholic and Protestant dependencies on the afterlife produce.

Cave also argues that

> most immortality narratives foster a profound selfishness. Such doctrines teach you to obsess about the infinite survival of your own individual personality; all actions are then measured by whether they make your personal survival more or less likely or the expected eternity more or less pleasurable. Outwardly admirable actions—such as giving to the poor—are performed for the sake of your soul. Even where this contributes to a more stable society, it does nothing to cultivate real virtues such as empathy or compassion for others but focuses all attention purely on the implications of an action for you.[29]

Here again, Davis would agree. What was most important for Davis was to live a life consecrated to improving the living world for others and for future generations—not to live a life consecrated to one's own survival post death.

Cave ultimately argues that there are two problems with immortality:

> On the one hand, the boredom and apathy that would result from having done and seen everything there is to do—that is, from having already lived a very long time—and on the other hand, the paralysis that would result from having an infinite future in which to do any further things. Both these problems, the backward looking and the forward looking, threaten to suck the meaning out of life and leave one wishing for a terminal deadline.[30]

An infinite life is not a life that prompts action, a life with urgency to take steps to do something worthwhile. On Cave's view, immortality does not prompt action in the world, and this Davis would find unacceptable. He might be very excited to learn the truth that scientific and technological research on aging provides. But he would be concerned if the consequence was to undermine our motivation for action.

28. Cave, *Immortality*, 261.

29. Cave, *Immortality*, 261.

30. Cave, *Immortality*, 263.

5. *Will a Belief in Immortality Survive?*

Now to Davis's sermon, "Will a Belief in Immortality Survive?" We can definitively answer the question posed in his title: Yes. A belief in immortality survives. Although perhaps it has not survived as Davis might have imagined. Among other things, it survives as a kind of holy grail of scientific and technological futurism.

I can imagine Davis would have conflicted feelings here. On the one hand, he would be excited by the advances in science and technology. We know more of the truth of the world, enough more to perhaps give us an idea about controlling our aging, perhaps even our mortality. But I don't know that he would be overly excited about the prospect of controlling our mortality—although I cannot be sure. I may be projecting my own concerns about "controlling our mortality" onto my grandfather.

So, Davis was confident that a belief in immortality would survive. What about his view about immortality itself? He was very clear at the outset of the sermon: "I do believe in personal immortality."[31] He provided a short argument to support his belief:

> The first point to be noted is this: that we live in a world that is orderly and understandable. Our minds seem capable of discovery and, in a measure, interprets its laws. On the basis of this belief in an intelligible world, inhabited by intelligible people, all of our educational and scientific attainments are based. This is the first step.[32]

Davis's next step concerned the existence of human purpose—human aspiration for a better world—in the evolving universe:

> The next step is that out of our knowledge and experience there is continually emerging the idea of a great and unifying purpose at the heart of all things. Into this stream of purpose human beings have come. They, by their efforts and fidelity, ideals, and devotions, have contributed to its significance and meaning.[33]

The philosopher in me notes a slippage in the argument here. As I have understood Davis's view, humans, with their ideals and aspirations, *bring purpose to* the world. Here, Davis argues that the world *comes with* a "stream of purpose," into which humans engage.

31. Davis, "Belief in Immortality" (192X), 1.
32. Davis, "Belief in Immortality" (192X), 1.
33. Davis, "Belief in Immortality" (192X), 1.

The third step to his argument concerned the importance of human personality:

> Now I believe that human personalities, conscious, thinking persons, are the highest expressions of the nature and character of the universe.[34]

With these three premises, he drew his conclusion:

> Believing therefore as I do, that the universe deals honestly with us and that human personality is an expression of its highest qualities, I am forced to a belief in immortality as the essential rounding out of a process in the midst of which we find ourselves. Otherwise, the whole process of human history becomes, when it has terminated, a meaningless episode in an intelligible world. This I take to be the foundation upon which all forms of belief in immortality exist.[35]

Immortality is real because of the importance of human personality—an expression of the highest qualities of the universe.

It is not my place here to refute this argument, although I do not find it persuasive. Where does "purpose" come from? I accept the idea that humans bring purpose to the universe. This seems a manifest truth based on our experience. We have aspirations, hopes, ideals, and these elements of our personalities add purpose to the development of the world. One could then argue that we were created with these purposes. That is, that purpose was built into the development of the world through it being built into the constitution of humans. But this—to me—suggests an external supernatural agent building purpose into humans. Instead, it seems more in keeping with Davis's naturalistic approach simply to observe that purpose evolved out of the processes of natural selection. Purpose—in humans and other life forms—is a natural product of evolution. It was not built into the world.

One could argue that the fact that purpose emerged through natural selection is a kind of argument for the conclusion that it was—naturally—built into the world. To my taste, however, I find this kind of argument and counterargument speculative, not conclusive. I don't conclude that Davis is wrong in his belief in immortality, only that, for me, his argument doesn't close the deal.

34. Davis, "Belief in Immortality" (192X), 1.

35. Davis, "Belief in Immortality" (192X), 1–2.

There are two further notable aspects to this sermon. First is Davis's surprising turn towards rationalism—finding truth based on the content of one's ideas—as opposed to empiricism—finding truth based on one's experience and empirical evidence. Descartes, in developing his rationalist approach (see chapter 2), would speak of "clear and distinct ideas" as the basis for certainty in thought. Davis concluded the first part of his sermon as follows:

> Therefore, my own personal belief is quite *distinct and clear* that the accumulated logic of life makes a belief in immortality the most natural and justifiable faith by which we live.[36]

The first part of this sermon is uncharacteristically "rationalist" in structure—and in the rationalist language of his conclusion: his belief is "distinct and clear," well-aligned with Descartes "clear and distinct ideas." For me, one of the most refreshing surprises that I discovered reading Davis's work was his consistent—or nearly consistent—focus on evidence and discovery. He did not argue his way to God. He found experience that spoke to him of God. Here, by contrast, it seems to me that he was arguing his way to immortality.

And this leads directly to the second curious feature of the sermon. The sermon could well have concluded with his distinct and clear conclusion in immortality. But the sermon continued,

> There is another phase of this question to which our attention has been called increasingly during the past 75 years, viz; the possible significance of psychic phenomena. In this field we have accumulated a vast amount of information and facts.[37]

Here we might have some possible empirical, experiential evidence for immortality. And Davis was correct; during the last decades of the nineteenth century and the first decades of the twentieth century there was substantial scientific interest in psychic phenomena and the possibility of communication with the dead. William James (see chapter 2) had a keen interest in research on psychic phenomena, phenomena that include—purportedly—communication between the living and the dead.

One of the more unusual documents that I found in the trunk of Davis's writings described his own experience, a "Record of Experience of a Psychic Phenomenon":

36. Davis, "Belief in Immortality" (192X), 2 (emphasis added).

37. Davis, "Belief in Immortality" (192X), 2.

> The following is a true report of an experience that I had last night while making a call at the home of Mr. James T. Rhodes, 241 East Street in this city.
>
> . . .
>
> I knew that Mr. Rhodes was an "impersonating medium," and in a conversation at my study he described some of his experiences. I also know that Mrs. Henckler was a Medium. She has never made use of her powers except in private circumstances and among friends.
>
> . . .
>
> Mr. Rhodes, having a defective sense of hearing, was sitting in the chair at my left, while the rest of us were talking. Suddenly he began to feel a sensation in his right hand, and his hand came under the power of some influence. It gave Mr. Rhodes the sense of great physical strength. Took him out of his chair, and twisted his arms and caused him to shake his fist at me, then he pounded the arm of the chair in which I was sitting. After that the control left.[38]

The "Record" continued relating in some detail all that went on during the evening, including further instances of "the control" taking over Mr. Rhodes's actions. Davis did not mention this experience in his sermon on immortality. But he did suggest that research into psychic phenomena could well provide "some of the most illuminating discoveries of mankind."[39]

Davis's sermon on immortality provided both a rationalist argument for immortality and a recognition of the empirical evidence that psychical research seemed to provide in support of the same conclusion. He couched his conclusion in the language of faith, not discovered or experienced fact: "The accumulated logic of life makes a belief in immortality the most natural and justifiable *faith* by which we live."[40] He did not take the conclusion of his "rationalist" argument for immortality as conclusive, but rather as significant enough to support a faith in immortality.

38. Davis, "Record of a Psychic Experience" (1908h), 1–2.
39. Davis, "Belief in Immortality" (192X), 3.
40. Davis, "Belief in Immortality" (192X), 2 (emphasis added).

6. What Davis Didn't Say About Immortality

Davis believed in immortality, both because he had an argument for immortality and because of the scientific evidence of psychic phenomena. This would appear to be a significant conclusion, a major element of his thinking and approach to religious matters. It is noteworthy, then, that, of the materials he left, this is nearly the only sermon that addressed immortality. Shortly, I will discuss a second sermon where immortality played a significant role, but these excursions into immortality were rare in Davis's writing.

There is much that Davis did not say about immortality. He did not discuss the nature of "the afterlife." He did not discuss questions of how one might gain entry into an afterlife or heaven. He did not discuss how one's personality might be experienced in an afterlife.

Davis did not discuss the resurrection of Jesus Christ. That, as we have already seen in chapter 5, was a critical issue for Davis. In keeping with Unitarian views common at the time, Davis argued that Jesus was a human, as all humans are human. Jesus was not special in that he was resurrected bodily. The final chapter of his *Lectures on the Origin and History of the Bible* was specifically about Jesus' resurrection—and why biblical accounts of it should not be trusted as historically accurate. He began that lecture with "Three General Remarks":

> First. It is frequently said that the truth or falsity of the doctrine of immortality is involved in this question of the resurrection of Jesus. There is no connection between the two. The idea of immortality is a faith in the value of human life. The question of the resurrection of Jesus is one of historical criticism based on evidence. If it can be demonstrated that Jesus was raised from the dead, that proves nothing about immortality, it simply proves that Jesus was raised from the dead. . . . If it proved that the stories are not true, what effect has it? It simply means that they are not true stories.[41]

The question of immortality for Davis concerned "the value of human life," or that "human personalities, conscious, thinking persons, are the highest expressions of the nature and character of the universe."[42] The

41. Davis, *Origins and History* (1916a) "Lecture XIV: The New Testament Story of the Resurrection."

42. Davis, "Belief in Immortality" (192X), 1.

question of immortality transcends the specific question of the accuracy of the stories about Jesus' resurrection.

Davis's sole contribution in his sermon "Will a Belief in Immortality Survive?" was to argue for immortality of individual personality. This conclusion expressed Davis's faith in the value of human life, human personality. But he did not consider what immortal life after death might be like. Considering how important immortality has been in religion, it is striking that Davis left the matter at this bare conclusion: Immortality of individual human personalities is real.

Making sense of these omissions brings me back to Davis's ultimate commitment to evidence and experience, and the fact that we, the living, arguably, have no experience of the afterlife. Davis's interest in psychic phenomena came from a need to fill this gap. In the years following Davis's sermon on immortality, written in the 1920s, psychical research lost its "scientific luster" or standing. The current consensus of the scientific community is dismissive of the reality of psychic phenomena. The Society for Psychical Research (SPR)—still active in 2024—describes itself as follows: "Founded in 1882, the SPR was the first organization to conduct scholarly research into human experiences *that challenge contemporary scientific models.*"[43] That is to say, "contemporary scientific models" do not support communication between the living and the dead, among other kinds of psychic phenomena.

This is how Davis closed his sermon:

> In conclusion, my own conviction is that the belief in immortality is grounded in the nature of things; that subject to all sorts of modifications and variations, it will continue into the future as it has in the past, to be perhaps the most potent belief cherished by the human race.[44]

Davis's conclusion returned to the framing of the sermon. *Belief* in immortality will survive. Davis couched his conclusion that individual human personalities are immortal in the language of faith. It is not something we know to be true because of our experience. To say more about the afterlife, about the resurrection, about a supernatural God and heaven—not heaven on earth—would have violated Davis's commitment to discovery, to experience.

43. https://www.spr.ac.uk/ (emphasis added).

44. Davis, "Belief in Immortality" (192X), 3.

7. Experience of an Afterlife

Experience of, or from, the afterlife would be world changing. The afterlife would not be a matter of faith, but of experienced evidential fact. The closest we come to this is with what are called "near-death experiences." There have been reports from some people who, for various reasons, come to the very edge of death—in some cases have been ruled brain-dead—and yet who return to life, and can report on their experiences while dead, or almost dead.

Consider one such narrative by Eben Alexander, an academic neurosurgeon who experienced his own near-death and wrote about it in *Proof of Heaven: A Neurosurgeon's Journey into the Afterlife.* Prior to his experience Alexander was a modern materialist about personality and consciousness. He writes,

> When your brain is absent, you are absent, too. As a neurosurgeon, I'd heard of many stories over the years of people who had strange experiences, usually after suffering cardiac arrest: stories of traveling to mysterious, wonderful landscapes; of talking to dead relatives—even of meeting God himself.
>
> Wonderful stuff, no question. But all of it, in my opinion, was pure fantasy. What caused the otherworldly types of experiences that such people so often report? I didn't claim to know, but I did know that they were brain-based. All of consciousness is. If you don't have a working brain, you can't be conscious.
>
> This is because the brain is the machine that produces consciousness in the first place. When the machine breaks down, consciousness stops . . . Pull the plug and the TV goes dead. The show is over, no matter how much you might have been enjoying it.[45]

Then Alexander had his own near-death experience.

Alexander was in a coma where it wasn't just that his brain was not working properly, "it wasn't working *at all*."[46] His book goes on to describe what he experienced while his brain "wasn't working at all."

Alexander provides an interesting, detailed narrative, compelling in many respects. For example, he touches on the shifting boundaries of self that he experienced:

45. Alexander, *Proof of Heaven*, 8–9.

46. Alexander, *Proof of Heaven*, 9 (emphasis in the original).

> Just as my awareness was both individual yet at the same time completely unified with the universe, so also did the boundaries of what I experienced as my "self" at times contract, and at other times expand to include all that exists throughout eternity. The blurring of the boundary between my awareness and the realm around me went so far at times that I became the entire universe. Another way of putting this would be to say that I momentarily saw an identity with the universe, which had been there all the time, but that I had just been blind to up till then.[47]

This is the bare tip of Alexander's extensive narrative. I have no doubt that having such an experience would radically shift one's thinking about immortality. Particularly for Alexander, because, as a neurosurgeon with scientifically supported views about what should have been or could have been possible in the medical condition he was in, this experience would be mind altering.

Most of us have not had such experiences, and the replicable scientific evidence for such is lacking. I do not dismiss Alexander's story, but neither can I endorse his conclusion. These were his experiences, not mine. And they are not scientifically replicable.

8. Easter, 1917

There is one other sermon where Davis directly discussed immortality. It was the Easter sermon he gave on April 8, 1917, two days after the United States entered "the Great War." What he said there is revealing, if enigmatic.

His interest in immortality was not tied to life after death, but rather to the here and now. The "purpose" of our immortal personalities was not to somehow ensure some kind of continued existence after death, rather it was

> to let the elements of immortality display themselves in the life that now is, in the integrity, and the quality of life that we live, its unconquerable buoyancy, its illimitable faith, its transcendent hope. This is where the elements of immortality must show themselves, here on this earth, in the lives that you and I live, here in Pittsfield, in this fellowship, in this year, not by

47. Alexander, *Proof of Heaven*, 160.

> and by but now, in our personal life, in our political, social, business relations.[48]

At first encounter this does not make sense. What does it mean for "the elements of immortality" to "display themselves in the life that is now?" Immortality—I would have thought—is about continued existence, existence beyond death, certainly beyond the here and now. It is not about what we do while living before death. Is it?

A little later Davis clarified what "living the life of an immortal being" meant for him:

> We are not playing a game but living the life of an immortal being, through whose soul shoots the shaft of life of a living god. That is the big thought, the big transcendent faith that through the ages man has gleaned by the travail of his soul in the midst of the mystery of life. Whatever language he uses, whatever symbol he speaks with, that is the song that he sings this day, the triumphant song of an unconquerable faith in the imperishable worth of his own soul.[49]

The big thought, the big transcendent faith is that our personalities—our souls—each of our individual souls—have "imperishable worth." They are the sites through which the living God acts in the world.

For Davis, the living God was not external to us. The living God existed in and through us, each of us individually. Our personalities—our characters, our virtues, our vices, our readiness to act or to hold back, our intelligence, ruminative or impulsive, but most important our hopes, aspirations, and ideals—this is what drives change in the world. This was the living God acting. This was the "worth of our souls," our immortality.

Immortality, as Davis understood it—or better, as best as I can understand how Davis understood it—lies in the ongoing human, all too human, effort to improve the world, the living world, the forever changing, never finished, always emerging, living world. These efforts reveal the living God acting in and through us—the immortal living God acting in and through us, each of us individually, each of our individual personalities. As each of us individually participates in this effort we secure our immortality. We become part of the living God.

What matters, what is important, is the action that one takes in this world, here and now—in Pittsfield in April 1917 in response to

48. Davis, "Church as a Fellowship" (1917a), 5.

49. Davis, "Church as a Fellowship" (1917a), 5.

entry into the Great War, or wherever and whenever one finds oneself responding to the challenges of one's world. What matters, what is important, is not whatever may or may not happen after death. Immortality, for Davis, was not about another world. Immortality was about our identification as a site of the immortal living God, our identification with the ever ongoing processes of change, of progress—processes that have been in place before our individual birth and processes that will continue after our death. We are part of this.

Immortality, for Davis, most assuredly was not sitting "about the throne and singing in the heavenly choir and living a life of idle purity."[50] It was about being part of the evolving universe: "The elements of immortality display themselves in the life that now is, in the integrity, and the quality of life that we live, its unconquerable buoyancy, its illimitable faith, its transcendent hope."[51]

9. Immortality Here and Now

This way of thinking of immortality is entirely consistent with Davis's enduring natural focus, on the here and now, on living on earth, heaven on earth, as opposed to some hypothetical supernaturally revealed world of heaven beyond death. But is this immortality? In what sense does this approach show human personality transcending death?

Cave's four-part analysis of immortality—four immortality narratives—offers some help. On the one hand, this could be immortality as a kind of legacy, Cave's fourth immortality narrative. While alive we participate in the ongoing work of driving change. To the extent afforded by our personalities, we leave a mark—our mark on the world. Something about the universe is different—some small thing, different because we lived. And in living, and in aspiring, we were part of, we participated in, the living God. The living God acted in and through us, in and through our personalities. The world changed because of our mark, our legacy, in Cave's terms.

Some of us leave "marks," that promote bigger changes, sometimes for the better—Jesus—sometimes worse—Hitler. Although in the universal scheme of things, all these marks are small, nearly infinitesimal.

50. Davis, "Demands of the New Year" (1911a), 4.

51. Davis, "Church as a Fellowship" (1917a), 5.

Most of us do not leave "big marks," we don't become part of recorded history. But we do leave a mark. One cannot live without leaving a mark. And, in this way, recorded or not, remembered or not, we participate in the ongoing work of change, we are part of the living God. We are immortal, but perhaps not immortal in the sense that we can anticipate personal experience beyond our deaths. We are immortal because of our legacy.

On the other hand, perhaps something stronger is suggested here. Davis could have been thinking of immortality as a kind of spiritual being, Cave's third immortality narrative. Perhaps Alexander's language from his near-death experience helps:

> The blurring of the boundary between my awareness and the realm around me went so far at times that I became the entire universe.[52]

This merging with the entire universe, but in a way that allowed Alexander's point of view, his personality, to recognize the merger, this could be one way of spelling out what Davis might mean by our identification with the living God.

In the final chapter of his book, *Why We Die*, Venki Ramakrishnan shared thoughts about death from a variety of points of view. One, that of linguist Ganesh Devy, is pertinent here:

> He said he himself did not fear death. I was skeptical, but he pointed out that on a field trip once he was bitten by a highly poisonous snake and he felt no fear or panic at the thought of dying. I asked him why. Devy said that we have to regard our individual selves as parts of larger entities like family, community, and society, just as all the cells in our body are part of tissues and organs and us. Millions of our cells die every day. Not only do we not mourn their passing, but we are not even aware of it. So even if we as individuals die, our society, and indeed life on Earth will go on. Our own genes will live on through our offspring or other family members. Life has been going on continuously for several billion years while we individuals come and go.[53]

Seeing ourselves as part of something bigger, something with a long past and a long future, this could be the immortality that Davis was seeking to describe.

52. Alexander, *Proof of Heaven*, 160.
53. Ramakrishnan, *Why We Die*, 236–37.

Whether "this immortality" is some kind of continued existence as a spiritual being—as a part of the living God—or is "only" our legacy, may be a matter that only death will reveal. But this picture of immortality does offer direction on how to live. It is in line with what Cave urges in his fifth "wisdom narrative," cultivating selflessness. It is the source of hope that Davis suggested to his congregation, as I shared in the first chapter:

> Age after age we have discovered some bit of insight into the nature of that life stream in which we move from age to age, but its steady flow, its unexhausted power still calls us, not from the past but from the age to come. However great the past may have been, in remote ages or in more immediate centuries, whatever of wisdom may have been gleaned from the experiences of the centuries, the startling truth faces us that we, the living and the generations to come after us, are the vital agents through which that life spirit, call it by whatever name you will, moves out of the past into the age to come. We should face it all not with fear and despair, but in faith and confidence, buoyant in spirit, strong in purpose, keen to contribute to the age to come whatsoever of the Life Spirit dwells within each one.[54]

This is immortality here and now.

54. Davis, "Not Revelation" (1947a), 5.

Chapter 9: **Natural Faith**

> The true theist is the person who has an ideal, who is working for the things that shall be, and has faith that the universe is with him. . . . I care not by what name he may call his ideal and his hope, but in that he has faith in its reality, and gives himself to its attainment, he has made, and has, a living god.[1]

1. Personality, the Living God, Progress

PERSONALITY LAY AT THE core of Davis's thought. We saw in chapter 5 that it was the personality of Jesus—not his beliefs, not his morality, not his alleged miracles, not his specific sayings, but his personality—that Davis, following Chicago theologian George Burman Foster, held to be the essence of Christianity. Personality is central not only because of the personality of Jesus, but because personality is primary for all humans. In our personalities lies the connective tissue of our thoughts, beliefs, hopes, desires, aspirations, ideals. Our personalities underwrite our capacity for action.

Davis found deity everywhere—in nature, with its awe-inspiring beauty and power, but also in human nature, in human personality. For Davis, it was through the power of human aspirations and ideals, found in human personality, that progress was made. Our personalities drive our choices, our free will, and through our free will, our capacity to lend direction to the world's unrelenting onrushing change (chapter 2). As

1. Davis, "Is Your God Dead?" (1909j), 5.

Davis saw it, it was through our "immortal personalities" (chapter 8) that the living God (chapter 6) acted in the world to make progress toward the creation of heaven on earth (chapter 7).

Davis found divinity—and depravity—in our personalities. We are mixtures of good and bad:

> The living God, the God that is Life, that is Human Life, that dwells in the individual men and women, with all their noble hopes, all their achievements, all their defeats and their limitations, all their mistakes, and selfish, cruel sins, the God that is all this and more, infinitely more, that is the totality of life, that God grips our souls.[2]

Noble hopes, achievements, but defeats and limitations, mistakes, and selfish cruel sins, "the living God is all this and more."

How, then, for Davis, could this mixture, this mash-up of good and evil, emerge as the living God in our individual personalities? It did so because humans can bend their wills toward good. That humans—some humans, some of the time—do bend their wills towards good was the core of Davis's faith, his faith in what he called the integrity of the universe and his faith in the progress he saw in the past and anticipated for the future (chapter 6).[3] This progress followed from our aspirations and ideals driving positive change in the world. Past progress was the observable, palpable evidence of the living God acting in and through our personalities. Future progress was Davis's faith.

It takes effort. Change always takes effort. It takes effort to resist our own temptations. In Davis's picture of things, "noble personalities" were noble because they faced and overcame challenge, including significantly, internal challenges, temptations, loss of faith, despair. We might say that the divinity Davis found in human personalities was where the better angels of our nature triumphed over our own doubts and temptations. Our "immortal personalities" revealed themselves "in the integrity, and the quality of life that we live, its unconquerable buoyancy, its illimitable faith, its transcendent hope."[4]

Personality was the ultimate good for Davis:

2. Davis, "Thirst for a *Living* God" (191Xa), 3.

3. In his September 19, 1909, sermon, "Two Great Principles of the Modern World," Davis argued for these two principles: (1) the integrity of the universe and, (2) progress, see Davis 1909b. See also ch. 6, section 8.

4. Davis, "Church as a Fellowship" (1917a), 5. See also ch. 8.

> Now I believe that human personalities, conscious, thinking persons, are the highest expressions of the nature and character of the universe.[5]

The ultimate goal of our efforts in the world should be to provide an abundant life for all human personalities. Other goals should be subservient to—instrumental to—the goal of supporting all human personalities.

Davis's most important belief about personality was his commitment to individual free will. It was through free will that humans could provide direction to change. It was because of free will that Davis's living God, living in each of our personalities, could drive positive, progressive, change in the world.

> The function of human personality, which gives to human life its most profound significance, is that of making reality. Whether we so wish it or not, the fact remains that the thoughts we think, and the conduct that expresses those thoughts goes to constitute the reality in the midst of which we live.[6]

Combine free will with our individual capacities for thought and action, with our individual hopes and aspirations, with our ideals, and put all of this in a messy complicated soup of millions—billions—of people and you have the living God in action, the God that is "Life, Life and evermore Life."[7]

2. Conscious Rational Personality

Davis's picture of personality emphasized our ability to learn from experience and to reason. We exercised our free will through our conscious reasoning. Davis was open to influence of unconscious. But it was our conscious powers of experiencing and thinking that mattered most to him. This he revealed in a side remark from a sermon he gave shortly after the United States entered the First World War:

> Last Friday morning I received a request to preach a patriotic sermon this morning. I propose to do so. But in so doing I must conform to a resolve, a habit, a conviction that is part of my very nature, I hope. I have never preached from this pulpit anything

5. Davis, "Belief in Immortality" (192X), 1. See also ch. 8.
6. Davis, "Making of Reality" (1909h), 1. See also ch. 6
7. Davis, "Thirst for a *Living* God" (191Xa), 3. See also ch. 6.

> that I was not willing to act upon myself. I have never uttered one word calculated to influence any one of you to believe in a doctrine, or to act contrary to your judgement. I have never tried to override your personality and stampede you into an emotional and mob action. I have stated my beliefs, my ideas, my motives of conduct as frankly, and as honestly as I could. I shall continue to do this unless perchance I too may be caught in the mob spirit and swept off my feet.[8]

He did not preach to "override your personality and stampede you into an emotional and mob action." His sermons aimed to appeal to the rational powers of his congregants. Although he recognized that there is the possibility that he too "may be caught in the mob spirit" and swept off his feet.

For Davis, experience, and one's conscious rational reflections on experience, fed into the complicated and deeply individual matrix of each person's personality—their hopes and fears, loves and hates, beliefs and passions, their ideals, and more—and then, through their free will, beliefs were formed, decisions made, actions taken, or not. Change was nudged forward.

3. Personality and Individual Versus Collective Ends

As I wrote in chapter 7, the whole point of Davis's heaven on earth was to provide a full abundant life for *all* individual personalities. The development of each person's personality was the ultimate goal, the final good.

It was the "rights of personality" that lay at the heart of Davis's argument for democratic socialism, over and against the "rights of wealth":

> It is an irrepressible conflict between the rights of personality and the rights of wealth. Shall the industrial system be the servant of human life contributing to its growth and development, and to the emancipation of personality? Or shall it remain the lord and master to whose command we must submit and upon whose altar we must place our sacrifices of degradation, poverty, debauchery, corruption, and even life itself? . . . Is society to remain plutocratic or shall it become democratic? Shall wealth remain monarchical, or shall it become socialized? That is the essence of the social question today.[9]

8. Davis, "Sermon on Patriotism" (1917b), 1.
9. Davis, "Churches and Socialism" (1910g), 7.

We still struggle with this conflict, personality versus the monarchy of money. If one is "modern," as Davis understood the term, one rejected authority and obedience of whatever sort, governmental or capitalistic, in favor of the primacy of personality.

And yet, chapter 7 exposed a challenge to Davis's focus on personality, the challenge of the relative emphasis on individual ends as opposed to collective ends. Davis's democratic socialism leaned toward collective ends, while Davis's good friend, Charles Edward Park,[10] reminded us that "our Founding Fathers were hungry for individual opportunity."[11]

We live this challenge every day—a robust notion and valuing of individual freedom and ends and a rather stunted notion and valuing of collective goals and ends. Indeed, it is fair to say that the challenge is more acute today in the 2020s than when Park was writing in the 1950s. Individual freedom comes hand-in-hand with individual responsibility—we have our burden to bear—in supporting collective ends.

For Davis there was a path through this dynamic between individual and collective ends. He took up exactly this issue in his November 14, 1909, sermon, "The Individual and Society." Ultimately, we must balance our purely individual ends with our collective ends.

In his sermon, Davis imagines a person purely focused on individual ends:

> I take the very forces of nature and make them work for me. I take men and make them work for me. . . . Grasping, eating, and devouring, I go about my life. But stop. Where shall I end if I carry this too far? Suppose by virtue of my industry, and my skill . . . I become the very ruler and king of all. What is my satisfaction? . . . In what is my happiness? Lo, I have all thought, all power, everywhere men have become my servants. I am alone. There is no one with whom I may talk, no one with whom I may share in my power, my cultured and refined ideas. I am alone on the heights, and I can tell no one of the beauty that I see. I am benumbed and un-human. . . . In my zeal for self-preservation, I have destroyed the only thing worth

10. Charles E. Park, minister of the First Church in Boston (Unitarian) from 1906 until 1946, was among Davis's closest friends. Among the artifacts I inherited from my grandfather was a Bible, inscribed and signed by Ed Park, a Bible he gave Davis in February 1942 "after the winter sojourn."

11. Park, *Way of Jesus*, 44. See also ch. 7.

> preserving, the power and the capacity for human fellowship. This is the stern logic of individual self-culture.[12]

A purely individualistic focus cuts off human fellowship, the possibility to interact with and enrich one's life with other human personalities.

Davis similarly argued that a person focused purely on collective ends also is untenable:

> Equally impossible is the man whose sole aim self-sacrifice. We come across occasionally a being who has been carried off his feet by the idea that he must do nothing for himself. Every thought, every deed must be directly for others. . . . He cannot take time to care for his body, because he must care for the body of others. He cannot take time to develop his mind, because he must see to it that the minds of others must be developed. . . . For others he will sacrifice all. But pray, what is that all? If he has nothing or is nothing in himself that he values, that he honors, that is dear to him, pray, what is the meaning of his sacrifice? It is nothing. It is worthless. . . . He who gives, must have something to give, besides sheer goodwill.[13]

A prosaic reading of this argument is found in the instructions that airlines provide to put on one's own oxygen mask before helping others to put on theirs. To give, we must have something to give.

Davis argued that the only way forward was to find a balance between one's individual ends—so that one has something to contribute—and the collective ends of one's society. For Davis this balance was found in discovery—of the world and one's place in it. It was through discovery that Davis found an individual's connection to the unfinished, ongoing, and never complete effort to realize human ideals on earth.

Davis took his direction from Jesus, as reported in John 6:28: "I came down from heaven, not to do mine own will, but the will of him that sent me." This was how Davis understood Jesus on this point:

> To this end have I been born and to this end have I come into the world that I should bear witness to the truth. I am here not merely to realize my own personal aims, but to grasp the meaning of human life, and let the high aims of human life find their expression in and through me. I am born, not to feed at the crib of a common idealism, but to translate that idealism

12. Davis, "Individual and Society" (1909k), 5–6.

13. Davis, "Individual and Society" (1909k), 6–7.

> into a living reality, personal and social, to bear witness to the beauty and the truth of human life.[14]

He continued, "History shows the truth of this," that the

> men who have become the milestones of human progress, are not characterized by what they have taken out of the common life, but by what of truth they have translated into reality.[15]

It was the strength of their personalities, "achieved at great cost and unspeakable toil," that has created the world we live in, "the very soil that we live on."

And so, for Davis, your

> end is not in yourself, nor is it in society, but it is in both. The truth comes when we realize that our true relationship is not expressed by the phrase, "me and the world," the one over against the other, the one sacrificing to the other, but rather when we realize that our relationship is expressed by the phrase, "myself in the world," when the world becomes ours, and is so engrained into us, and we into it that every least bit of its wellbeing or its ill-being we know as our wellbeing and our ill-being.[16]

For Davis the pathway through the dynamic between individual and collective ends was found in the identification of oneself with the collective, of one's individual ends with collective ends. Such an identification was not a simple matter of a singular commitment, but an ongoing moment-by-moment, decision-by-decision, action-by-action legacy of living in the world.

For Davis, personality lay at the core of this pathway—this unending sequence of decisions and actions—where individual and collective ends were reconciled. It is through an individual's personality that an individual connected personal ends with collective ends. "Noble personalities," as Davis used the term, found pathways of integrity, pathways that supported human flourishing, pathways that supported the abundant life for all human personalities.

Reconciling individual and collective ends, for Davis, turns on individual personalities. Davis's "noble personalities," are those that have consecrated themselves to working for the abundant life for all, all

14. Davis, "Individual and Society" (1909k), 7.
15. Davis, "Individual and Society" (1909k), 7.
16. Davis, "Individual and Society" (1909k), 7–8.

personalities. This was where Davis found progress towards heaven on earth. And this raises the question: what characteristics were central to Davis's noble personalities?

4. The Modern Pioneer

On November 20, 1904, Davis, preached a sermon, "The Modern Pioneer" at the Unity Church in Pittsfield, Massachusetts.[17] He was twenty-eight years old and recently had graduated from Harvard with his "Bachelors of Sacred Theology," or STB, degree. This sermon, along with another, "Man's Responsibility,"[18] preached a week later on November 27, 1904, were part of his candidacy for the ministry at the Unity Church in Pittsfield.

"The Modern Pioneer" was a Thanksgiving sermon, a sermon given to recognize and speak to the Thanksgiving festival of the harvest. In 1904, Thanksgiving was celebrated four days after Davis's Sunday sermon, on Thursday, November 24th. Thanksgiving, as the name suggests, is usually seen as festival of thanks, thanks for the successful harvest, thanks for the successful accomplishments of the past year.

Not so for Davis. What if the harvest was not successful? What if the year has been one of struggle and setback? He observed that

> others, whose life has been one continual period of hardship, disappointment, suffering, and sorrow, such people seem to look forward to a day like this with a far greater sense of appreciation and expectancy than those who have been most favored.[19]

Davis wrote a note on the top of the sermon's manuscript, "Written to give courage and independence and faith to people just recovering from a period of discouragement."[20]

With hardship and challenges in mind, Davis thought that Thanksgiving should be more about hope for the future than thanks for the past:

> Not what we love, or what we have done, or what we are is the basis of our thanksgiving, but what, through God's grace and our own effort, we hope to have, and hope to do, and hope to

17. Davis, "Modern Pioneer" (1904b).

18. Davis, "Man's Responsibility" (1904c). I have discussed "Man's Responsibility," among other places in ch. 1.

19. Davis, "Modern Pioneer" (1904b), 1.

20. Davis, "Modern Pioneer" (1904b), 1.

> become in the magic ever-alluring, but unknown future which stretches out before us. It is a consecration to the things undone rather than an exaltation over the things done. Today we face, not the past but the future.[21]

For Davis himself, he most certainly was thinking about what he hoped "to become" in "the magic ever-alluring, but unknown future." He was making the very first moves in his alluring, but unknown, future career as a Unitarian minister. He needed to secure a ministry, and as any person on a job search knows, doing so is taking a leap into the unknown. There can be hardships, challenges, setbacks.

But Davis's sermon did not follow a self-reflective path. Instead, he first looked to the past, to the early pioneers arriving in "the New World," and to their character traits, as he imagined them, character traits that he thought lay behind their hope for the future through years of struggle, privation, and uncertainty. He wanted to understand their personalities.

5. Pioneers in the New World

Davis got into the body of his sermon as follows:

> In solving the problems of the future, we often avoid many foolish mistakes and embarrassing blunders by going back to the past for help and wisdom. I often try to picture to myself the kind of men they were, those pioneers who first settled in this country, and held their thanksgiving festivals on the shores of an unknown continent thanking God for the things that had been vouchsafed to them and consecrating themselves to the unsolved problems of a new world with all its hardship. I try to get some conception of the mental and moral equivalent of those men who in the middle of the 18th century picked their way through the Hoosac mountains leaving behind the comforts of the settlements near the coast, and resolutely faced the vast unknown and unexplored . . . From our ease and safety and quiet we can look back to those days of hardship and danger, and read the stories of their adventures, and try to glean from them something of the spirit, something of the character which led them through days of discouragement and darkness, to days of victory and rejoicing.[22]

21. Davis, "Modern Pioneer" (1904b), 2.
22. Davis, "Modern Pioneer" (1904b), 2–3.

Let us own that Davis was a man of his times—as we are all of the times we live in—and he was not sensitive to or attentive to the points of view of the indigenous Americans that these pioneers were engaging. Indigenous Americans already had explored, knew, and occupied this land. He wrote in a gendered way, but he was clearly thinking of both men and women. The first person he considers is Sarah Deming, who at the age of twenty-six, joined her husband, Solomon Deming, in coming to Poontoosuck—now Pittsfield—"the first white woman who ever called it home."[23] These deficiencies and gaps in Davis's thinking about the early pioneers and the challenges they faced do not undermine, I don't think, the central point he makes about their personalities.

It was an interesting and instructive exercise that Davis followed here, speaking to some of the 1904 Pittsfield descendants of these early pioneers. He was right that it took great courage to strike out into the wilderness towards an unknown future, "no ordinary courage,"[24] as he put it. But he noted that even this great courage alone was not enough. It took independence, a willingness to break with the customs and routines of settled life and do something different. Courage and independence were key character traits that Davis saw as important inheritances that these pioneers passed on to their descendants. Without courage and independence, exploration into the unknown world would not happen. Discovery would not happen. Courage and independence were necessary virtues for Davis's picture of progressive change.

6. And Faith

And yet, Davis argued, courage and independence were not enough. Davis told his congregation that "there is the still more profound characteristic, which is the basis upon which all else rests, that is faith."[25] Courage, independence, *and faith.*

And here, as I read this sermon for the first time in the summer of 2021, early in my acquaintance with my grandfather's thought, I was

23. Davis, "Modern Pioneer" (1904b), 3. Here Davis is quoting material from *The History of Pittsfield (Berkshire County) Massachusetts, From the Year 1734 to the year 1800,* compiled and written, under the general direction of a committee, by J. E. A. Smith in 1869. The Hoosac mountains form the western edge of the northwest Berkshire plateau of Western Massachusetts. Davis is writing here specifically about the British and European pioneers that settled Pittsfield and the Berkshire mountains of Western Massachusetts—where he hoped to be hired for his first ministry.

24. Davis, "Modern Pioneer" (1904b), 3.

25. Davis, "Modern Pioneer" (1904b), 4.

stopped short. The philosopher in me—specifically the philosopher concerned with rationality, with knowledge, belief, decision theory—was not ready for the role of faith—my grandfather's "still more profound characteristic." Surely, I thought, faith cannot be the solution. We need evidence and reason, anything but—blind?—faith.

Easily enough I had followed my grandfather's line of thought. I could appreciate the immense psychological challenge that these pioneers had had to face as they struck out into the unknown. Courage, absolutely. Independence, yes. But the problem is that they did not have—could not have had—the evidence and reason to underwrite their trek into the unknown. Hence, faith. But still, my contemporary—"postmodern"—mind rebelled.

Faith is all well and good when engaged with personal matters or one's individual spiritual commitments. But surely whether, where and how to go—into the wilderness—should be matters of weighing the evidence, of thinking through probabilities of risks and rewards. We need decision theory, not faith.

I have had to think about my grandfather's recipe—courage, independence, and faith—to wrestle with what I think about faith. Faith has not been part of my conscious thinking about living life. Should it have been? Should it be?

In 1946, Davis's friend Charles E. Park published a book of two hundred short—one page each—sermons. His 110th sermon concerned faith. He began with a puzzle from Josh 24:19:

> Joshua urges his people to commit themselves to Jehovah. Just as they are about to make the promise, he suddenly declares, "Ye cannot serve the Lord: he is too holy." It is a curious inconsistency; urging them in one breath to do the very thing that, in the next breath, he tells them they cannot do. . . . What strange guiding have we here? The things we cannot do, and must.[26]

Here was the puzzle animating Park's short sermon.

What was the solution? What pathway did Park find through this puzzle? Park found the limits of rationality and the beginning of faith:

> Reason based on experience outlines what we can do, what we can know. Faith leaps far ahead and beckons us to things beyond reason's cautious limits, both to do and to believe. If we followed reason, we should go right but never get far or do much. It is just because our souls, tutored by faith, are reckless

26. Park, *Inner Victory*, sermon #110. The biblical quote, "Ye cannot serve the Lord: he is too holy," that serves as the Scripture for the sermon is from Josh 24:19.

> enough to bite off more than we can chew that we clothe our fate in raiment of hope and promise. The entire glory of life lies in the courage with which we embrace these inconsistencies; to believe that which is beyond knowledge, to attempt that which is beyond ability.[27]

For Park, to live a life of pure rationality, a life without faith, would be an unpardonable sin:

> The unpardonable sin is to repudiate that guidance of faith and surrender to reason. The supreme act of manhood is to trust the unreasonable something in us which is More-than-Man, and follow its guidance into the glories that eye hath not seen nor ear heard.[28]

There is more than a whiff of William James's "Will to Believe" here—"to believe," as Park put it, "that which is beyond knowledge."[29] James argued that there are situations where a failure to believe, because of a lack of evidence, could be as dangerous—if not more so—than the adoption of a belief on faith.

Reason is not enough. It makes sense to me that Davis's "early pioneers" would never have ventured forth without some kind of faith underwriting their courage and independence. Reason wouldn't have been—couldn't have been—enough.

What about today? We live in a world that is awash in evidence. It is an overused trope today to say that one's conclusions, one's recommendations, one's policies are "evidence based." Bringing evidence to bear on our problems is an essential part of how we can reasonably, rationally, properly think, dialogue, and act. Reason and evidence can also provide a shared common ground from which antagonistic beliefs and actions might be assessed, mutually improved upon, brought into greater consilience. Reason and evidence bring civilization to difference. This is better than violence.

And yet Davis, and his friend Park, shared the view that reason and evidence were not enough. Faith was necessary. But doesn't this invite violence? If your faith differs from my faith, and they point in different directions, how are we to engage with this difference? As we are here engaged in matters of faith, reason and evidence would seem not to bear. What tools, besides bombast and violence, do we have? This

27. Park, *Inner Victory*, sermon #110.

28. Park, *Inner Victory*, sermon #110.

29. James, "Will to Believe" in James, *Will to Believe*, 1–31, and Menand, *Pragmatism*, 69–92. See also ch. 2.

question seems to me even more pressing in the twenty-first century America that I live in.

7. Davis's Modern Faith

Faith is not the only virtue. Even in the context of "The Modern Pioneer," faith sits alongside courage and independence. But of course, there are yet other virtues that engage our thought and action, other virtues that temper faith.

Furthermore, genuine faith for Davis was not just some random thing one might believe completely independently of reason and evidence. Neither Davis nor Park was advocating a random or credulous—a blind—faith. Both appreciated the important roles that evidence, and reason brought to the table.

In a 1922 sermon that goes into detail on the then current neurobiology, Davis looked to discover where our "ideas, reasoned judgements, moral purposes that determine our conduct" come from.[30] The neurobiology he read pointed to the cerebral cortex. But he continued, "Thus far science. But our mind does not rest satisfied."

> The answer is one of faith, not a blind credulous faith, but a faith that carries us forward in the direction to which all known facts point, a faith so confirmed by all that we know and experience, that it becomes a great compelling conviction.[31]

Faith, for Davis, followed in the wake of knowledge, and yet, as Park suggested, leads us forward beyond knowledge.

Davis's sermon on neurobiology has the surprising title of "The Essential Christ." After a quick sketch of the nervous system, Davis came to his point:

> Here in this cerebral cortex, as it is called by the scientists, where consciousness makes the selection of incoming messages, and establishes the connections for outgoing messages to the world, takes place all those marvelous developments of ideas, reasoned judgements, moral *purposes that determine our conduct*.[32]

The connection to Christ emerged from his conclusion that

30. Davis, "Essential Christ" (1922), 3. Davis's information on neurobiology is taken from George Howard Parker's (1864–1955) *Biology and Social Problems*.

31. Davis, "Essential Christ" (1922), 4.

32. Davis, "Essential Christ" (1922), 4 (emphasis in the original).

> somehow in that wonderful mystery of conscious personality that operates in the central exchange of our cerebral cortex, there is a central urge that reaches out towards the truth, goodness, and beauty of the world. . . .
>
> Within us is the urge that responds to the temptations, to truth, goodness, and beauty without. "I and my father are one," said Jesus. The God without and the God within are of like life. Purpose registers in us because it is grounded in the world without.[33]

As Davis understood the neurobiological research the key elements of personality operated in and through the cerebral cortex, and this was where he found "the temptations to truth, goodness and beauty." But we humans are part of the world (chapter 6, section 10): "the God without and the God within are of like life." The fact that progress is possible, and has been achieved through human effort, shows, for Davis, our inner divine selves reflecting an outer divine world. Our temptations to truth, goodness, and beauty, was the nub of the living God, or "the essential Christ."

Put aside whether Davis had the details of the science correct. His point was that within our personalities, which were under scientific investigation, Davis found "temptations to truth, goodness, and beauty." This urge to "truth, goodness, and beauty" was, for Davis, the manifestation of the divine in human personalities. It propelled human life forward, and upward. Here were the ideals to which we should bring courage, independence, and faith, the ideals for which we should abandon safety, for which we should be willing to sacrifice.

8. Faith, Among the Virtues, and Not a Credulous Faith

Davis was always interested in what experience taught us, what we learned from science and human experience more generally. Hence his close reading of the neurobiology of his day. He believed that faith could and should be responsive in an ongoing way to new knowledge. For him the church—at least his church—should be a place to engage new discoveries with faith.

In a sermon Davis gave in 1942, "Remarks at Tenth Anniversary," he spoke directly to his congregation:

33. Davis, "Essential Christ" (1922), 4–5. The quote from Jesus is from John 10:30.

> This fellowship, which we call a Church, means many things to me. It is the center of many dear associations. It is the holy ground of many high thoughts, of many moments of illumination when you have felt the spirit of the living God playing about your own personalities—moments which mark epochs in your lives. You have told of these facts. But one thing more. I hope that during the years that are before us, this place will stand in the eyes of this community, not only as a place of spiritual power, but as a place of keen intellectual influence, a place where great problems, great questions may be presented, discussed with sincerity and freedom, a place where, with malice towards none, and with charity for all, we may sift the gold of modern thought, as well as ancient thought from the dross, and carry the gold of truth and place our just contribution at the disposal of this community.[34]

Davis's church was a place where, "with malice towards none, and with charity for all," the congregation could think through the implications of modern thought—science, technology, and the rest—with the wisdom of the ages to arrive at a reasoned faith, not a blind credulous faith.

Among the virtues, faith lives with charity and benevolence. Before resorting to violence, which would violate charity and benevolence, we should engage each other in reasoned dialogue; we should discuss—with sincerity and freedom—both our differences and what we share. We may not find our way to agreement, but we can do better than violence. Faith need not be the end of reason and the beginning of violence.

Davis's conception of democracy played an important role here too. Democracy was not just about voting, counting and majorities. Democracy was—is—about social engagement. Here Davis followed John Dewey, who argued in his essay "The Ethics of Democracy" that democracy is not a "mere weighing of numbers."[35] Humans are fundamentally social creatures and this bears on the practice and meaning of democracy:

> A man when he comes to vote does not put off from him, like a suit of old clothes, his character, his wealth, his social influence, his devotion to political interest, and become a naked unit. . . . He votes, not as a mere unit, but as a representative of the social organism. . . . A vote, in other words, is not an impersonal

34. Davis, "Remarks at Tenth Anniversary" (1942b), 4–5. The "Tenth Anniversary" of the title refers to Davis's tenth anniversary as minister of the First Congregational Church (Unitarian) in Petersham, Massachusetts.

35. Dewey, "Ethics of Democracy," in Menand, *Pragmatism*, 188.

> counting of one; it is a manifestation of some tendency of the social organism through a member of that organism.[36]

Many of Davis's sermons spoke to the importance of engaging in the political matters of the day, one's civic duty. This engagement set the stage for which issues and which candidates came before voters. This engagement is Dewey's "social organism" in action.

The result is messy, full of compromise, and does not move in a straight line. But it is the avenue of discovery, freedom, and consent. Democracy allows for constructive engagement between differing opinions, differing faiths, without resorting to violence.

> The Giant of Democracy is rising. It is no respecter of persons, of nations, or of Churches. It may be turbulent and rugged in its fresh energy, but in the long run, it is the voice of the living God in life and in reality. That voice of the living God will speak to us as men have spoken all through the ages. "To this end, have I been born and to this end am I come into the world, that I should bear witness to the truth."[37]

9. Courage, Independence, and Faith

Davis's 1904 sermon initially concerned itself with the early pioneers, the early white explorers who found their way from the East Coast west to Pittsfield and beyond. But the title of his sermon is "The Modern Pioneer." He was principally concerned with modern times—his "modern times," the beginning of the twentieth century. Turning from past to present and future, he recognized that

> it is true that nearly all the lands of the world have been explored. It is true that our country is quite thoroughly settled. It is true that the dangers and heroisms of early days no longer offer themselves as fields for our courage, independence and faith.[38]

Many of the difficulties and challenges that the early settlers faced were past.

> I am fully aware of the tremendous gains that have been made. I know that there is no warrant for a cup of despair, and I am

36. Dewey, "Ethics of Democracy," in Menand, *Pragmatism*, 188–89.
37. Davis, "Religion in Life and in Reality" (1918e), 6. The quote is from John 18:37.
38. Davis, "Modern Pioneer" (1904b), 5.

> certain that this world as it is this minute is a very genial comfortable sort of a place in which to live.[39]

At least this was true for (some of) the white settlers. Nonetheless, Davis recognized that very significant challenges remained.

Writing in 1904, Davis identified four significant challenges: (1) "crime, carelessness and disease"; (2) political corruption; (3) "warfare between labor and capital"; (4) "conditions of things in the religious affairs." These challenges called for modern pioneers:

> If ever there was a time when pioneers were needed, that time is now. In whatever direction one may turn there is the demand for a pioneer with courage, independence and faith enough to launch out into the unknown, and undiscovered, leaving behind the traditions and accumulations of custom which have become too much of a hinderance to the normal growth of man.[40]

Not geographic exploration, but social, ethical, economic, and scientific exploration called for courage, independence, and faith.

Courage, independence, and faith were needed—Davis argued—by anyone actively seeking to explore, to discover, to create, to prompt change in the world. While Davis's world of 1904 seemed a "genial comfortable sort of a place in which to live," he was aware that work needed to be done, work that would require striking out into the unknown—the social/political/scientific unknown. Work that required abandoning comfortable traditions and customs for uncertainties, uncertainties reaching for a better world. This too would take courage, independence, and faith.

And today. Davis's world of 1904 and the world of the 2020s present similar, serious problems. Davis was painfully aware of the many people living in his time who were confronting significant hardships. His sermon was aimed at "people just recovering from a period of discouragement." Today too, with our "deaths of despair." Many people need help; they need a pathway forward from hardship and discouragement. For Davis the core problem came from structures that infringed upon some people's pursuit of an abundant life. Today, just as much as the early settlers, just as much the inhabitants of 1904 Pittsfield, we need courage, independence, and faith to face these challenges.

39. Davis, "Modern Pioneer" (1904b), 5.

40. Davis, "Modern Pioneer" (1904b), 6.

10. Natural Faith

Our "evidence-based" world hides our faith. With our rationality and our data, we believe that the future can be known; it will emerge as our best evidence tells us. But this is a matter of faith. There is no proof. Somehow, we think that the evidence is the proof. But the evidence is only the proof if the universe "obeys the evidence," or, perhaps better, if the universe operates in a regular "law-like" manner. This is an age-old philosophers' problem, the "problem of induction." No amount of evidence from past regularities guarantees that things will continue to be so in the future. Our pretense of a future that can be rationally known is a matter of faith, a hidden faith. We hide our faith behind our rationality.

In the first draft of this chapter I titled this section, "Hidden *False* Faith." I was thinking that—rationally—we cannot know the future, that the evidence is always insufficient. I was thinking like a philosopher, mindful of the fact that past performance is no guarantee of future performance.

I wrote the first draft of this chapter before I had encountered Davis's September 19, 1909, sermon, "Two Great Principles of the Modern World," which I have already discussed in chapter 6. Recall these principles:

1. "the substantial integrity of the universe," that the universe is knowable, and
2. "progress," that human effort in pursuit of human ideals can make things better.[41]

These principles were the core to Davis's "modern faith," a faith to be distinguished from an early "faith" tied to revelation. Davis's modern faith underwrote Davis's modern world—a world of discovery, freedom, and consent. There can be no discovery without the substantial integrity of the universe—as Davis understood that concept. Progress too. For Davis, discovery, freedom, and consent were the doors that allowed progress.

For Davis, faith in the "integrity of the universe" and "in growth, development, progress" was not something one argues for. One either had this faith or not.

When I read this sermon, I realized that this is the faith behind science and discovery. This is the faith that we can improve the world. I

41. Davis, "Two Great Principles" (1909b), 2.

agreed—I agree—with these principles. Without realizing it, I have this faith. I do believe that the universe is knowable, that we can learn more about the universe—indeed, that we already have learned more. I believe that progress is possible, that human effort can improve the world—indeed, that human efforts already have improved the world.

Is the world perfect? Do we know everything? Certainly not. It is an ongoing process. As I shared at the end of chapter 2, Davis's picture of humankind was of a process of centuries, of millennia:

> Half in blind obedience to instincts that are the essential characteristics of his [humankind's] nature, and half in a semi-conscious following of a purpose, he sets out on his long journey over the centuries . . . through hardship and toil unspeakable, he has climbed the stairway of the centuries, and . . . today we still find ourselves climbing those same stairways, whose foundations are lost from our view in the utter darkness of the past, and whose uppermost steps are beyond the reach of our wildest imagination. Yet we climb on and on, allured by the light of our radiating visions of truth, goodness and beauty, and impelled by the great power of human life.[42]

Through hardship and toil unspeakable we have continued forward—and we continue forward—in the faith that we are getting somewhere.

Do I have reason to agree with Davis's principles? This is a complicated question. I think there is evidence that the universe is knowable. I think there is evidence that we have made—and continue to make—progress. But is there proof? No. I discovered my faith. It was, indeed, hidden. I didn't see it, until my grandfather's sermon put it smack down in front of me.

Is this a "false faith"? This too is a complicated question. It could be false. But that is just the thing with faith. There is no guarantee, no proof. It is a question of where we believe the evidence points, and it is a question of where we believe the best path into the future may be found.

This is a "natural faith." It is natural in that it fundamentally derives from nature, from one's experience of nature, the regular—if also irregular—passing of the seasons, and the regular—if also irregular—behavior of people. The integrity of the universe, of nature—human nature included—is knowable, if not perfectly. It is knowable fallibly, humbly.

This also is a natural faith because it would be challenging to live without some such faith, consciously or not. It comes naturally to us, at

42. Davis, "Inevitable Compensation" (1909d), 4–5.

least to me. We need to assume that food will continue to nourish us, that life and the universe can be—at least partially—known. It underwrites our "evidence-based" culture. It provides reason to strive into the future.

11. Atheism or Theism Is a Matter of Fact

Shortly after I read Davis's "Two Great Principles of the Modern World" sermon I read his December 5, 1909, sermon, "Is Your God Dead?" There he claimed that the "question of atheism or theism is not a question of philosophy, but of fact."[43] Wait, what? The philosopher in me was struck dumb by this claim. Isn't atheism just exactly a matter argument, of philosophy—or perhaps of expressed faith? Argument is how philosophers have always approached this question: What are the arguments for the existence of God?

One of the first philosophy papers I wrote in my first undergraduate philosophy course concerned classic arguments for the existence of God. I found the arguments unsatisfactory. I still find them unsatisfactory. They all, it seems to me, sneak something into their premises by way of how "God" is defined that leads to the conclusion that God exists. But it seemed to me then, and it seems to me now, that you don't get much by defining a God that you can then prove exists. Definition is hardly evidence of existence. The professor replied to me that a definition would not be a compelling source of conviction either. I agree.

But Davis claimed that one's belief in God's existence was—is!—simply a matter of fact. How could this work? Davis asked, what, *in fact,* are one's convictions, what lies behind one's actions? Is one committed to the integrity of the universe and to progress, or not? It does not matter what one says about God—or even what one says about the universe and progress. What matters is how one acts with respect to the universe:

> The true theist is the person who has an ideal, who is working for the things that shall be, and has faith that the universe is with him. . . . I care not by what name he may call his ideal and his hope, but in that he has faith in its reality, and gives himself to its attainment, he has made, and has, a living god.[44]

For Davis, a person who believed in the principles of the modern world, in the integrity of the universe, and in the possibility of

43. Davis, "Is Your God Dead?" (1909j), 5.

44. Davis, "Is Your God Dead?" (1909j), 5.

progress—me!—was a theist. I didn't know! These beliefs betrayed my faith in what Davis understood as the divine living in me—along with all of nature and human nature, his pantheism.

Ironically, if you think things are not as they should be, if you can imagine a better future—and you are willing to work for this better future—in Davis's view, you betray your theism:

> When we find our place and see the outline of the world that shall be, and the vision of that which is not becomes to us as real [as] the world in which we live, then our God lives, and life is real and life is true.[45]

Atheists, who argue that organized religion has caused—and continues to cause—unbearable suffering and human harm and should be eliminated, are, in Davis's view, theists. They are imagining a better future, and in so doing, they betray their "living God." Natural deity, natural faith.

12. Natural Faith, Divine Faith

This natural faith seems so obvious that one doesn't even realize one has it. I certainly didn't. It just is there. But not always. Davis's principles make demands on our behavior, our integrity, our contributions to the progress of the world. Much of the time these demands are trifling. But not always. This is why Davis's sermon, "The Modern Pioneer," provided a three-part recipe: *courage, independence,* and *faith.*

This three-part recipe is the central message of the story of Jesus in the garden of Gethsemane.[46] I have already written about Davis's admiration for the story of Jesus in the garden of Gethsemane. It was a key element of his "personal bible," which I wrote about in chapter 4. It is worth revisiting for the light it sheds on the more demanding elements of Davis's natural faith, faith in the integrity of the universe and in progress.

In the final day leading up to Jesus' crucifixion, Jesus had the Last Supper and then retired to the garden of Gethsemane with his closest disciples. He went there to pray for the courage, independence, and faith he knew he would need to respond to the challenge ahead. Davis shared with his congregation:

45. Davis, "Is Your God Dead?" (1909j), 6.

46. See Matt 26:36–45.

> It is easy to declare our faith in the face of the applauding multitude; it is easy to stand in the church surrounded by precious memories and dear friends and say that we believe in the moral values of life, and that we believe in God. But when the tide of approval has run out, and the tide of angry opposition and violence is already lashing against the walls of life's most precious possessions, then the test of faith comes. When the multitude has vanished, when friends have been left behind, and, alone under God's open sky, you are called upon to make the decision of sealing your faith with your own life's blood, then you really declare your faith. Did you mean business or were you just talking when you so glibly recited your credo?[47]

Jesus' struggle in the garden of Gethsemane brings together his courage—courage unto death—and his independence—he faced this trial alone as his disciples slept[48]—and his faith, "O my Father, if it be possible, let this cup pass from me: nevertheless, not as I will, but as thou wilt."[49]

> In the Garden of Gethsemane men measure the quality of their own soul, whether or not they have the moral courage to face the ignominy of trial, condemnation and death for truth's sake, for that spiritual value that we call integrity. In Christ's Gethsemane he made that choice. That is the supreme moment of his life. He had staked his life on the faith, the conviction, not the proven knowledge, but the conviction that God exists, that truth counts, that life has eternal qualities. That faith, that conviction held good in the Garden of Gethsemane. He came through clean.[50]

Jesus' integrity held. For Davis, the point was not to be found in the specifics to Jesus' faith. The point of the story of the garden of Gethsemane was in Jesus' personality, in Jesus' integrity, in his courage, independence, and faith.

For Davis the message of the garden of Gethsemane was the most important message in the Gospels:

> You may have the rest of the Gospels, and all the rest of Christianity to do what you please with, provided you leave only the scene in the Garden of Gethsemane, the power to choose to bear witness to truth at any cost, and the rest is easy.[51]

47. Davis, "Did Christ Have the Power" (1923b), 8–9.
48. See Matt 26:40–45.
49. Matt 26:39.
50. Davis, "Did Christ Have the Power" (1923b), 9.
51. Davis, "Review of Androcles and the Lion" (1913b), 9.

Here is the core of Jesus' personality. And here, for Davis, was the most important message of the Gospels, courage, independence, and faith, acting together in support of one's belief in a better—truer, more just, more beautiful—tomorrow. Here, for Davis, was the supreme example of a noble personality. As Davis put it in his thoughts about his personal Bible (see chapter 4), "One of the great human moments of history. I love to read that when I hear of a man or a woman who has done the brave deed and faces the condemnation of the world alone. Its human. Its divine."[52]

Jesus is not unique. Davis celebrated Jesus because of his personality, his deep core integrity, his love, and empathy for his fellow human beings—irrespective of their status—and his willingness to give all he had for his beliefs. Davis well recognized that there have been others in history.

In his January 8, 1911, sermon, "The Essence of Manhood," Davis wrote of great human personalities found in history. He opened with Charles Sumner (1811–74) "perhaps the greatest of Massachusetts' senators,"[53] who was a vigorous leader of the anti-slavery forces prior to and through the Civil War. He moved on to Theodore Parker (1810–60) nineteenth-century reform-oriented Unitarian minister and ardent abolitionist. He discussed other examples from church history, the prophets from the Old Testament, Amos, and Hosea. Then Jesus, of course, but also Girolamo Savonarola (1452–98), who was executed for refusing to join Pope Alexander VI's efforts against the French and instead led protest processions, "bonfires of the vanities."[54]

Davis's argument was always that these humans, whom we remember and applaud as heroes, provided us insight into the essence of humanity:

> You may keep from me all the superficial secrets of your life, but once let me know your hero, I have entered the secret chambers of your personality. Take humanity then . . . and what do you find? What kind of men does it honor, respect, and love? Here the record of history is absolute. Men of courage, men of faith, integrity, men who have born witness to the truth that was in them. Men who have cast behind them all conformity and acquainted men at first hand with deity.[55]

52. Davis, "Democracy of the Bible" (1910b), 6.
53. Davis, "Essence of Manhood" (1911b), 2.
54. Davis, "Essence of Manhood" (1911b). 3.
55. Davis, "Essence of Manhood" (1911b), 5.

These were the people whose characters drove what Davis saw as positive, progressive change through history, through their courage, independence, and faith. Davis:

> Courage, love, integrity, wisdom, honor, we have cherished as life values in our heroes of the past, because they have born witness to our own unrealized longings and possibilities.[56]

Davis concluded his sermon looking to the future:

> Let the dead past bury its dead, while we honor and cherish the living present, and with courage, integrity, and wisdom and love press on to the tasks and the life that is before us. . . .
>
> Our task is . . . to bear witness to the manhood and womanhood that is in us.[57]

13. Natural Religion

Davis developed his theology piecemeal, sermon by sermon. He came to it out of a liberal, but still traditionally theist, tradition. His nineteenth-century hero, William Ellery Channing, argued for the deity in humans, but Channing's deity was not divorced from Jesus' God of spirit and truth. Davis came to his theology as part of the struggle between "modern materialism" and the "spiritual power" of humans,[58] a struggle put into crisis by Darwin's *Origin of Species.*[59]

Davis was not willing to abandon science—Darwin included—for supernatural revelation. Instead, he found a natural religion in human personality, in human ideals, and the power of human ideals to make a better world. Davis's "modern faith," his "natural faith," was a faith in the power of human ideals to make a better world. It was connected to his faith in the integrity—the knowability—of the universe. Humans—natural humans, not supernatural humans—are part of the universe, and so our human ideals are themselves part of the universe, part of the evolution of the universe.

How did these ideals get there? In Davis's writings there are hints of a kind of divine power behind them—something like Jesus' God of spirit and truth. Davis called it the "Indwelling Goodwill." He wrote, for

56. Davis, "Essence of Manhood" (1911b), 7.

57. Davis, "Essence of Manhood" (1911b), 7.

58. See ch. 5, section 4.

59. Darwin, *Origin of Species.*

example, "The God without and the God within are of like life. Purpose registers in us because it is grounded in the world without."[60] This, I think, betrays Davis's cultural inheritance. For myself, I don't know that it matters how these ideals became part of human nature, part of the universe. The fact is that they did.

The fact also is that humans are complex mixtures of virtues and vices. Throughout history, up to and including our own day, there has been—and remains—much human depravity, human suffering, people falling short of these ideals. The ideals—the virtues—may be there, but they do not always rule.

Indeed, we are not completely clear what the virtues are, what the vices are. Improving our understanding of these matters is itself part of the history of humankind, part of human progress. The universe is not finished. There remains work to do. It always will be so.

But natural religion is underwritten by a natural faith that we can—with effort—make the world better. Through our efforts to do so, we are part of the evolution of the universe.

Natural religion does not itself answer difficult knotty problems that vex us. It provides guides. Jesus' second commandment to love thy neighbor as thyself, with some conceptual work, turns into Immanuel Kant's "Categorical Imperative": "Act in such a way that you treat humanity, whether in your own person or in the person of any other, never merely as a means to an end, but always at the same time as an end."[61] But this leaves much more work to do.

What natural religion does do is connect individual human lives to the long history of the evolution of the universe. In this sense we are immortal beings. Natural religion's natural faith in the integrity of the universe and the possibility of progress gives meaning and purpose to this connection between individual lives and the history of humanity. This natural faith says we do not struggle in vain:

> I am born, not to feed at the crib of a common idealism, but to translate that idealism into a living reality, personal and social, to bear witness to the beauty and the truth of human life.[62]

60. Davis, "Essential Christ" (1922), 4–5.
61. Kant, *Metaphysics of Morals*, 36.
62. Davis, "Individual and Society" (1909k), 7.

Chapter 10: **Afterword**

> Half in blind obedience to instincts that are the essential characteristics of his [humankind's] nature, and half in a semi-conscious following of a purpose, he sets out on his long journey over the centuries. . . . Through hardship and toil unspeakable, he has climbed the stairway of the centuries, and . . . today we still find ourselves climbing those same stairways, whose foundations are lost from our view in the utter darkness of the past, and whose uppermost steps are beyond the reach of our wildest imagination. Yet we climb on and on, allured by the light of our radiating visions of truth, goodness and beauty, and impelled by the great power of human life.[1]

1. What, Then, Is Religion?

As I come towards the end of my journey into my grandparents' lives and into my grandfather's thinking, I wonder what I have learned. How might this change my life? Should it change my life?

Starting from near zero, I certainly have learned an immense amount about religion, about the central role of religion in history, and in particular—and surprisingly—in the development of governance. My grandfather's understanding of the emergence of American democracy from medieval royal entitlement and authority—the so-called divine right of kings—and his robust enthusiasm for American democracy

1. Davis, "Inevitable Compensation" (1909d), 4–5.

have re-inspired my own appreciation for American democracy. Discovery, freedom, and consent is much better than revelation, authority and obedience. This appears to be a lesson that needs to be learned and re-learned and re-re-learned. Authoritarianism in its many beautiful raiments has not disappeared.

I have learned that, at its core, religion is not about specific institutions and/or beliefs—churches and creeds. It is not about the many and diverse speculations and practices that might engage deity or support a possible afterlife. My grandfather did not believe in the permanency of religious institutions—any religious institutions—nor the permanency of specific religious beliefs—any religious beliefs or creeds. "Not forms," he said, "but the Holy Spirit":[2]

> The Holy Spirit, the whole, healthy life, life with values and standards, life with purpose, life healthy and vigorous with its eye on some better tomorrow, some better age, some better world.[3]

He believed in permanent values. He believed in a life lived by these values, a life with standards, purpose, a life lived toward a better world, a better tomorrow. As my grandfather understood it, religion is more about living, living in the world, and living with values and purpose.

Truth, beauty, and goodness, this is where my grandfather found deity. What are truth, beauty, and goodness? Here again, he did not believe in permanent answers. "Not revelation," he said, "but discovery":[4]

> The open mind, ready for new truth, ready to risk that truth in the open arena. To this principle, to this method above all else we are dedicated.[5]

He believed in the ongoing *and fallible* effort to understand truth, beauty, and goodness—along with everything else. While he believed in the permanency of religious questions, in the permanency of the human need to understand—and appreciate—our universe and our place in it, he did not believe in permanent answers; the answers are never final, but always subject to ongoing test "in the open arena." And in this open arena, we must always be ready for new truth.

2. Davis, "Not Revelation" (1947a).
3. Davis, "Not Revelation" (1947a), 2.
4. Davis, "Not Revelation" (1947a), 2.
5. Davis, "From Copernicus to Galileo" (1942a), 8.

2. *Living in Darwin's World*

Change was my grandfather's constant. No surprise. He grew up in the full flush of Darwin. Growing up two generations later, in the wake of "the Atomic age," Darwin didn't have the same grip on my imagination. But reading through his sermons I can begin to appreciate how revolutionary Darwin was—*is*. Change. Ongoing, unstoppable change. And the remarkable power of natural selection to produce an amazing, astonishing diversity of life forms.

Three score and ten. Now beyond my seventieth birthday and life and death come into a different kind of focus. I am in good health—at least I think I am—but the numbers mean something. And I can feel some diminishment in my strength—time for more strength training! A year ago, I tripped and fell while jogging, dislocating my shoulder. I experienced a new and more intense kind of pain, and it has taken months of physical therapy to get something like normal functioning back. Then six months ago out of the blue I had a small stroke, fortunately without any enduring disabilities.[6] All the tests and all the medical intelligence has yet to identify a cause. I now have an internal "loop recorder" that monitors my heart rhythms and sends the information to my doctors for analysis. So far nothing, and, for the most part, I feel myself to be in good health, but I also hear a faint knocking of mortality at the door.

As I think about this I am struck by the astonishing miracle of my life, of any life, of life. There are so many things that can go wrong in this amazing, complicated body in which—through which—I exist. Listening to doctors consider the various things that could have caused my stroke, it is a wonder that strokes are not more common. But not just strokes, all the innumerable things that can go off course in the proper functioning of a body. It is incredible that it all works as well as it does. And, yet, for most of my life—three score and ten—it has all ticked along beautifully. Thank you, Darwin. Thank you, period. For this I am most grateful.

This miraculous body of mine—but, of course, not just mine—is the result of generations and generations of evolution by natural selection. I think of all the "failed experiments," untold numbers of bodies, over generations, "selected against." Some element of the whirling complexity that makes a human life—or any kind of life—didn't work well enough to support reproduction. How to think of these people, "proto people"—earlier life forms—from thousands—millions—of years ago?

6. I have written about my experience of this stroke; see Baird, "My TIA."

"Life experiments" that died without reproducing, life experiments that evolution "selected against." "Proto people" selected against. Yet these "failed experiments" allowed natural selection to create the quite marvelous, yet imperfect, body of mine. Some of the "failed experiments," I imagine, must have suffered terribly. I must owe these earlier generations something for their suffering.

Then there are the "successful experiments." I would not exist if not for the efforts—and the luck—the successful reproduction of the generations and generations of my ancestors. Anywhere along this long thread of "A begot B begot C begot . . . begot me," something could have intervened to break the thread. When I think about my life from this perspective, it seems most unlikely, infinitesimally probable. But, of course, here I am. Stephen Cave (see chapter 8) captures my feeling perfectly:

> An unbroken chain of many millions of ancestors over billions of years all managed to do their bit to bring us into existence, that is our blessing. And it is an extraordinary one, involving more strokes of luck and cosmic coincidences than are possibly countable. . . .
>
> Complex life—and in particular—the life of any individual—is remarkable. Astonishing. Wondrous.[7]

I agree. We should—I should—hold a large measure of gratitude for our lives, my life. It has been—and continues to be—a huge privilege to have had—and to have—a first-person perspective on the glorious world of ours. And not just "a perspective." I have been—I am—part of this evolving chain of life.

My grandfather looked at this long chain of life and he saw something additional. He saw the power of ideals. Perhaps this starts with primitive preferences. But humans have concepts. We have ideals, and ideals can drive action. With our ideals we become agents of change. Direction emerges out of Darwinian evolution.

> Half in blind obedience to instincts that are the essential characteristics of his [humankind's] nature, and half in a semi-conscious following of a purpose, he sets out on his long journey over the centuries. . . . Through hardship and toil unspeakable, he has climbed the stairway of the centuries, and . . . today we still find ourselves climbing those same stairways, whose foundations are lost from our view in the utter darkness of the past, and whose uppermost steps are beyond the reach of our wildest

7. Cave, *Immortality*, 281.

> imagination. Yet we climb on and on, allured by the light of our radiating visions of truth, beauty and goodness, and impelled by the great power of human life.[8]

Onward we climb, learning more about our world, learning more about truth, about beauty, about goodness. And as we climb, my grandfather was buoyed by the faith—the natural faith—that we are getting somewhere, getting closer to *the* truth, to goodness, to beauty. Perhaps my grandfather would have said we are getting closer to God. The word doesn't matter so much. But to be part of this evolution, that, for my grandfather, was a kind of immortality.

3. Where Do Truth, Beauty, and Goodness Come from?

There is a story in the history of ideas, a story commonly told as I was growing into my academic career. It is a story of the de-centering of humans—the de-centering of "Man," as the story is usually told. In the ancient and medieval worlds, the earth was the center of the universe and humans were the center—or better, the apex—of life on earth. Copernicus and Galileo decentered the earth, putting it in orbit around the sun. Darwin knocked humans off the apex of life. The result is the materialist modern world we currently inhabit. This is a world where humans are one curious outcome of evolution—one of a near infinite diversity of life forms that developed out of the physical, chemical, and ultimately biochemical reactions that have evolved through natural selection over millennia.

One way of reading my grandfather is that he was working to re-center humans—specifically human ideals, aspirations, and hopes for a better world. While the materialistic universe of Copernicus, Galileo, Newton, and Darwin may be directionless, simply following materialistic laws towards no particular end, human ideals, aspirations, and hopes do aim for—presumably—desirable ends. Human actions in response to these ideals and aspirations move the world towards these—presumably—desirable ends. Humans, with their ideals, bring direction to the flow of history. Progress becomes possible. Indeed, it seems to me that there is ample evidence that progress has been made over the centuries. But clearly we still have a long road ahead of us.

8. Davis, "Inevitable Compensation" (1909d), 4–5.

The human ideals behind the pursuit of truth, beauty, and goodness are significant, powerful elements of the world. Where do they come from? I think my grandfather would have provided a deistic answer: Here is the living God, active in the ongoing lives of humans—day by day and century by century—active in the development of the universe:

> The true theist is the person who has an ideal, who is working for the things that shall be, and has faith that the universe is with him. . . . I care not by what name he may call his ideal and his hope, but in that he has faith in its reality, and gives himself to its attainment, he has made, and has, a living god.[9]

This answer may be enough. From a practical standpoint, it is enough, enough to focus our time and energy on taking steps to improve the world and to put aside niggling concerns about what this "living God" might "really be."

I can imagine speculative philosophical arguments about the evolutionary origins behind the pursuit of truth, beauty, and goodness. Knowing at least certain truths surely has survival value. Similarly, sociality has survival value, as flocking demonstrates. It is a matter of conceptualization and generalization to get from these survival values to permanent values of truth and goodness. And conceptualization and generalization—human rationality at work—itself has survival value. Beauty too.

Thus, I can imagine that these ideals are themselves the result of evolution. On this view, these ideals are not simply human ideals, but ideals that evolved into and out of life itself. My grandfather's living God is embodied in the laws of the universe, in the action of evolution. There is direction in the evolution of the universe.

Pure speculation. At best gestures toward "just so stories."

Does it matter? This is not clear to me. The idea that there is a direction to the evolution of the universe has been a powerful idea through history. Frequently enough, however, we have come up with over-narrow notions of this direction and used these notions to support implausible theories and outright evil actions. Genocides have been supported by such ideas.

There may be direction in the evolution of the universe, but we must be humble in our appreciation for what this might be. Our tools for discovery—our ways to experience the world, our instruments and methods of investigation, indeed our tools for thinking, our concepts,

9. Davis, "Is Your God Dead?" (1909j), 5.

our arguments—all are changing and developing along with our conclusions. There is always more to learn, more to learn about the world, more to learn about how we conceptualize the world, indeed, more to learn about how to learn about the world. Change remains the constant.

Towards the end of his fascinating narrative of members of the Blood family across centuries, John Kaag quotes the last paper William James wrote, "A Pluralistic Mystic." In the paper, James quoted Benjamin Blood: "Ever not quite!" wrote Blood. To which James added,

> This seems to wring the very last panting word out [of] . . . philosophy's mouth. . . . There is no complete generalization, no total point of view, no all-pervasive unity, but everywhere some residual resistance to verbalization, formulation, and discursification, some genius of reality that escapes from the pressure of the logical finger, that says, "hands off," and claims it privacy, and means to be left to its own life. In every moment of immediate experience is somewhat absolutely original and novel . . . there is no conclusion. . . . Farewell![10]

Discovery is always and ever ongoing: Ever not quite!

4. The Universal Consecration of One's Personality

I was surprised by my grandfather's view that the foundation of Christianity is found in the personality of Jesus—not in Jesus' beliefs, not in his morality, not in what he said, and certainly not in his alleged messiahship. Indeed, when I first read this, I was mystified. What could this mean? As I came to understand my grandfather's thinking better, it became clear that this ties back to how human ideals bring direction back to the evolution of the universe.

Personality—perhaps better put today, "character"—lies behind specific beliefs, deeds, moral commitments. It is what drives these beliefs etc. Specific beliefs and deeds respond to particular—historical and individual—circumstances. Behind these particularities is personality. It is one's personality that leads to one's beliefs and actions when responding to specific circumstances. And so:

> Christianity is a religion in which we are religious, not because we read a bible, but we write a bible because of the inner power of our personality. We are not the doers of good deeds, and the

10. James, "Pluralistic Mystic," quoted in Kaag, *American Bloods*, 231.

> livers of the noble life, not because some book or clericus or whatnot tell us to, but because we are dominated by the power of some ideal.[11]

As my grandfather understood him, Jesus provides us a model "heroic personality." A person committed to truth, beauty, and goodness, committed to love for his fellow humans and love for his world, but also a person of courage, independence and faith enough to stand for these ideals against a tidal wave of opposition, unto his death. Thereby Jesus initiated positive change in the world.

Jesus did not finish the job. The job is ongoing. Change is constant. And the world continues to respond to "heroic personalities"—grand and less grand—personalities that drive positive change in the natural world:

> Others have had it [Jesus' heroic character]. Their gracious and holy lives have lighted the way of human history. They have kindled fires of noble purpose in thousands of souls. They have stimulated and confirmed that greatest of all human adventures, the faith that God is, and that life has eternal meaning. That is the power of God in the human soul. It was in Christ. It is in you.[12]

As my grandfather saw things it is the combined effects of all the millions—billions—of human personalities that together drive change:

> However great the past may have been, in remote ages or in more immediate centuries, whatever of wisdom may have been gleaned from the experiences of the centuries, the startling truth faces us that we, the living and the generations to come after us, are the vital agents through which that life spirit, call it by whatever name you will, moves out of the past into the age to come.[13]

All our personalities come together to move from the past and present into the future. It can feel overwhelming, but history teaches us that it can be done, done by staying true to our ideals:

> We should face it all not with fear and despair, but in faith and confidence, buoyant in spirit, strong in purpose, keen to contribute to the age to come whatsoever of the Life Spirit dwells within each one.[14]

11. Davis, "Finality of Christianity" (1906d), 6–7.
12. Davis, "Did Christ Have the Power" (1923b), 9.
13. Davis, "Not Revelation" (1947a), 5.
14. Davis, "Not Revelation" (1947a), 5.

I never quite thought of my life in such terms, never as part of a grand, centuries-long effort to make things better. Yes, I thought I could contribute. I have always valued education and have done what I can to be a good educator: to promote and teach the joys of discovery alongside thoughtful, reflective consideration. As I've come to know myself, I am clearly a child of the Enlightenment, an advocate for the liberalism that characterizes Enlightenment thought. But I never quite saw myself as part of a millennial effort of human progress. Before reading my grandfather that would have seemed overly grand, a gargantuan overplaying of my humbler abilities.

My grandfather gives this a different reading. We should all—and always—bring humility to our efforts. But we should also all and always "contribute to the age to come whatsoever of the Life Spirit dwells within." Whether we recognize it or not, we are part of the process of creating the future. Not to aggrandize oneself—but to see oneself in the long flow of history, out of the past, into the present and towards the future—this perspective contributes meaning to life. In all our human personalities, this was where my grandfather's hope for the future, his faith in the future, lay.

5. Not Only Ideas, but Actions

As I have been writing this "Afterword" I have also been sharing earlier chapters with friends—willing, I hope interested, first readers. One response stopped me dead:

> One aspect of Davis's thinking surprises me. . . . My first-hand religious experience . . . makes ritual a key element of religious life. Creeds exist in religions, but ritual has the central role in services. A man's religious identity grows and shows from the ritual he practices. Jews sing the whole of the Torah each year-end on Simchat Torah. . . . Catholics have rituals for the sacraments—baptism, confession, communion, confirmation, marriage, holy order and extreme unction—and Mass itself is a skein of rituals. . . .
>
> Davis was, by comparison, fixated on ideas rather than practices. I was somewhat surprised you didn't take up the topic . . . since your philosophy of science is so attentive to what scientists do and the instruments they rely on when conducting

> experiments. . . . Anyway, if you look for group identities or unities in creeds or thoughts, I think it is hard to find them.[15]

Have I abandoned my own philosophical commitments, my own focus on actual practice and not just on theories and ideas? Is my grandfather himself focused on ideas and creeds—or their absence—instead of ritual and practice? Have I misrepresented my grandfather?

Many—mostly defensive—responses came to mind as I read this email. What material have I been working with? My grandfather's writings, particularly those where he was working out his thinking, *his ideas*. The texts I started with—his sermons—are only a part of the Sunday services he led. Again, ideas, not rituals. But truth be told, as religious ritual has never been a part of my life, I was not looking for ritual. I was more aware of ideas about religion, ideas that one finds in elementary philosophy texts—juvenile and primitive ideas to my mind now. I went looking for ideas, and ideas are what I found.

Towards the end of my time transcribing my grandfather's documents, I worked my way through the service notes for his time in Petersham. Here I came across plenty of evidence of ritual. Here is typical entry.[16]

15. Mike Lavin, email to the author, July 11, 2024.

16. Davis, *Sermon Notes* (1947b), sermon notes for January 5, 1947, 1.

Petersham, Mass.
Jan. 5, 1947

Service 1. Page 3 88
Litany, Page 5. 99
320

Readings:
Psalm 24
Matt. 23/27-- 39.

The Lord mighty in Battle
or the Lord of Hosts.

The conflict of the Ages.

A picture of contrasts.

The pathetic figure of Senator Bilbo

Emerson Guild in Budapest

"With God Against Hitler."

Szent Ivanyi. Jamaica Plain
Wife from Lexington Etc.

Service Notes for Sunday January 5, 1947

Like nearly every set of service notes there are readings—Ps 24 and Matt 23:37–39; there are hymns—numbers 88, 99, and 320 from the shared hymn book; there is a structure—Service 1. Page 3. Litany, Page 5. Clearly there was structure and ritual to the service.

There also is information about the sermon in these notes, "The Lord Mighty in Battle or the Lord of Hosts." But the notes can be opaque. I don't really know what my grandfather had in mind bringing together Senator Bilbo, Hitler, Szent Ivanyi, and Emerson.[17] I could speculate, but

17. Theodore G. Bilbo (1877–1947) was an American politician who twice served as governor of Mississippi (1916–20, 1928–32) and then served as US Senator from 1935 to 1947. Bilbo was an outspoken supporter of segregation and white supremacy. Alexander Szent-Ivanyi (1882–1960), Harvard STM, 1926, was a former minister in Kolozsvár. In 1947 he became deputy-bishop of the Unitarians in Hungary, responsible to a Transylvanian bishop. During World War II he worked to bring relief to refugees and prisoners in Budapest.

his full-text sermons are much clearer in their meaning and intent. And so, I have paid my closest attention to the full-text sermons. This led me away from the Sunday services with their rituals in which the sermons were embedded. It led me to my grandfather's ideas.

In a few instances even more structure was presented. Here are the service notes for May 25, 1941:[18]

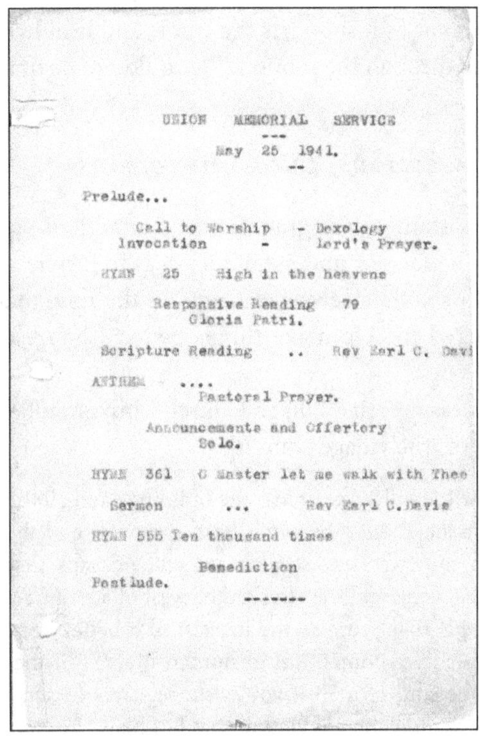

UNION MEMORIAL SERVICE

May 25 1941.

--

Prelude...

Call to Worship - Doxology
Invocation - Lord's Prayer.

HYMN 25 High in the heavens

Responsive Reading 79
Gloria Patri.

Scripture Reading .. Rev Earl C. Davi

ANTHEM ....
Pastoral Prayer.

Announcements and Offertory
Solo.

HYMN 361 O Master let me walk with Thee

Sermon ... Rev Earl C.Davis

HYMN 555 Ten thousand times

Benediction
Postlude.

Service Notes for Sunday May 25, 1941

These notes provide a clear agenda: Prelude—Call to Worship—Doxology—Invocation—Hymn 25—Responsive reading—Gloria Patri—Scripture reading by Rev. Earl C. Davis—etc. Part of the reason for the more detailed agenda is that this was a shared—or "Union"—service bringing together both Petersham congregational churches, the "North Church" and my grandfather's church, "the First Congregational

18. Davis, *Sermon Notes* (1941), sermon notes for May 25, 1941, 1.

Parish."[19] It was necessary for the two churches to be clear with each other who was doing what when.

So, the ideas in my grandfather's sermons were only one element of the Sunday services he presided over. Having noted the fact of these Sunday service rituals, I am also aware that these Unitarian rituals are pale and loose reflections of their pre-Reformation Catholic origins. I think for my grandfather, this is as it should be: Not forms but the Holy Spirit. Ritual is fine insofar as it supports the whole and healthy life. Empty ritual—just "going through the motions"—would not be of interest to him.

6. Not Only Actions, but Connections

Ideas were important to my grandfather. But actions spoke louder for him. His goal—so far as I understand it—was to inspire members of his congregation to see themselves as agents in the long march of history, agents empowered to help make things better. Change comes through action.

In a 1944 essay, "The Village Church," my grandfather shared his understanding of "the village church":

> Somehow the village church—the buildings and all the imponderable associations—becomes both a symbol and the witness of a faith, imperfect and somewhat vague perhaps, that our human lives, even amid the wrecked harvest of a tragic era, are the fertile seeds that promise the harvest of a better age to come. This irresistible momentum of human life, call it the spirit of God in the soul of man if you wish, registers in some human lives as a compelling conviction that has been the cloud by day and the pillar of fire by night in the long trek through history.
>
> The primary function of the village church, as indeed of all churches, is to be aware of this quality in human life, to understand its meaning, to stimulate its development in the lives of persons and in the community. This is the essential

19. There is an interesting history behind these two churches. The "First Congregational Church," originally called the "Church of Christ in Petersham," was established in 1735 shortly after the town was settled. In 1819, Reverend Luther Willson (1783–1864) was called to the ministry of this church. Willson was a religious liberal, who among other things referred to Jesus as "the son of God" and not "God, the son." Willson's liberal theology prompted a schism in the congregation and in 1823 about twenty congregants left the church to form the "Orthodox Congregational Church" otherwise known as the "North Church." Willson retired from his ministry in 1834, but he continued to reside in Petersham until his death.

> soul of a church, and it cannot be sacrificed for the advantages of the hour.[20]

The primary function of the village church—or any church—was to be found in the degree to which the church instilled what my grandfather here called "the spirit of God in the soul of man." It was about helping people to see themselves as part of the long progressive development of life, helping them to take a part in making things better for future generations. Action for a better world was the goal.

Ideas may support this function of a church, but ideas are instrumental. Perhaps more powerful than ideas are the forces of fellowship.[21] After defining the function of a church, Davis asked how effectively village churches are achieving this function. In response, he wrote,

> In addition to the imponderable changes that the war is producing we feel in a very intimate way the impact of those forces upon persons and homes: ten per cent of the population in service; forty names of men and women on the Honor Roll of one village church; almost every available man and woman at work in factories. "Lloyd was in the battle of Bougainville;" "Roger is in Italy;" "Horace sent a cable from England;" "Arthur is in Alaska;" "Charles received a D.S.C. in New Guinea;" "Herbert goes tomorrow"—members of the village church; they sang in the choir, went to the church school, danced at the socials. They are our boys—flesh of our flesh, spirit of our spirit.[22]

It is through a collection of human relationships that the church can achieve—or fail to achieve—its goal.

Davis concluded his 1944 essay,

> Why do young people want to stand alone in the village church to be married by its minister? Why do they bring their children from distant cities to be christened? Why do boys who are going into the Marines and Navy shyly express a desire to become a member of the village church? The thoughts of youth are long, long thoughts. One suspects that here are the vital seeds of the

20. Davis, "Village Church" (1944), 92. Also note Davis's borrowing from Exod 13:21–22, "the cloud by day and the pillar of fire by night."

21. While I am here attending to Davis's 1944 essay, it is worth noting that the first sermon he ever gave, July 21, 1901, before he had entered Harvard Divinity School, was on "The Church as a Social Institution." See Davis (1901).

22. Davis, "Village Church" (1944), 92. Note, the "DSC" is the "Distinguished Service Cross"; it is rated just below the Medal of Honor and is given for extraordinary bravery.

> great tradition planted in the good soil of youth. As one gets the comeback from conducting services of public worship year in and year out, one cannot escape the conviction that here . . . is the vital seed of promise that lifts the life of the individual to the plane of its universal consecration. The integrity of individuals so touched . . . are the seeds of promise, even in a war-torn world. To this the village church bears witness.[23]

He wrote this essay in a time of extreme darkness, before D-Day, before the liberation of Rome, during a time when the intensity, the horror and the uncertainty of the war were at their peaks. During this time, Davis observed that people wanted hope, they wanted to believe in the possibility of progress. Here was the kernel of "the seeds of promise, even in a war-torn world."

Mike Lavin, my reader who prompted this reevaluation of my focus on my grandfather's ideas, shared this with me:

> I do, as an aside, think it has proved much harder for non-denominational Christians to attain and retain distinctive identities than it is for groups that are ritual heavy. In fact, in my dark moments, I think it is hard for groups without strong identities to mobilize and stay mobilized for community action.[24]

Much as I want to resist this idea, I think there is a significant amount of truth in what Lavin writes here. It is psychologically much easier to identify with a tribe that is ritual heavy; the rituals help to establish the tribe's coherence and shared identity. And it is then easier to mobilize for action, action that supports tribal goals.

It is harder to support a broader identification with the Enlightenment notion of "humanity." This was the aspiration of the various post-World War II institutional efforts, the United Nations (1945), the Universal Declaration of Human Rights (1948), the Geneva Conventions on warfare (1949), etc. While there is no question that these institutions and efforts have been significant, indeed transformational, they have not erased the power of more tribal identities. If anything, tribal power is ascendant in our current time.

Shortly after I finished a draft of this chapter I began "clean-up work" with the manuscripts I inherited from my grandfather. I had—I thought—worked my way through all the complete manuscripts. What

23. Davis, "Village Church" (1944), 93.

24. Mike Lavin, email to the author, July 16, 2024.

was left was a collection of perhaps seventy-five individual sheets that had gotten lost from their full manuscripts. "Orphans," I called them. As I began to work with the orphans I discovered to my surprise and joy that four orphan sheets that had been separated were in fact together a full sermon, "God and My Neighbor," delivered at the Church of Our Father in Lancaster, Pennsylvania, on September 21, 1919. This likely was the first sermon Davis preached there as minister.

The sermon speaks to exactly what I had been—and am now—writing about. Davis urged the members of his congregation to get to know their neighbors. History shows, he argued, that sometimes the people least admired at the time turn out to be the most interesting or important. They turn out to be the people with the most to offer. Jesus and John the Baptist were his examples. Why do we turn away from people? Davis wrote,

> The trouble is that we do not meet men as men. We meet them as types, as classes, and groups. "Do you know your neighbor," you are asked. "No, I do not. He does not interest me. He is not associated with the people whom I know. In fact, I do not think he amounts to much. I do not care to know him." But he is just an ordinary man. The associates are accidental. . . . All of us are human under our skins.[25]

In keeping with the pantheism I have attributed to Davis, he told his congregation that getting to know your neighbor was getting to know God:

> The essence of all this is the simple truth that the revelation of God in our times is in and through those very people whom we call neighbors. What we learn of our neighbor is just so much knowledge of God. All the knowledge we have of God is through this common experience of life in the interchange of human experience. . . .
>
> God and my neighbor are pretty much one and the same thing. If I do not know my neighbor whom I have seen, I certainly cannot know God who dwells in my neighbor.[26]

25. Davis, "God and My Neighbor" (1919d), 2. It is perhaps worth noting that getting to know his neighbors was exactly what Davis had to do, arriving as he was, as the new minister in a town far from his New England roots.

26. Davis, "God and My Neighbor" (1919d), 3.

6. Earl Clement Davis, Annie Foster Davis

Earl Clement and Annie Foster Davis got to know their neighbors. They were deeply embedded in the communities in which they lived. If I focus only on their time in Petersham, I find that Earl C. Davis was:

- President of the Petersham Village Improvement Society
- President of the Petersham Memorial Library
- President of the Petersham Handicraft Society
- Chairman of the Petersham Branch of the National War Fund Council
- Member of the Petersham Farm War Council
- Member of the Petersham Timber Salvage Committee

He was deeply and extensively engaged in the life of the village. Prior to his time in Petersham he was also actively engaged in the civic life of the various communities he lived in, including his socialist political activism in Pittsfield, Massachusetts, during the early years of the twentieth century.

It has been a great joy to get to know my grandparents, to know them as real dimensional people, dealing with the world as they found it. Most of my resources—principally my grandfather's writings—do not speak to more personal elements of their lives. But there are some clues.

My grandfather was an avid gardener, who each year planted and tended a large vegetable garden.

Earl Clement Davis and his Petersham garden

I have been told—although I have no way to verify this—that my grandparents helped to feed their village with their garden during the Depression. He took many lessons from his garden and the natural life cycles in which it partook. These lessons appear repeatedly in his sermons.

Farming and gardening was the primary metaphor—or is it a metaphor?—behind his essay on "The Village Church." The fact that villagers lived "close to the land" provided them vital insight into life:

> We may not know much about "The Sovereignty of God" and we may be a little careless in our use of language, but we have learned much by living so close to the land. On our farms and in our gardens we have shared in the productive process of nature. We have learned that we live in the midst of powerful and constant forces. We have learned that we may work with them, and, to a small degree, may come to understand them, but that we cannot escape their exacting standards. Either by the way of education and training or by the "hard way" we know that "The Will" of those forces must be discovered and obeyed or we perish.
>
> We meditate upon this exacting process of which human beings are at once products and transmitting agents—first the

> blade, then the ear, and then the fertile grain in the ear. Just how we may not know, but the fertile fruit of the past contains the promise of harvests to come.[27]

And so, he concluded his 1944 essay speaking of the "long, long thoughts" of the youth of that time. Here he found the "seeds of promise" in a war-torn world.

My grandfather was also an avid woodworker. One of my most valued possessions is a footstool he made for my grandmother, Christmas 1933.

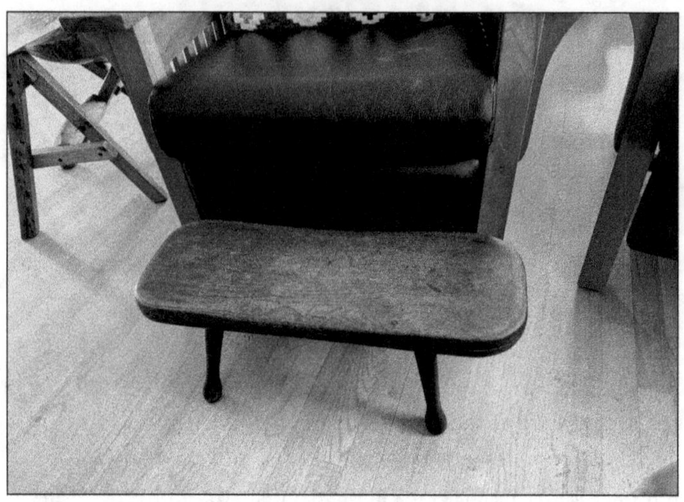

A footstool made by Earl C. Davis, given to his wife, Annie F. Davis, Christmas, 1933

Turning the stool over there is a message.

27. Davis, "Village Church" (1944), 92.

The underside of the footstool with note

"A.F.D."—Annie Foster Davis—"Xmas 1933"—and a curious code: "I•II•III•III•II•I." Years ago, I learned from my mother that this was my grandparents' private code for "I love you; you love me."

My grandmother was a weaver. I have quite vivid memories from my time as a child of a massive and endlessly fascinating loom—that I was not to mess about with! It came with her when she moved in with my family after her husband died.

Annie F. Davis at work at her loom

I noted above that my grandfather was president of the Petersham Handicraft Society. In fact, he founded this society during the Depression. It was, he thought, a way for community members to earn some additional income, and both he and his wife were very active in their crafts—woodworking and weaving—as ways to generate additional income.

After my mother died in 1987, my sister Brinna managed to rescue several items that our grandmother had kept when she moved from Petersham. These included a large salt crystal and a tiny stuffed bear, which I am told sat together on my grandfather's desk.

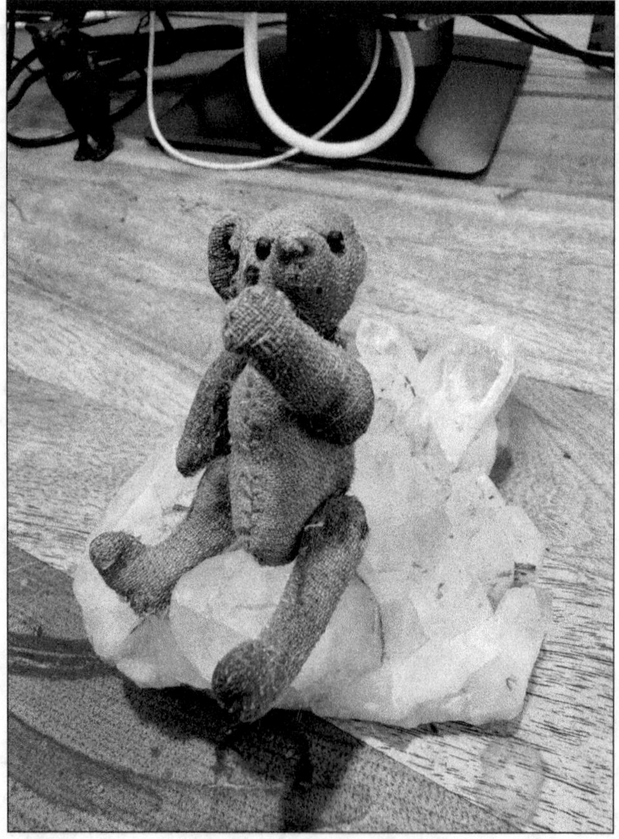

Earl C. Davis's teddy bear on his salt crystal—as it was on his desk

One can see here—or I can see here—my grandfather's love of the natural world with its curious mixture of chaos and order. But also, just his love—saving what was a small handmade stuffed bear from his youth. They now sit in front of my computer screen.

My sister also rescued a letter basket filled with my grandmother's memorabilia of a lifetime.

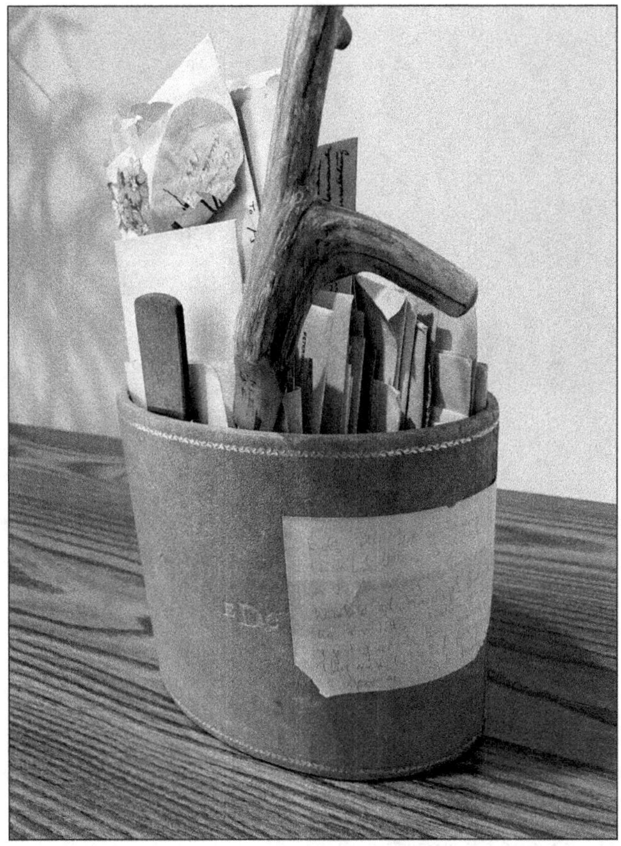

Earl C. Davis's letterbox as left by his widow, Annie F. Davis, with the mementos of her life

These were left largely undisturbed from the time of my grandmother's death in 1964 until I pulled them out of the basket and began to inventory and appreciate the items my grandmother saved. The contents go back to an 1890 letter that my grandmother's mother wrote to her. There were numerous birthday and Christmas epistles that my grandfather wrote to my grandmother. There were letters and other memorabilia from her children, including an arithmetic exercise done by my mother as a child:

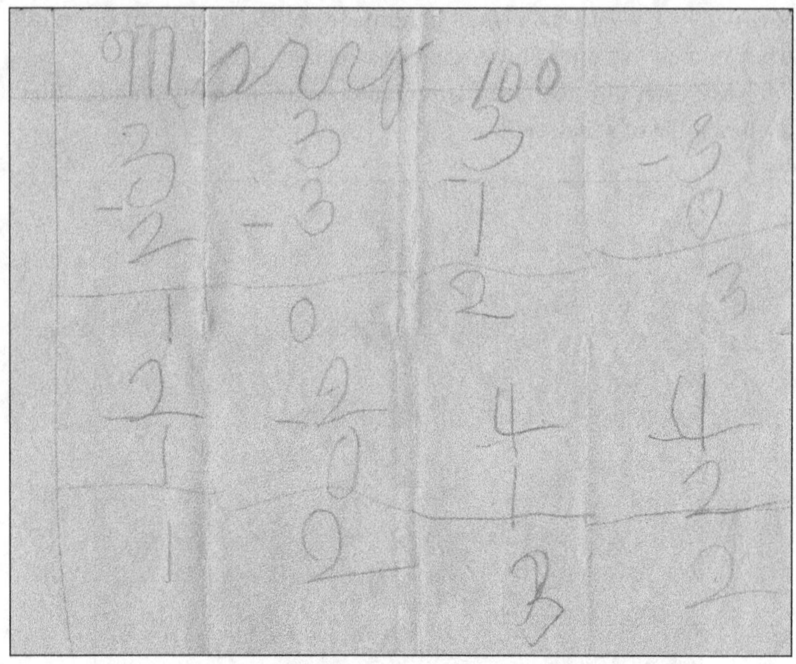

Arithmetic homework by Mary W. Davis—the author's mother—
saved by her mother, Annie F. Davis

How amazing to see evidence of my long-dead mother's efforts as a child to master elementary arithmetic. I found here a powerful sense of the seasons of life—my grandparents' lives, my parents' lives, my life.

What emerges most powerfully from these mementos is the depth of my grandfather's love of my grandmother. Numerous letters, notes and hand-crafted cards attest to this. Let me touch on three, one early, one mid-marriage, one towards the end.

First is a letter my grandfather wrote my grandmother on June 22, 1905, three days before they were married. The letter begins:

> Dearest,
>
> It was many letters ago that we first began to write these little love messages that have carried so much comfort and happiness. The first letter of that sweet happy period of betrothal I began with "dearest," I begin this last one with the same word. . . . It seemed then as if I were saying all that life and love could say. But tonight, I can see the almost infinite growth. The presence of a power and a sweetness in life tonight, such as I did

> not and could not know then, and the almost infinite vista of hope and vision that is stretching out before us beckoning us to follow its lead into the unknown seems to say, "without end." Out of the fulness of my heart I am going to preach Sunday on the subject, "Without End."[28]

Unfortunately, Davis's sermon, "Without End," did not make it into the trunk.

Thirty-one years later my grandfather wrote a birthday letter to his wife:

> My own dearest sweetheart,
>
> Last night while you were asleep, cuddled up to me, I had one of the gloriously happy moments of life in thinking over the throws of the shuttle that you have made in weaving the pattern whose design and texture Mary [their daughter, my mother] so well described in her letter. Not quite because you paddle a canoe in good form, or can walk on the seashore with understanding, or because the smile of your childbirth pains still haunts me as with a divine beauty, or because you have been so wise in selecting your children, or because of [the] thousand and one things that you have done; or even because you do not sidestep but see things straight and face them, and your children see in your dependable and understanding character, but back of it all is a personality of dignity, or strength, integrity, and charm. So, because you are you, I love you, and because you have always been you, I respect and admire you. And because I respect, admire and love you, I gain for myself a certain hope that in a measure I may have become like unto her whom I and my children love.[29]

The letter Davis mentioned "from Mary" also survives. There, among other things, Mary W. Davis, age twenty-one and about to graduate from Smith College, wrote,

> I think we were pretty darn lucky to have a mother as fine as you are. Perhaps what we admire you the most for is your clear thinking, and straight outlook on life—you face things and work them out without side-stepping.[30]

28. Davis (1905b), Letter from Earl C. Davis to Annie F. Dodge, June 22, 1905.

29. Davis (1936a), Birthday note from Earl C. Davis to Annie F. Davis, May 6, 1936.

30. Davis (1936b), Birthday letter from Mary W. Davis to Annie F. Davis, May 6, 1936.

And finally, another sixteen years further on, another birthday note. As this birthday note from May 1952 makes clear, sometime during the previous year my grandfather was diagnosed with—and treated for—a serious illness. He wrote his wife of forty-seven years:

> Many happy returns of the day to:
>
> 1. My most attractive scholar.
> 2. My partner in the "minuet of life."
> 3. My canoe-mate.
> 4. My wonderful wife.
> 5. My adored mother of four well-brought up children.
> 6. My wife who is adored by her lovely grandchildren.
> 7. My best cook.
> 8. My best nurse.
> 9. My beloved dictator.
> 10. My chauffeur
> 11. My companion of many years.
> 12. My reason for coming through the events of 1952.
>
> Twelve reasons why you are to me, as to many, one of the great women of the years through which we have lived.
>
> The patient. The parson. E. C. D.[31]

I have never known the details of my grandfather's final illness. I know he died of intestinal cancer. Clearly, his wife, my grandmother, had had to take the burden of care—cooking, nursing, driving for him.

On January 1, 1953, my grandfather wrote to the American Unitarian Association resigning his Petersham ministry effective August 16, when he would have completed twenty years as minister in Petersham. At this point he was dictating his letters to be handwritten by his wife.

He did not make it to August, dying on May 19, 1953. His good friend, Charles E. Park—Ed Park, retired minister of the First Church in Boston—spoke at his funeral service on May 21:

> What Emerson said of Abraham Lincoln is another of those sayings we think of in connection with Mr. Davis: His heart was as wide as the world, but there was no room in it for a single unkind thought. And the consequence was that he habitually

31. Davis (1952), Birthday note from Earl C. Davis to Annie F. Davis, May 6, 1952.

> lived in a world that was peopled by noble women, and by men for whom he had his favorite expression, royal good fellow . . .
>
> Just by being himself, in Petersham, Mr. Davis made the whole town a better, a sweeter, a happier place. . . .
>
> He was as clear as crystal. His mercy was as plain as the day. His honor was as hard as stone. . . .
>
> For twenty years Petersham has enjoyed the ennobling experience of being loved by one who was true to his God, and true to his fellowmen, and true to himself.[32]

Annie F. Davis and Earl C. Davis, Petersham, early 1950s

A few years earlier in his 1947 sermon, "Not Revelation but Discovery; Not Forms but the Holy Spirit" my grandfather wrote:

> In my yard stands a noble white Ash tree, sometimes called the Tree of Heaven. Two feet in diameter at the base, planted about 1875 by a former minister on the day a child was born in his

32. Park, "Eulogy for Earl C. Davis," 7–9.

> family. . . . Under its shade we sit on a summer's day. Children climb its drooping branches, and laugh as they swing. . . . In fertile years it produces a crop of flowers and seeds. Not far from half a million seeds cling to its branches. Ash trees, years younger, grow about the place. All of this life presses forward to the prize of its high calling in the forests of the world. But the day will come when this noble ash tree will have rounded the years of its living process. The Life Force will no longer flow through branches. It will be cut down, worked up into lumber and wood. If could speak it might, say "I have run my course, I am content. My life still lives on in the forests to come."[33]

I imagine my grandfather writing this—age 71—mindful of his own mortality. And indeed, his life still lives on in all the people he touched, his fecund family, his writings. However, improbably, it has lived on in me.

33. Davis, "Not Revelation" (1947a), 3–4.

References

Earl C. Davis Archives

1893–1953. "Earl Clement Davis Papers." Robert H. Goddard Library Digital Commons. https://commons.clarku.edu/earl_davis/.

1901. "The Church as a Social Institution." https://commons.clarku.edu/sermons_-1902/1/.

1903a. "Sermons I: The Leadership of Jesus." https://commons.clarku.edu/education/8/.

1903b. "Philosophy V: The Country Manufacturing Plant; A Solution of One Aspect of Housing the Poor." https://commons.clarku.edu/education/9/.

1904a. "A Prophet of Democracy." https://commons.clarku.edu/education/2/.

1904b. "The Modern Pioneer." https://commons.clarku.edu/sermons_1902_04/8/.

1904c. "Man's Responsibility." https://commons.clarku.edu/sermons_1902_04/9/.

1905a. "A Plea for the Principle of a Creedless Church." https://commons.clarku.edu/pittsfield_sermons/2/.

1905b. Letter from Earl C. Davis to Annie F. Davis. June 22, 1905. Unpublished letter.

1905c. "Origins of Modern Religion, Modern Charity and Modern Labor Problems." https://commons.clarku.edu/history_manuscripts_1/.

1906a. "Rise and Development of the Congregational Polity and Spirit." https://commons.clarku.edu/history_manuscripts_2/.

1906b. "Temptation." https://commons.clarku.edu/pittsfield_sermons/25/.

1906c. "Abraham Lincoln and the Needs of the Times." https://commons.clarku.edu/pittsfield_sermons/1/.

1906d. "The Finality of Christianity." https://commons.clarku.edu/pittsfield_sermons/19/.

1906e. "Growth and Salvation." https://commons.clarku.edu/pittsfield_sermons/3/.

1906f. "Industrial Cooperation." https://commons.clarku.edu/pittsfield_manuscripts/16/.

1908a. "The Religion of Humanity." https://commons.clarku.edu/pittsfield_sermons/94/.

1908b. "The Significance of Count Tolstoi." https://commons.clarku.edu/pittsfield_manuscripts/22/.

1908c. "The Moral Significance of the Evolution of Religious Faith: From the Idea of God as an Occasional Visitor, to the Idea of God as the Indwelling Goodwill." https://commons.clarku.edu/pittsfield_sermons/85/.

1908d. "The Bearing of Burdens." https://wordpress.clarku.edu/dbaird/the-bearing-of-burdens-july-19-1908/.

1908e. "The Need for Extending More Rational Methods in Dealing with the Small Offenders Against the Social Order." https://commons.clarku.edu/pittsfield_sermons/88/.

1908f. "Practical Politics and Civic Righteousness." https://commons.clarku.edu/pittsfield_sermons/64/.

1908g. "The Social Unrest." https://commons.clarku.edu/pittsfield_manuscripts/21/.

1908h. "Record of Experience of a Psychic Phenomenon." https://commons.clarku.edu/pittsfield_manuscripts/3/.

1909a. "The Travail and Pain of Human Life: What Can it Mean?" https://commons.clarku.edu/pittsfield_sermons/99/.

1909b. "Two Great Principles of the Modern World." https://commons.clarku.edu/pittsfield_sermons/92/.

1909c. "The Adventurous Task of the Church." https://commons.clarku.edu/pittsfield_sermons/69/.

1909d. "The Inevitable Compensation of Thought and Conduct." https://commons.clarku.edu/pittsfield_sermons/80/.

1909e. "The Value and the Limitations of Allegiance to Religious Leaders." https://commons.clarku.edu/pittsfield_sermons/101/.

1909f. "Our Debt to Thomas Paine." https://commons.clarku.edu/pittsfield_sermons/61/.

1909g. "John Brown and the Passion for Justice." https://commons.clarku.edu/pittsfield_sermons/56/.

1909h. "The Making of Reality." https://commons.clarku.edu/pittsfield_sermons/83/.

1909i. "What to Do." https://commons.clarku.edu/pittsfield_sermons/89/.

1909j. "Is Your God Dead?" https://commons.clarku.edu/pittsfield_sermons/54/.

1909k. "The Individual and Society." https://commons.clarku.edu/pittsfield_sermons/79/.

1910a. "Socialism: A Reply to the Common Assertion That the Socialist Movement is Atheistic, Irreligious, and a Menace to the Family." https://commons.clarku.edu/pittsfield_manuscripts/39/.

1910b. "The Democracy of the Bible." https://commons.clarku.edu/pittsfield_sermons/75/.

1910c. "The Social Unrest." https://commons.clarku.edu/pittsfield_manuscripts/21/.

1910d. "Is There Any Sense in Praying?" https://commons.clarku.edu/pittsfield_sermons/53/.

1910e. "The Democracy of God." https://commons.clarku.edu/pittsfield_sermons/74/.

1910f. "The Social Ideal of the Modern World." https://commons.clarku.edu/pittsfield_manuscripts/31/.

1910g. "The Churches and Socialism." https://commons.clarku.edu/pittsfield_manuscripts/30/.

1910h. "The Class Struggle." https://commons.clarku.edu/pittsfield_manuscripts/27/.

1910i. "Churches for Truth and Justice." https://commons.clarku.edu/pittsfield_manuscripts/25/.

1911a. "The Demands of the New Year." https://commons.clarku.edu/pittsfield_sermons/73/.

1911b. "The Essence of Manhood." https://commons.clarku.edu/pittsfield_sermons/77/.

1912. "Socialism." https://commons.clarku.edu/pittsfield_manuscripts/32/.

1913a. "The Influence of Democracy on Religious Thought and Practice." *Christian Register* 92, Oct. 9, 1913, 970–73. See also https://commons.clarku.edu/pittsfield_sermons/81/.

1913b. "Review of 'The Introduction of Androcles and the Lion' by George Bernard Shaw." https://commons.clarku.edu/pittsfield_manuscripts/8/.

1914. "The New Era." https://commons.clarku.edu/pittsfield_sermons/11/.

1916a. *The Origins and History of the Bible.* https://commons.clarku.edu/origin_bible/.

1916b. "The Other End of a Shad Dinner." https://commons.clarku.edu/pittsfield_manuscripts/9/.

1916c. "The Dream of a Christmas Shopper." https://commons.clarku.edu/pittsfield_manuscripts/33/.

1917a. "The Church as Fellowship for Common Purpose." https://commons.clarku.edu/pittsfield_sermons/71/.

1917b. "A Sermon on Patriotism." https://commons.clarku.edu/pittsfield_sermons/43/.

1918a. "The Great Tradition Becomes the Great Faith." https://commons.clarku.edu/pittsfield_sermons/13/.

1918b. "Democracy and Socialism." https://commons.clarku.edu/pittsfield_sermons/31/.

1918c. "Peace Service Sermon: A Dynamic Peace." https://commons.clarku.edu/pittsfield_sermons/14/.

1918d. "The Significance of Labor Strikes from the Point of View of Evolution of Religion." https://commons.clarku.edu/pittsfield_manuscripts/34/.

1918e. "Religion in Life and in Reality." https://commons.clarku.edu/pittsfield_sermons/30/.

1919a. "Channing, the Apostle of Liberty." https://commons.clarku.edu/pittsfield_sermons/15/.

1919b. "Five Months at Camp Devens." https://commons.clarku.edu/pittsfield_manuscripts/12/.

1919c. "The Strike of the General Electric Company Employees." https://commons.clarku.edu/pittsfield_manuscripts/10/.

1919d. "God and My Neighbor." https://commons.clarku.edu/lancaster_sermons/17/.

191Xa. "The Thirst for a *Living* God." https://commons.clarku.edu/pittsfield_sermons/35/.

191Xb. "Sermon on Labor." https://commons.clarku.edu/pittsfield_sermons/34/.

1920. "Notes on Everett Dean Martin, *The Behavior of Crowds*." https://commons.clarku.edu/lancaster_manuscripts/6/.

1922. "The Essential Christ." https://commons.clarku.edu/lancaster_sermons/5/.

1923a. "The Need for a Spirit of Broad Fellowship. What Shall We Do with the Heretics?" https://commons.clarku.edu/lancaster_sermons/6/.

1923b. "Did Christ Have the Power of God?" https://commons.clarku.edu/lancaster_sermons/7/.

192X. "Will a Belief in Immortality Survive?" https://commons.clarku.edu/lancaster_sermons/10/.

1931. "The Results of Protestantism." https://commons.clarku.edu/concord_manuscripts/2/.

1932. "Alumni Tribute." In *In Memoriam: William Wallace Fenn, 1862–1932*, 33–38. Cambridge: Theological School in Harvard University, 1932.

1936a. Birthday note from Earl C. Davis to Annie F. Davis, May 6, 1936. Unpublished letter.

1936b. Birthday letter from Mary W. Davis to Annie F. Davis, May 6, 1936. Unpublished letter.

1941. *Sermon Notes*. https://commons.clarku.edu/petersham_sermons/9/.

1942a. "From Copernicus to Galileo." https://commons.clarku.edu/petersham_sermons/2/.

1942b. "Remarks at Tenth Anniversary." https://commons.clarku.edu/petersham_sermons/1/.

1944. "The Village Church." *Christian Register, Unitarian* 123:3, Mar. 1944, 92. See also https://commons.clarku.edu/petersham_publications/5/.

1947a. "Not Revelation but Discovery; Not Forms but the Holy Spirit." https://commons.clarku.edu/petersham_sermons/4/.

1947b. *Sermon Notes*. https://commons.clarku.edu/petersham_sermons/7/.

1950. Letter from Earl C. Davis to his grandson, Jock Davis, Mar. 2, 1950. Unpublished letter.

1952. Birthday note from Earl C. Davis to Annie F. Davis, May 6, 1952. Unpublished letter.

No Date-a. "Permanent Characteristics of Liberal Religion." https://commons.clarku.edu/pittsfield_manuscripts/17/.

No Date-b. "The Ethical Aspect of Socialism." https://commons.clarku.edu/pittsfield_manuscripts/15/.

Davis, Earl C., and Carl H. Kopf. 1936. "Democracy Versus Authority in Church (and State)." https://commons.clarku.edu/petersham_manuscripts/4/.

Works Consulted

Alexander, Eben. *Proof of Heaven: A Neurosurgeon's Journey into the Afterlife*. New York: Simon and Schuster, 2012.

"American Eugenics Society." Wikipedia. https://en.wikipedia.org/wiki/American_Eugenics_Society.

Ames, Charles Gordon. *Five Points of Faith*, Boston: George H. Ellis Co., 1903.

———. *Sermons of Sunrise*. Boston: George H. Ellis Co., 1901.

"Anthropocene." Wikipedia. https://en.wikipedia.org/wiki/Anthropocene.

Armstrong, Karen. *A History of God*. New York: Ballantine, 1993.

Aslan, Reza. *God: A Human History*. New York: Random House, 2017.

———. *Zealot: The Life and Times of Jesus of Nazareth*. New York: Random House, 2013.

Baird, Davis. "Histories of Baird Associates." In *From Classical to Modern Chemistry: The Instrumental Revolution*, edited by Peter Morris, 129–48. London: National Museum of Science and Industry, 2002.

———. *Thing Knowledge: A Philosophy of Scientific Instruments*. Berkeley: University of California Press, 2004.

———. "Earl Clement Davis." Davis Baird: Philosophy Pages, 2022. https://wordpress.clarku.edu/dbaird/home/earl-clement-davis-pages/.

———. "My TIA." Davis Baird: Philosophy Pages, Jan. 29, 2024. https://wordpress.clarku.edu/dbaird/essays/.

Baird, Davis, et al., eds. *Heinrich Hertz: Classical Physicist, Modern Philosopher.* Boston Studies in the Philosophy and History of Science. Dordrecht: Springer Books, 1997.

Baird, Davis, and Ashley Shew. "Probing the History of Scanning Tunneling Microscopy." In *Discovering the Nanoscale*, edited by Davis Baird et al., 145–56. Amsterdam: IOS Press, 2004.

Brooks, David. "The Canadian Way of Death." *Atlantic Monthly*, June 2023, 84–96.

Burge, Ryan. *The Nones: Where They Came From, Who They Are, and Where They Are Going.* 2nd ed. Minneapolis: Fortress, 2023.

Capps, John. "The Pragmatic Theory of Truth." *Stanford Encyclopedia of Philosophy*, May 22, 2023. https://plato.stanford.edu/entries/truth-pragmatic/.

Cave, Stephen. *Immortality: The Quest to Live Forever and How It Drives Civilization.* New York: Crown, 2012.

Channing, William Ellery. "Introductory Remarks." In *The Complete Works of William Ellery Channing Including the Perfect Life*, 57–64. London: Routledge & Sons, 1884.

Chesterton, G. K. *Orthodoxy.* London and New York: John Lane, 1908.

Church, Forest. *The American Creed: A Spiritual and Patriotic Primer* New York: St. Martin's, 2002.

Darwin, Charles. *On the Origin of Species: By Means of Natural Selection by the Preservation of Favored Races in the Struggle for Life.* London: John Murray, 1859.

Descartes, René. *Meditations on First Philosophy*. 1641. Translated by Michael Moriarty, Oxford: Oxford University Press, 2008.

Dewey, John. "The Ethics of Democracy." In Menand, *Pragmatism*, 182–204.

Dexter, Henry Martyn. *The Congregationalism of the Last Three Hundred Years.* Boston: Thomas Todd Congregational House, 1880.

Douthat, Ross. "The Americanization of Religion." *New York Times*, Dec. 21, 2022. https://www.nytimes.com/2022/12/21/opinion/america-religion-christianity.html.

———. *Bad Religion: How We Became a Nation of Heretics.* New York: Free Press, 2012.

Ehrman, Bart. *Misquoting Jesus: The Story Behind Who Changed the Bible and Why.* New York: HarperCollins, 2005.

Foster, George Burman. *The Finality of the Christian Religion.* Chicago: University of Chicago Press, 1906.

French, David. "'Shiny Happy People': Fundamentalism and the Toxic Quest for Certainty." *New York Times*, June 13, 2023. https://www.nytimes.com/2023/06/13/opinion/shiny-happy-people.html.

Friedman, Thomas. *The World Is Flat: A Brief History of the Twenty-First Century.* New York: Farrar, Straus and Giroux, 2005.

Goff, Philip. *Why? The Purpose of the Universe.* Oxford: Oxford University Press, 2023.

Gregory, Caspar René. *Canon and Text of the New Testament.* New York: Charles Scribner's Sons, 1907.

Grose, Jessica. "What Churches Offer That 'Nones' Still Long For." *New York Times*, June 28, 2023. https://www.nytimes.com/2023/06/28/opinion/religion-affiliation-community.html.

Hacking, Ian. *Representing and Intervening.* Cambridge: Cambridge University Press, 1983.

Hertz, Heinrich. *Principles of Mechanics.* 1899. Translated by D. E. Jones and J. T. Walley. Whitefish, MT: Kessinger, 2010.

Hobbes, Thomas. *Leviathan.* 1651. New York: Penguin Classics, 2017.

Hochschild, Adam. *American Midnight: The Great War, a Violent Peace, and Democracy's Forgotten Crisis.* New York: Mariner, 2022.

Huneven, Michelle. *Search: A Novel.* New York: Penguin, 2022.

Hunting, Harold B. *The Story of Our Bible: How It Grew to Be What It Is.* New York: Charles Scribner's Sons, 1915.

Hyde, Lewis. *The Gift: Creativity and the Artist in the Modern World.* New York: Vintage, 1979.

James, Montague Rhodes. *The Apocryphal New Testament.* Oxford: Oxford University Press, 1924.

James, William. "The Pluralistic Mystic." *Hibbert Journal* 8 (1910) 739–59.

———. *A Pluralistic Universe: Hibbert Lectures at Manchester College on the Present Situation in Philosophy.* London: Longmans, Green and Co., 1909

———. "Pragmatism's Conception of Truth." *Journal of Philosophy* 4:6 (1907) 141–55.

———. *The Varieties of Religious Experience.* New York: Longmans, Green and Co, 1905.

———. "The Will to Believe." *The New World*, June 1896, 327–47. Repr. in James, *Will to Believe*, 1–31; Menand, *Pragmatism*, 69–92.

———. *The Will to Believe and Other Essays in Popular Philosophy.* New York: Longmans, Green and Co., 1897

"The Jetsons." Wikipedia. https://en.wikipedia.org/wiki/The_Jetsons.

Kaag, John. *American Bloods: The Untamed Dynasty That Shaped a Nation.* New York: Farrar, Straus and Giroux, 2024.

———. *Sick Souls, Healthy Minds: How William James Can Save Your Life.* Princeton: Princeton University Press, 2020.

Kant, Immanuel. *Groundwork of the Metaphysics of Morals.* 1785. Translated by James W. Ellington. Indianapolis: Hackett, 1993.

———. *Critique of Practical Reason.* 1788. Translated by Mary Gregor. Cambridge: Cambridge University Press, 2015.

Kuhn, Thomas. *The Structure of Scientific Revolutions.* 50th anniversary ed. Chicago: University of Chicago Press, 2012.

Kurzweil, Ray. *The Singularity Is Nearer: When We Merge with AI.* New York: Viking, 2024.

Kurzweil, Ray, and Terry Grossman. *Fantastic Voyage: Live Long Enough to Live Forever.* New York: Rodale, 2004.

Lakatos, Imre. *The Methodology of Scientific Research Programmes, Philosophical Papers.* Vol. 1. Edited by John Worrall and Gregory Currie. Cambridge: Cambridge University Press, 1978.

Lippmann, Walter. *Drift and Mastery.* 1914. Madison: University of Wisconsin Press, 1985.

Martin, Everett Dean. *The Behavior of Crowds.* New York: Harper & Brothers, 1920.

Menand, Louis, ed. *Pragmatism: A Reader.* New York: Vintage Books, 1997.

Miller, Perry. *The New England Mind: The Seventeenth Century.* Ann Arbor: University of Michigan Press, 1939.

Nolan, Albert. *Jesus Before Christianity*. New York: Orbis, 1976.

Park, Charles E. "Address at the Memorial Service." In *In Memoriam: William Wallace Fenn, 1862–1932*, 1–8. Cambridge: Theological School in Harvard University, 1932.

———. "Eulogy for Earl Davis," 1953. https://commons.clarku.edu/funeral/1/.

———. *The Inner Victory: Two Hundred Little Sermons*. Cambridge: Harvard University Press, 1946.

———. *The Way of Jesus*. Boston: Beacon, 1956.

Parker, George Howard. *Biology and Social Problems*. Boston: Houghton Mifflin, 1914.

Parker, Theodore. "Justice and the Conscience." In *Ten Sermons of Religion*, 66–102. Boston: Crosby, Nichols, and Co, 1853.

Peirce, C. S. "The Fixation of Belief." *Popular Science Monthly* 12 (1877) 1–15. Repr. in Menand, *Pragmatism*, 7–25.

Phillips, Stephen. *Herod: A Tragedy*. London: John Land, 1901.

Pinker, Steven. *The Better Angels of Our Nature*. New York: Vintage, 2011.

"Postmodernism." Wikipedia. https://en.wikipedia.org/wiki/Postmodernism.

Putnam, Robert. *The Upswing: How America Came Together a Century Ago and How We Can Do It Again*. New York: Simon and Schuster, 2020.

Ramakrishnan, Venki. *Why We Die: The New Science of Aging and the Quest for Immortality*. New York: William Morrow, 2024.

Reagan, Ronald. "Inaugural Address 1981." Ronald Reagan Presidential Library and Museum. https://www.reaganlibrary.gov/archives/speech/inaugural-address-1981/.

Rorty, Richard. *Philosophy and the Mirror of Nature*. Princeton: Princeton University Press, 1979.

———. "Postmodernist Bourgeois Liberalism." *Journal of Philosophy* 80 (1983) 583–89. Repr. in Menand, *Pragmatism*, 329–37.

Rossel, Greg. "The Other Swan Island: A Jewel on the Kennebec." *Maine Boats, Homes and Harbors*. https://maineboats.com/coastal-adventures/swan-island-jewel-on-the-kennebec/.

Smith, J. E. A., ed. *The History of Pittsfield (Berkshire County) Massachusetts, from the Year 1734 to the year 1800*. Boston: Lee and Shepard, 1869.

"Socialists Pleased: Believe That Vote Cast Was Mostly a Pure and Simple Socialist Vote. *Berkshire Eagle*, Dec. 13, 1911, 9.

The Societal Implications of Nanotechnology: Hearing Before the Committee on Science, House of Representatives, 108th Cong. 108–13 (2003). https://www.govinfo.gov/content/pkg/CHRG-108hhrg86340/pdf/CHRG-108hhrg86340.pdf.

Spong, John Shelby. *Jesus for the Non-Religious*. New York: HarperCollins, 2007.

"Transhumanism." Wikipedia. https://en.wikipedia.org/wiki/Transhumanism.

Unitarian Universalist Association. "Leader Resource 1: A History of Covenant." https://www.uua.org/lifespan/curricula/river/workshop7/175913.shtml.

Worcester First Unitarian Church. "Our Covenant." https://www.firstunitarian.com/who-we-are/.

Worcester Unitarian Universalist Church. "Our Mission and Beliefs." https://www.uucworcester.org/about-us-welcome/uucw-our-mission-and-beliefs/.

Williams, L. Griswold. *Antiphonal Readings for Free Worship*. Boston: Murray, 1933.

Wittgenstein, Ludwig. *Tractatus Logico Philosophicus*. 1922. Translated by C. K. Ogden. New York: Dover, 1998 .

Wright, Conrad. *Congregational Polity: A Historical Survey of Unitarian and Universalist Practice.* Boston: Skinner House, 1997.

Zenou, Theo. "The Long and Gruesome History of People Trying to Live Forever." *Washington Post*, May 1, 2022.

Zhong, Raymond. "Geologists Make It Official: We're Not in an 'Anthropocene' Epoch." *New York Times*, Mar. 20, 2024. https://www.nytimes.com/2024/03/20/climate/anthropocene-vote-upheld.html.

Name Index

Earl Clement Davis's name appears on nearly every page, and consequently I have not indexed his name. His views on any of a variety of subjects—religious and otherwise—can be found by following the index entries for those subjects. Otherwise, I here provide some brief biographical details:

Earl Clement Davis was born on June 3, 1876, in Auburn, Maine. He graduated from the Edward Little High School there in 1893 and from Bowdoin College in 1897. After graduating from Bowdoin, he took the job of Principal of the Howe School (the public high school) in Billerica, Massachusetts, a job he held for five years. In 1902 he enrolled in the Harvard Divinity School where he graduated with a Bachelor of Sacred Theology in 1904. He was called to four ministries over a nearly 50-year career: Unity Church, Pittsfield, Massachusetts, where he was ordained on April 7, 1905 and served until 1919; Church of Our Father, Lancaster, Pennsylvania, 1919–1924; Unitarian Church of Concord New Hampshire, 1924–1933; First Congregational Church (Unitarian) in Petersham, Massachusetts, 1933–1953. He married Annie Foster Dodge—in whose family home he had boarded while Principal of the Howe School—on June 28, 1905. They had four children, John (1906–1959), Foster (1908–1958), Byron (1912–1998) and Mary (1915–1987). Earl C. Davis died on May 19, 1953, of complications from intestinal cancer. His widow, Annie F. Davis, died on December 24, 1964.

Subject Index

Scripture Index

www.ingramcontent.com/pod-product-compliance
Lightning Source LLC
Chambersburg PA
CBHW071244230426
43668CB00011B/1577